ON EMERGING FROM HYPER-NATION

Purdue Studies in Romance Literatures

Editorial Board

Íñigo Sánchez-Llama, Series Editor
Brett Bowles
Elena Coda
Paul B. Dixon

Patricia Hart
Gwen Kirkpatrick
Allen G. Wood

Howard Mancing, Consulting Editor
Floyd Merrell, Consulting Editor
Susan Y. Clawson, Production Editor

Associate Editors

French
Jeanette Beer
Paul Benhamou
Willard Bohn
Gerard J. Brault
Thomas Broden
Mary Ann Caws
Glyn P. Norton
Allan H. Pasco
Gerald Prince
Roseann Runte
Ursula Tidd

Italian
Fiora A. Bassanese
Peter Carravetta
Benjamin Lawton
Franco Masciandaro
Anthony Julian Tamburri

Luso-Brazilian
Fred M. Clark
Marta Peixoto
Ricardo da Silveira Lobo Sternberg

Spanish and Spanish American
Maryellen Bieder
Catherine Connor
Ivy A. Corfis
Frederick A. de Armas
Edward Friedman
Charles Ganelin
David T. Gies
Roberto González Echevarría
David K. Herzberger
Emily Hicks
Djelal Kadir
Amy Kaminsky
Lucille Kerr
Howard Mancing
Floyd Merrell
Alberto Moreiras
Randolph D. Pope
Francisco Ruiz Ramón
Elżbieta Skłodowska
Marcia Stephenson
Mario Valdés

 volume 62

ON EMERGING FROM HYPER-NATION

Saramago's "Historical" Trilogy

Ronald W. Sousa

Purdue University Press
West Lafayette, Indiana

Copyright ©2014 by Purdue University. All rights reserved.

∞ The paper used in this book meets the minimum requirements of American National Standard for Information Sciences—Permanence of Paper for Printed Library Materials, ANSI Z39.48-1992.

Printed in the United States of America
Template for interior design by Anita Noble;
template for cover by Heidi Branham.

Cover photo: *The Second Death of António de Oliveira Salazar in Santa Comba Dão in 1975*. In 1965 a statue was erected to Oliveira Salazar, creator and leader of Portugal's fascist regime. Seemingly designed to echo the Lincoln Memorial, it stood outside the municipal courthouse of small Santa Comba Dão, Salazar's birthplace. With the 1974 overthrow of the regime, the statue was both covered with denunciatory graffiti and decapitated. In multiple ways, the image of the statue in this state (it was later further destroyed with explosives) serves as a metaphor for the argument advanced in this book. The photograph was taken on February 20, 1975, photographer unknown. (Reproduced with the permission of Keystone-France/Gamma-Keystone/Getty Images.)

Library of Congress Cataloging-in-Publication Data

Sousa, Ronald W., 1943–
　On emerging from hyper-nation : Saramago's "historical" trilogy / Ronald W. Sousa.
　　　pages cm. — (Purdue studies in Romance literatures ; 62)
　　Includes bibliographical references and index.
　　　ISBN 978-1-55753-697-6 (paperback) — ISBN 987-1-61249-349-7 (epdf) — ISBN 978-1-61249-350-3 (epub)
1. Saramago, José.—Criticism and interpretation. 2. Historical fiction, Portuguese—History and criticism. 3. Literature and history. 4. Discourse anlysis. I. Title.
　PQ9281.A66Z8666 2014
　869.3'42—dc23   2014033969

For Joyce—
To remember forever
what Simon said …

As a group of rules for a discursive practice, the system of formation is not a stranger to time. ... [I]t ... outlines the system of rules that has to be put into operation if a change in other discourses (in other practices, in institutions, in social relations, and in economic processes) is to be transcribed within a given discourse, thus constituting a new object, giving rise to a new strategy, giving place to new enunciations or new concepts.
—Michel Foucault
The Archaeology of Knowledge

It ought ... to be possible to link the immanent analysis of works with reception research in such a way that they illuminate each other and not merely present a marginal reception history of individual authors *alongside* the interpretation of individual works ... the institution functions within the work, just as the work functions within the institution.
—Peter Bürger
The Institutions of Art

Contents

xi **Acknowledgments**

1 **Introduction**
What's in a Smile?

11 **Chapter One**
Portuguese Fascism and Literary Institutionality

39 **Chapter Two**
Baltasar and Blimunda: The Readership Pact and the Release of Pleasure

79 **Chapter Three**
Reading the Labyrinth: Text as Obstacle in *The Year of the Death of Ricardo Reis*

123 **Chapter Four**
Mastering the Culture's Tool Kit, or "Is the City Still Taken?": *The History of the Siege of Lisbon*'s Self-Invited Reader

171 **Conclusion**
What Has the Smile Brought with It?

181 **Notes**

185 **Works Cited and Consulted**

193 **Index**

Acknowledgments

Many people, colleagues, students, and others, have participated, willingly or not, in the making of this book, having done so in ways ranging from basic support and simple comment to probing question to full-blown critique. Those (former and forever) colleagues of whose support in one or more of those modalities I am most aware in drawing this project to a close are Elena Delgado, Michael Palencia-Roth, Rolando Romero, Nicolau Sevcenko, Hernán Vidal, Anthony N. Zahareas, Russell Hamilton, and Rodolfo Cardona. Amongst students I am most grateful to are Saulo Gouveia, Derek Pardue, and Selma Vital, all now, happily, professorial colleagues. Especially Saulo, who not only provided both insightful questions and practical observations but also carried out much of the original spadework for what follows. I am similarly indebted to my wife, Joyce Sousa, and our son Benjamin Sousa for their work with the illustrations. I owe thanks as well to Gwen Ashburn, Dean of Humanities at University of North Carolina Asheville for her support, personal and financial. These are, however, but a few. As you will see, I am indebted as well to literally hundreds more, from undergraduate university students to colleagues to nonprofessionals, both Portuguese and other, who have made remarks and initiated conversations that have moved this project forward. Some of you may glimpse yourselves in the ensuing pages. To all of you, my thanks.

Some materials in this study have been drawn from projects I have published previously. A distant cousin to some portions of Chapter 4 is to be found in my "José Saramago 'Re-vises,' or Out of Africa and into Cyber-History," *Discourse* 22.3 (Fall 2000): 73–86. © 2001 by Wayne State University Press. Reprinted with the permission of Wayne State University Press. Another part of that same chapter has appeared as "José Saramago and the Modalities of History, or Dragging Their Telos behind Him," *Da Possibilidade do Impossível: Leituras de Saramago,* ed. Paulo de Medeiros and Jose N. Ornelas (Utrecht: Utrecht Portuguese Studies Series, 2007), 315–23.

Introduction

What's in a Smile?

This is an unconventional little book—deceptively so, I think. At its core it is the record of my working through a problem, though in these pages that record appears reworked to produce a linear presentation for the purposes that I shall here introduce. In what follows I express that problem in the form of a question: "Why my smile?" Because, in point of fact, that is how the problem first presented itself to me: I found myself smiling and wondered exactly why I was doing so. Expressed in longer form, the problem has a number of facets to it: Why did I react as I did on first reading what I refer to as the "historical" novels of José Saramago? Why do I still react to them in a roughly similar manner? Have other readers reacted similarly (the quick answer to that question is "yes")? In what ways can that similarity be accounted for? How can I seek to understand that reaction in historical terms—i.e., what investments in Portuguese history are at play in my own and others' reader reactions? How can I seek to describe and understand those reactions in critical terms? That short list by no means exhausts the content of the problem, but it does set forth its principal dimensions, thus providing an idea of what the ensuing pages are about.

This study is, then, in effect, my attempt to read critically key aspects of my own reception of specific literary texts. That statement, however, is more complicated than it sounds. Allow me to explain. First of all, by "reception of specific texts" I mean something very precise: the initial operation in production of what follows has been my working through the texts in *epoché*, my goal being to understand the basic features of the reception that occasioned my initial smile and leads to smiles even today in myself and in others. That is my base operation—creation of a simple phenomenological inventory. But in the ensuing pages the results of that first gesture seldom appear unalloyed, and even when they

Introduction

do—largely at the outset of Chapter 2 but decreasingly thereafter—they are selected, contextualized, and rendered rhetorically (I shall demonstrate what that means as we move on), all to the end of my attempt to address the various facets of what I shall henceforth call my "smile question." Normally appearing on the page are, then, the results of a second, very different operation. By "reading my reception" I mean something much less precise than the first gesture—because, like the sundry elements that compose the smile question, it is hopelessly compound. I mean "analyze, present, discuss, and draw conclusions from a select subset of the features that that initial reception points out and do so through recourse to established literature- and culture-analytical modalities" (which, for the purpose, I sometimes push a bit beyond their usual application). This bipartite process involves, then, in gesture number two, something akin to an ongoing translation of the principal results of gesture number one into a number of different registers, one after the other, as I deem necessary and appropriate to my "smile" pursuit. For me (it may not be so obvious to you, the reader), the major chapters of this book—namely, chapters 2, 3, and 4—represent little more than my moving from one analytical modality to another in a curious narrative process narrowly focused by the texts in question and by the smile pursuit. Mine is what might be called a narrative in critical modalities. It is not a study grounded in conventional literary criticism, or even conventional reader-response analysis (if there is such a thing as conventional reader-response analysis), though it contains passages that, read in isolation, can easily function as one or the other.

One always wonders "Why this project?" and not that one, or yet another, to work out in extended form. Again, like the genesis of the project itself, my response moves into the area of the self-referential. I think I chose "this" project because carrying it out at some length has helped me formulate and/or consolidate ways to deal with a number of the specifics of post-revolutionary Portuguese writing—principally but not exclusively literary writing—in a way that does not abandon the actual, immediate readerly reception of writing for a reductionist sociology or para-sociology on the one hand or for a "historical" explanation conceived post-festum on the other. It thus works for me as a sort of master reference for my ongoing work with much else that went on in the post-revolutionary moment.

What's in a Smile?

Now my second gesture, the "narrative in critical modalities," obviously comes grounded in some general orienting convictions that I bring to the analytical task as operating premises and is carried out through use of allied expository strategies and conventions, all of which come with their specific entailments. I should point out at least the most central of those premises and strategies, leaving the specific critical modalities to be introduced each in its turn as my odd narrative moves along.

First point. There have, of course, been others before who have analyzed literary texts in roughly the manner I outline above, and I rely upon them. It is to one chief among that group, the late Wolfgang Iser, that I owe the basics of the intellectual framework that I employ as I "read my reception" (I think especially of the studies contained in Iser, *Implied Reader*). Iser's readings of literary texts, however, by and large move from the phenomenological (i.e., his "reception") to the formal (his "reading of his reception")—that is, his work is in the main devoted to explicating readerly activity within individual texts. I, by contrast, take the liberty of wandering far afield, adding an array of psychological, socio-historical, and other analytical currents and often changing analytical-discursive stances quite abruptly, given that my goal is to explain not a text but a ... smile. Consequently, my study has a very different texture from that which Iser creates in his work. In the main, I focus on the text's general positioning of the reader rather than on explication.

Second point. One of the prominent touches that I "add" to what I take from Iser is the "institutional critique" of Peter Bürger, which I have found to be necessary to broaden Iser's philosophical/formal focus and thereby facilitate investigation into the social power bound up with practical hermeneutics—into, then, some of the effects of the historical within the act of reception. I consider the amalgam of Iser's work and Bürger's (from the latter, especially his *Theory of the Avant-Garde*) to be the principal sources for my critical practice in these pages, though—again—the texture of my practice differs from either. Iser would, I believe, approve of the combination, while Bürger, I know, would utterly reject it. In any case, since that combination lies at the core of my work here, I am responsible for the representation within it of what each of those thinkers brings to the task of scholarship about cultural production as well as for the slippages that I inherit in bringing the two together in the manner that I do.

Introduction

My little book's third basic starting-point is the judgment on my part that case study, albeit an idiosyncratic sort of case study, can be an effective form for tackling problems such as I have heretofore outlined. Not unaware that the term has been used before for a somewhat different kind of scholarly work, I have therefore dubbed what follows a "local study." While my sources are fetched from several diverse fields of critical work, they come in relationship to questions posed by three texts only, and it is on the basis of the answers produced that I carry out a text-based investigation, quite limited in scope, into some of the contours of the milieu within which those texts were created and, most particularly, within which they were received.

* * *

As to the texts themselves. I have confessed publicly before that my first reading of a post-revolution-era novel by then-future Nobel Laureate José Saramago—indeed, my reading of its first twenty pages or so—represented an experience that both astonished me at the time and has since proved indelible. The novel was *Memorial do Convento* (1982; translated into English as *Baltasar and Blimunda* [1987]). I recall very clearly my immediate reaction as the narrative voice, in a breezy and irreverent tone that was unlike anything I had read in Portuguese literature before, began setting the background of early-eighteenth-century Portugal and the events that would lead up to the construction of the convent-palace complex at Mafra. As a student of Portuguese history and society and someone familiar with the geography and local history of Mafra (my status as a legal entity in Portugal is recorded in a notary's office in Mafra), I could see that the historical representation was accurate and thus surely the product of research. But every time the narrator reached a point where the material unearthed by research could be speculated upon, a fancy took over that did something extraordinary to the "historical facts" (I shall eventually disown that term) and did it overtly, often outrageously. The result: I found myself smiling as I finished the successive sections of the book. I still smile as I think back on the experience. I am smiling now.

Hence the question that serves as the central guide, both intellectual and methodological, for what follows. Clearly the smile came not just in recognition of a clever mixture of historical accuracy and irreverent imagining. I had read works before that were built on that combination of elements. Indeed, works that, like Saramago's, as a part of the outcome of the Revolution of 1974 and its overthrow of the long-standing fascist regime, were involved in contesting the constituted Portuguese imaginary. I think particularly of José Rodrigues Miguéis's two-volume *O Milagre Segundo Salomé* (1975), which, also entertaining in a highly irreverent way, nonetheless did not engender anything like a recurring smile as a part of my reception. Nor did the smile come just in relation to Saramago's complex and entertaining playing with narration and narrative point of view, which has caught the attention of international criticism and, along with other textual features, has led to categorization of his work as "post-modern." To be sure, both of those elements played a role in eliciting my smile, but, as I thought about it, I was sure that other, more basic factors lay at its core.

As I read further in Saramago's work of the 1980s, discussed it with others, and read the pertinent criticism, both Portuguese and international, I realized two things. First, while several of his works had something about them that touched my "smile button," those that dealt in detail with Portuguese history, indeed, those that by dint of their construction would generally qualify as "post-modern" "historical novels"—or, what one strand of contemporary criticism, following Linda Hutcheon (*A Poetics of Postmodernism* [1988]), would prefer to label "historiographical metafiction"—did so much more definitely than did the others. Second, my smile was not mine alone. A number of Saramago readers with whom I spoke identified similar reactions to his work in general and to the "historical" titles in particular. Those novels are, in chronological order, the aforementioned first source of the smile, *Memorial do Convento*, along with *O Ano da Morte de Ricardo Reis* (1984) (*The Year of the Death of Ricardo Reis* [1991]), and *A História do Cerco de Lisboa* (1989) (*The History of the Siege of Lisbon* [1996]). The first two titles, along, perhaps, with the later novel *Blindness*, are the best-known and most read of Saramago's novels. They are the works from which public readings of his novels most frequently excerpt and to which analysis of his writing practice regularly refers. *The History of the Siege of Lisbon*, published five years after its closest "historical" predecessor and after another major novel, *A Jangada de Pedra* (1986) (*The Stone Raft* [1994]), completes a historical trilogy of sorts.

Introduction

* * *

I propose to give my "answer" to the smile question in three principal chapters, one focused on each novel in turn. As is by now obvious, I shall not be engaging in a conventional reading to discuss what each novel is "about" or, for that matter, stylistic analysis or, really, any other traditional text-analytical modality. The path I shall make will be one largely *sui generis* as described above. Nor do I intend the chapters to constitute discrete units each "about" its corresponding novel. Instead I intend to have each chapter develop the focus most appropriate to it for reception-side exploration of the "smile question" and also both to reach back to prior chapters and to project forward into coming ones. That process of reference back and forth will serve to shed light on the complexity and the density of the issues being examined. Those three chapters are preceded by an introduction that presents socio-historical concerns, launches matters of methodology, and establishes analytical terminology for the ensuing chapters, some of it fashioned within the exigencies that this project itself has imposed.

As is obvious from the preceding paragraphs, my "answer" to the "smile question" is one that ranges far. Indeed, it reaches to historical, socio-psychological, and institutional considerations that transcend any précis of literary works—and thus also transcend my own personal case and presumably that of others who too have "smiled." Indeed, that answer involves, among other matters, the many dimensions of that complex activity that is the reading of literature. It is my intent not to allow any one front to take precedence over the others—especially as they are closely interdependent. In the ensuing pages my goal is to be engaging simultaneously in literary analysis of the sort that the aforementioned Peter Bürger calls the "functional analysis" of art (and I prefer to call "analysis of the social operativity" of—in this case—literary texts), a reflection on the institutional dimension of hermeneutics grounded in that analysis, and a variety of institutional critique articulated with both of the preceding. I thus think of *Emerging from Hyper-Nation* as not only, not even primarily, a contribution to Saramago criticism—though I hope it will be of interest to those engaged in that criticism. I think of it as work on the deployment and functioning of the social symbolic of post-revolutionary Portugal carried out through examination of texts that can be seen to articulate that deployment and that functioning.

What's in a Smile?

There is a particular set of issues to which the relationship of what follows here must be made specific—primarily lest I be thought not to understand them. This even though, paradoxically, the key feature of that relationship will be the degree of non-relationship between them. I refer to the issues bound up with the concept—or concepts—of the literary "post-modern." One who reads the following chapters may well remark that "this is (just) the now-stock literary interrogation of historiography that we are all familiar with," or "this is (merely) an example of the well-known literary exploding of 'modernist' narrative practices," or even "this is (just) one version of the Euro-novel." As far as they go, all such statements are accurate—save, of course, for the qualifiers. But my purposes are different from ones that they imply. It is the case, however, that all of what follows has been conceived in implicit dialogue with the purveyors of the literary "post-modern" (critical touchstone: the aforementioned Hutcheon)—or its referentialist variety, "cultural production under late capitalism" (similar touchstone: Fredric Jameson, *Postmodernism* [1991], implicitly conflated with his prior work on literature). Either of the two camps—which, as is well known, stand in partial opposition to one another—is likely to grow impatient with these pages. The former will doubtless be impatient with especially my second chapter, significant portions of which will, for them, just replicate, with what will seem unnecessary deliberateness, categories and issues and analyses they long have recognized and consider obvious. Moreover, they will interpret that activity as being carried out from a hopelessly "modern" viewpoint. Both points are totally accurate if one accepts the premises of those I imagine advancing them. I urge those people to read on so they can see where I am taking the results of the exercise. The latter group will doubtless become exasperated on a different score: with my refusal to move my focus from literary text to society-as-text. I urge them too to read on, for they will discover that I have already all along made that move, though not in the register they expect. In reference to both camps, my refusal to adopt expectable critical gestures is intended to resist, to the extent possible, the robbing of the novels under scrutiny of their aforementioned "local" functionality through my own act of analysis, in effect the turning of the texts into neutered artifacts of my own critical activity. I shall allude to "the post-modern"/"late capitalism" and other allied matters

Introduction

only when either my analysis benefits from the direct linking or it seems to me derelict not to do so. And even then, in the main, by bibliographical reference or short allusion rather than by textual treatment. Some issues in this connection will, however, re-"emerge" in my Conclusion.

Another matter must be addressed as well. Because this book ends up touching on a number of issues in criticism and consequently cannot but entertain at least some of their implications, I occasionally take the liberty of indicating points of departure not taken and sometimes of meditating briefly and schematically upon them when my analysis points them up. Sometimes in so doing I am in effect pointing out but simultaneously closing off paths that lead away from my principal direction. I think of the passages thereby produced as jumping-off places for possible exploration. The many other such points that arise I simply bypass in the name of sticking to my principal inquiry. What follows, then, as regards implications for issues of criticism and critical theory, is something akin to a road map that shows forks and crossroads and occasionally even puts up a signpost to mark one or another of them, even though its route is one straight ahead.

Virtually needless to say after such a description, I shall not in what follows be dealing in any way whatsoever with authorial intentionality. Nor, when I talk about readership in general, shall I be talking about readers' consciousness of the nature of their own readerly undertaking. I shall instead, I repeat, be treating the social operativity of the literary texts themselves within and upon the horizon within which they were launched in the 1980s and, conversely as well, about what their operativity tells us about that horizon.

* * *

Several procedural issues should be clarified here at the outset. First, since this study is written in English, I shall present material from the novels, and occasionally from other sources, in that language, with the originals provided to serve those who can read them and for the facilitation of reference. For sources well established in English-language critical circles but originally written in another language, I do not reproduce the non-English originals. Nor do I in instances where I do not see it as germane to my argument to do so. Where I do reproduce translations, I use published translations, duly referenced, whenever possible or practical. I translate myself when no published translation exists and, occasionally, when the published translation misses the point that I am making in referring to the passage in question. All unattributed translations are my own. When I refer to a passage from a Saramago novel I give the page numbers for the English translation and the Portuguese original, in that order.

Because this study is ultimately an idiosyncratic one rather than one seeking to account for a specific literary or critical corpus, the apparatus reproduced in the ensuing pages is intended only to support and contextualize my line of exploration, my "narrative in critical modalities." Indeed, given the wide range of the wanderings contained in the ensuing pages, the creation of a comprehensive bibliography to encompass the terrain that those wanderings traverse would amount to another project in and of itself—and one of dubious utility. The ensuing bibliography, then, is most assuredly not a consistent one of the criticism on the three Saramago novel titles. This study not being, in a strict sense, literary criticism, my references to Saramago criticism—and they are relatively few—are made only for the purpose of squaring my narrative with the major lineaments of the critical record when my project touches upon them and, on occasion, conversely using pieces of the critical record as convenient rhetorical touchstones for the fashioning of my narrative. In carrying out my first "reading" gesture, my main endeavor with regard to the critical record has, of course, been to eliminate it from consideration. It is only with my "reading of my reception" that critical references appear. In any case, such references as there are are made to the title(s) where in my judgment the issue I am discussing is best developed for the purposes for which I make the reference. Often, but not always, those titles are ones in which that issue was first introduced in developed form. It should be understood as well that, unlike standard critical practice, my citing of a given piece of criticism does not imply my agreement with it. I am merely mapping my work here onto the critical record.

Some final, mundane matters. First, I assume that there is no need to bibliograph mere mention of key thinkers—e.g., Kant, Freud, Habermas—made with the intent to signal their overall intellectual gravitation. I do cite relevant sources when referring

Introduction

to specific argument on the part of such figures. Conversely, as a second point, I take the liberty of including among my Works Cited and Consulted several titles that have had an orienting value for me even though I may not actually have ended up employing specific citations from them.

Chapter One

Portuguese Fascism and Literary Institutionality

> Similar to various others on more scores than our knights errant of hypernationalism are willing to imagine, our national mythology is nonetheless in the last analysis specific to us. That specificity, however, does not take the form that we give out in the international assemblies where we are directly challenged to account for ourselves (since we do not challenge ourselves to do so).
>
> —Eduardo Lourenço
> *This Little Lusitanian House*

As a step preliminary to beginning my smile pursuit, I shall need to present and discuss several interrelated matters of historical import, as well as some of their implications for the study of contemporary Portuguese literature. The need comes on several fronts, principally, under present circumstances, to provide a sense of the historical and hermeneutical conditions under which my initial reading of the Saramago novels took place. My plan is to address those matters in a series of separable but interconnected fragments. I would not like to have them seen as conceptually complete presentations of the subjects that they involve but rather merely as ad-hoc expositions fashioned for present purposes.

I shall begin with reference to a familiar Portuguese literary figure.

* * *

In his novel-based social critique—in, say, *The Illustrious House of Ramires* (*A Ilustre Casa de Ramires* [1900])—Eça de Queirós implicitly trades upon several matters whose specification will provide a fundamental starting point for this study. The first of those matters is that he and his reader are more or less free to communicate about the social issues that they share, as a result of presumed cultural/linguistic commonality, if nothing more. That is, the novel's reader is expected to see Gonçalo, its protagonist, and the issues that the narrative develops around him as postulations about Portuguese life in a kind of open communication from Eça de Queirós, the by-then-famous practitioner of the social novel. This is, in its broad contours, the same contract that was in force between reader and author in the cases of, say, Dickens in England, Flaubert in France, Galdós in Spain, and so on. Second is that such issues are appropriately and effectively expressed in imaginative form. The reader is expected to read successfully through the fictional plot and understand that its content and dynamics identify and work with questions of the day while not therefore ceasing to read it as a self-contained imaginative narrative. Third is that the communication thereby effected represents participation in ongoing public debate, carried out within the sphere of literature and beyond, about questions of the day. Fourth, that at the same time that debate is acknowledged, the specific characteristics of the symbolic construction of this particular arena set it apart from other arenas in which debate on the same subject or subjects may occur, imparting to it a very specific status, one in which engagement, expressed through general reference to contemporary society, and detachedness, expressed in the self-contained character of the literary work, coexist (more about that "co-existence" presently).

This contract between writer and reader in force within the literary sphere in the late nineteenth century in Portugal and elsewhere is grounded in a set of general enabling conditions. Among them are the presence of a more-or-less self-governing sphere of communication, functional autonomy of producer and receiver within that sphere, and the capacity of art to provide models for the conceptualization of issues pertinent to other social spheres. Those features characterize what criticism of a generally Habermasian bent calls the bourgeois "sphere of autonomous art" (Bürger, *Theory* xxxv ff.). The concept of such a sphere is grounded in an historical analysis that says, in summary overview, that in Europe prior, generally, to the mid-eighteenth century, artistic production and reception followed a courtly arrangement: artists functioned mostly on the basis of patronage by the wealthy and powerful, and they produced objects to be received within the artistic-productive sphere created by such patronage. The conditions within which were fashioned the rules for what Bürger (*Theory* 13) has called "commerce with" artistic production and reception were provided by that arrangement. With the historical movement to a bourgeois-centered societal mode, that system gave way to one in which creation and reception/consumption of cultural products, as well as their reproduction and exchange, came to be conditioned by the rules of a self-governing sphere modeled on a market economy. In short, as society became bourgeois-centered, "art" entered the marketplace, in terms of its wider social functionality as well as in terms of direct exchange.

This transition—it is admitted to be a gradual one and one not synchronous in all its constituent aspects—brings with it a myriad of concomitant changes in the mode of artistic production and in its products, as well as in the expectations that the receiver is implicitly asked to bring to the reception process. For instance, the sort of communication in force in Eça de Queirós's *The Illustrious House of Ramires* involves a focus on representation of daily life and on the working of societal processes that would not have found favor—i.e., would not have been considered "artistic"—even a hundred years before, let alone earlier. The outlook inscribed in the novel bespeaks an approach to experience that is one of the key ingredients in the configuration of the bourgeois "sphere of autonomous art" in its late-nineteenth-century form: the "literature market" of the time is to a considerable extent based on the bourgeois reading public's seeing itself, and especially its problems, presented in some detail and addressed analytically within the literary product.

In order to analyze the functioning and historical movement of the sphere of autonomous art, Bürger, drawing on work in social theory, in socio-historically oriented art criticism, and in reception aesthetics, creates the concept of "institution of art" (*institution-kunst*). His *Theory of the Avant-Garde* sets forth that concept—more through exemplification than in theory. He explains that in his thinking "the concept 'art as an institution' ... refers to the productive and distributive apparatus and also to the ideas about art that prevail at a given time and that determine the reception of works" (22). In effect, then, the "institution," in Bürger's usage, is the composite of the understandings and practices that govern the sphere of art, thereby constituting the ground of his aforementioned phrase "commerce with art." He elaborates: "it is not in and of themselves that works of art have their effect but rather … [their] effect is decisively determined by the institution within which the works function" (31). According to that concept, works of art are, in the final analysis, effects within an institutional horizon constituted in great part according to the rules and expectations for their reception.

The concepts developed in *Theory of the Avant-Garde* and elaborated in some of Bürger's subsequent work (e.g., "Institution") are enormously suggestive beyond that single thesis. Indeed, one set of his observations will be of great use in the present study. It reads as follows:

> Autonomy … defines the functional mode of the social subsystem "art": its (relative) independence in the face of demands that it be socially useful. But it must be remembered that the detachment of art from the praxis of life and the accompanying crystallization of a special sphere of experience (i.e., the aesthetic) is not a straight-line development (there are significant counter-trends), and that it cannot be interpreted undialectically (as the coming into its own of art, for example). Rather, the autonomous status of art within bourgeois society is by no means undisputed but is the precarious product of overall social development. That status can always be called into question by society (more precisely, society's rulers) when it seems useful to harness art once more. Not only the extreme example of the fascist politics of art that liquidates the autonomy status, but the large number of legal proceedings against artists for offenses against morality, testify to that fact. … Art in bourgeois society lives off the tension between the institutional framework (releasing art from the demand that it fulfill a social function) and the possible political content … of individual works. This tension, however, is not stable but subject to a historical dynamics that tends toward its abolition. (*Theory* 24–25)

Amongst its several effects, the passage pinpoints the core "tension" (the term representing a further elaboration of the "coexistence" I refer to above) constitutive of the sphere of autonomous art: art's potential for critical functioning in tension with the tenet that art serves "merely" an "aesthetic" function within its specialized "aesthetic" sphere. ("Aesthetic" in this sense implies an understanding of receptor enjoyment as largely self-enclosed and therefore irrelevant to social critique.) Both the critical function and the "aesthetic" function of art are, of course, susceptible of being configured in many different ways, and their configuration evolves over time. As we have seen, in the case of Eça de Queirós and *The Illustrious House of Ramires* the dominant mode of reception, that is, that area of the "literary institution" (that term designating a sub-sphere of the "institution of art") that includes the rules for literary reception—which I shall hereafter call simply "the hermeneutic rules"—still included principal attention to a critical function, namely, novel-based social critique. By 1900, however, when *The Illustrious House of Ramires* was published, not only in Portugal but in many other places in Europe as well, those hermeneutic rules were moving away from focus on social critique and toward a mode emphasizing "aestheticist" concerns. Thus *The Illustrious House of Ramires*, manifesting though it does some effects of that ongoing institutional-sphere transformation, likely seemed a bit dated to the readers of its time because it retained the basic markers of the nineteenth-century social novel, then becoming old-fashioned.

The root tension between engagement and "aesthetic" functioning is, according to Bürger, a constituent part of the very development of the modern realm of aesthetics. "Aesthetics," used in this sense, is, structurally speaking, Kant's concept (*The Critique of Aesthetic Judgement*) of an apprehension that is disinterested—in the sense that its object is being looked to not for any practical ends or analytical value but rather for the sensory pleasure that it provides (many terms here are definable in divergent ways—and then lead to divergent lines of thought—without that divergence doing any substantial harm to this basic assertion). Seen in the light of these considerations, Eça de Queirós's *The Illustrious House of Ramires* comprises a series of representations in language that, apprehended by means of that specific, acquired mode of reception that is the reading of literature, provides pleasure through, among other dimensions, both its form and its allusion to society, and that pleasure comes precisely because direct practical connections do not have to be made. "Aesthetics" in this sense (please recall that I am speaking in structural terms) involves the concept of "aesthetic distance," in which the receiver understands him- or herself to be in the position of disinterested apprehension of the object and derives a measure of the "aesthetic pleasure" from that awareness.

The tension between engagement and "aesthetic" functioning that defines this complex social subsystem is realized in multiple ways. Enter here the issue of the possible reciprocally compensatory relationships that can come to exist between those two gestures. Most commonly dealt with is the phenomenon in which the "aesthetic" dimension of the reception of a work that challenges some aspect of received modalities comes to compensate for critique or, in general terms, for art's entire critical potential (e.g., Marcuse 95–101). Such compensation, it must be understood, while the terms with which it operates are lodged in the institutional sphere, is carried out in practical reception, wherein the "aesthetic pleasure" derived through reception of the art object comes to allay the psychological impact of the critique. In effect, one aspect of the mode of reception compensates for the other. Indeed, it can be argued that one aspect is always structurally available to intercept, displace, or undermine the other (Jusdanis 77–104).

Thus, according to Bürger, "autonomous art" is the contradictory site of critique of experience on the one hand and the aesthetically based relieving of "the pressure of those forces that make for social change" on the other (*Theory* 50). What he does not add in any significant way, perhaps because it is a dimension that such figures as Hans Robert Jauss and the aforementioned Wolfgang Iser—with agendas somewhat different from his—were already exploring with regard to literature, is consideration of the degree to which the reception of a work within such an economy must be conceived of as an experience that has psycho-social constructive implications. That reception constitutes an active arena of psycho-social structuration and change. In that regard, invoking the aforementioned concept of "aesthetic distance" employed variously by many contemporary theoreticians of aesthetics, Jauss analyzes the interaction between reader and text as one in which "aesthetic enjoyment that … occurs in a state of balance between disinterested contemplation and testing participation is a mode of experiencing oneself in a possible being other which the aesthetic attitude opens up" (32). That is, for Jauss, a part of the readerly creation of the aesthetic object involves the reception of another's construction of experience in the world in such a way both that the reader, in the act of reading, is the (co)producer of that experience and that the productive process provides the site for the reader's (potential) (re-)configuring of her/his own experience and/or manner of experiencing.

Jauss grounds the dynamics of this concept of reception in Jean-Paul Sartre's phenomenology of imagination, according to which imagination is, precisely, a model-building activity. Jauss capsules the concept, for himself and for Sartre:

> ... [aesthetic experience] progressively expand[s] and maintain[s] its area of meaning at the expense of bordering experiences of reality [i.e., experiences in other social (sub-)spheres], and this by usurpations and compensations, the crossing of boundaries, the offer of competing solutions. (111–12)

> ... The achievement of the aesthetic in living praxis can be recognized by its capacity to dynamically organize the experiences of reality [i.e., experiences in other social spheres] and the interests of other provinces of meaning. (115)

Using more traditional phenomenological terminology, Iser analyzes the mechanisms of the reader's symbolic-sphere self-construction in the act of reception. He argues that when we receive an art object—for present purposes, when we read literature—we in effect make our (socio-historically constructed) subjectivity available to the cues advanced by the text, thereby, metaphorically, giving ourselves to the text virtually as an instrument for it to play. Our subjectivity furnishes emotionality, provides cultural content, and fills in blanks that the text presents it with for the precise purpose of their being filled by us in reading (*Act* 152–59). It is in that way that we "construct" the text in the act of reading and simultaneously are aware of our so doing. For Iser, following Husserl, a primary result of that process is that "... the reader himself, in constituting the meaning, is also constituted" (*Act* 150)—that is, our socially based self-construction is impacted in some way: revived and/or ratified and/or modified in some combination. In investing our subjectivity in the reception process, we are thus also leaving it open to reconstitution through that process. Indeed, such reconstitution is a constituent part of literary reception. In sum, reception functions as a shaper/reshaper of the individual's dynamic connections with and within the social-symbolic realm.

It is of particular interest for us here that the passage from Bürger reproduced above (p. 14), in its reference to the "fascist

Chapter One

politics of art" and in commentary on the "precarious" state of art's autonomy, points to the radical historicity of the above concepts. Indeed, in *Theory of the Avant-Garde,* Bürger makes it clear that within the wide concept of "autonomous art" there can be many modalities corresponding to specific local/epochal situations. The entire construction of art as autonomous can itself be attacked—from, in the example he gives, outside the institution itself, as in the "fascist" "liquidation of autonomy status."

Let us take that matter of autonomous art's precariousness as a starting point from which to explore aspects of literary institutionality in fascist Portugal. (I should make it clear that I am avowedly using the term *fascist* as a period term, thereby seeking to avoid engaging in the knotty, much-debated question of the similarities and differences between the Portugal of 1930–74 and Nazi Germany, Fascist Italy, etc.)

* * *

A useful beginning-place for this exploration—one of many that might be taken up—is to be found in examination of the concept of "Portuguese philosophy." Pronouncements about that concept flourished within the culture from the early years of the twentieth century on through the fascist period (and beyond). In the late 1950s and early 1960s, an exchange took place in intellectual circles about whether or not the concept of "Portuguese philosophy" had merit, and, if it did, what "Portuguese philosophy" might be supposed to be. In 1960 the *Diário Popular,* a Lisbon daily newspaper, became the focus for concerted dialogue on the subject, though it was to be found in other newspapers and in magazines, journals, and books of the time as well.[1] More importantly, the concept (if we grant it concept status) directly or indirectly inflected much of the cultural production, especially the political thought, of the time.

The partisans of the position that there is something distinctive called "Portuguese philosophy" present a specific set of arguments—with, to be sure, considerable diversity among them. For them, first of all, "Portuguese" thought has a specific character: it is characteristically "intuitive" and "messianic." According to that view, "Portuguese philosophy" brings into play a human essence that escapes "European" rationalistic/positivistic thought processes, constitutes an attitude toward experience that intuitively grasps points in common even though they may at first glance seem antithetical, and brings them into a productive relationship with each other. It is creative in ways that are superficially diverse but ultimately unified. And its praeter-rational genius for creating unity out of superficial diversity, harmony out of apparent antagonism, underpins a supposed inherent Portuguese "mission" as a unique cultural force, especially a uniquely positive colonizer. As a corollary to this argument came the discourse of "Lusotropicalism": a set of assertions about Portuguese uniqueness in making its colonial holdings oases of social harmony and progress. For example, through much of the 1960s the Lisbon daily *Diário de Notícias*—which held the status of unofficial news organ of the fascist regime, called the *Estado Novo* ("New State")—published a weekly column called "Paragraphs on Overseas Literature" ("Parágrafos de Literatura Ultramarina"). The underlying premise of the series and other critical gestures like it is perhaps best summed up in the title of one of the articles appearing under that heading, by one Afonso de Lima. "Unity and Cultural Revelation in the Portuguese World" ("Unidade e Revelação Cultural no Mundo Lusíada") (Lima) suggests that there is somehow a coherence in cultural values throughout the Portuguese colonial world that is the result of the inherent Portuguese "genius."

Spokesmen (and they are all "spokes*men*") for this outlook are quite capable of listing a preferred canon of "Portuguese philosophers" whose thought they claim manifests the supposed peculiarly "national" features. The most frequently mentioned are: José Pereira de Sampaio (Bruno) (1857–1915), António Sardinha (1888–1925), Leonardo Coimbra (1883–1936), Teixeira de Pascoais (1877–1952), and Fernando Pessoa (1888–1935). The last is the now-internationally acclaimed poet whose profile was being constructed in Portugal at this same time—in substantial part, in and through these very debates. Indeed, "Pessoa" served as a prime cultural battleground upon which many of the issues of the day—in effect, issues in the constitution of the sphere of literary institutionality—were contested. The "Pessoa debates" thus illuminate those issues (Sousa, "Europe"; "Pessoa Criticism"). As a consequence, much of what follows in the next few pages as regards "Portuguese philosophy" comes from the struggle around "Pessoa."

Chapter One

Much of the Pessoa criticism of this period practiced by exponents of the line of thought that accepts the notion that there is a "Portuguese philosophy" clearly has it as one of its purposes to inscribe Pessoa in the aforementioned list; indeed, it is fair to see such writings as those of Agostinho da Silva (who would later be added to the list himself), António Quadros, and Amândio César in just that light. It should be noted that not all of the figures cited in this gesture of canonization can be labeled politically "conservative" in any superficial sense. Indeed, Sampaio Bruno, who is the first name uttered in most short-form recitals of the canon, was the prototypical ardent Republican. The principal factor linking these figures would seem to be some degree of conviction about Portuguese uniqueness and active publicity of that conviction. Even with that factor in hand, however, supporters of this line of thought have problems capturing some of the figures for their outlook. Indeed, one of the more interesting arguments set forth in an effort to achieve that end posits, in effect, that "national thought" constitutes the only common element, while all else may vary dramatically, even to the point where the figures stand in stark opposition to each other on specifics, this deployment—again, this bringing of unity out of diversity—being itself the ultimate hallmark of Portuguese thought (see, e.g., Quadros, *Teoria*).

This outlook is one set of outgrowths from the conservative social and political movements spawned throughout Europe in the first part of the twentieth century and most powerfully in the 1920s and 1930s. To use the fascist leadership as a source of examples, it might be noted that the dictator Salazar himself had been a prominent member of a right-wing Catholic political party and, in the early 1920s, the prime reformulator of its orientation. He also maintained a long correspondence with the imprisoned French Monarchist thinker Charles Maurras, founder of Action Française, which, in turn, clearly had an influence on especially Sardinha of the canonical line outlined above (see Weber 485–86). Suffice it to say that this line of thinking represents the narrative backbone of fascist discourse, both official and unofficial.

The kind of argumentation advanced for this outlook should be exemplified in some detail so that its texture can be apprehended. Let me do so through recourse to the works of Álvaro Ribeiro, in which some of the main lines of the argument are clearly set out. Ribeiro stands as a bridge between such earlier figures as Sampaio

Bruno and Sardinha on the one hand and such younger followers as Quadros and César on the other. Ribeiro is also a key canon-creator, for primarily to him are owed the first descriptions, if not the very concept, of the canon of "traditionalist Portuguese philosophers" running from Sampaio Bruno down to his (Ribeiro's) present day. The line would later be extended, especially by Quadros, to include Ribeiro himself.

Ribeiro's argument is decidedly abstract: for him, the very conceptualization of human knowledge as described in the epistemological tradition of Western philosophy has marginalized what he identifies as the a-rational faculties of knowing. He cites as significant missteps those taken in the philosophies of the Pythagoreans, Descartes, and the nineteenth-century positivists. To this direction he, in general terms, opposes a variety of thought, scholastic in its basic structure, that sees faith and intuition as constituent features of knowing; indeed, he argues that vital knowledge cannot be reached without the active participation of such capacities. In this sense, he is a traditional Catholic thinker, though his discourse is not in the least theological; it is rather a blend of an idiosyncratic understanding of the discourse of epistemology of his day, history of philosophy, and varieties of cognitive psychology and vitalist philosophy. For him it follows that philosophy is not properly thought of as a systematic undertaking; it is rather a mode of intellection—which he terms "existential." A tight definition: "philosophy is not ... a body of doctrine ... but rather the human process of, through love, transforming belief into knowledge."[2] Ribeiro then adds that the partly a-rational process that is philosophy properly understood varies among peoples, since "languages" (which he understands, in Rousseauean terms, as the effective instantiations of ethnic specificities) articulate experience differentially and also are the products and preservers of the "tradition" (his term) of each people: "... not being pure and complete rationalism, [philosophy] is conditioned in the soul of each man and in the tradition of each people. The means by which each man animates his reason in seeking to move from his 'I' to the 'not-I' depends upon various factors that characterize his ethnicity" (*Arte* 130–31). "Soul" is by and large the Christian concept inflected in specific ways by Ribeiro in the creation of his analytical lexicon. The terminology, of course, reflects reading in existentialist thought (Kierkegaard seems to have been the preferred figure for these thinkers, though they use concepts taken from Sartre and likely Buber as well, usually without attribution). Thus, in sum, the melding of specific "national" thought processes and the term *philosophy*.

Ribeiro adds that this national-philosophical expression comes most frequently in "aesthetic processes" (*Arte* 133), by which he means both artistic creation and also its analysis. Indeed, in his terminology, "aesthetics" usually refers to the latter—though, in a parallel to his understanding of "philosophy," what is referred to is not systematic aesthetics but rather virtually any pronouncement reflecting upon creative activity. Poetry is seen as a cultural form in which the two sorts of activity come very close to each other, and Ribeiro dedicates considerable effort to dealing with both the distinction between poetry and philosophy and also what he sees as their close proximity as modes of understanding (Prefácio 7–15). From that starting point he describes a theory of aesthetic production and reception: there is in effect a national symbolic realm that underlies and informs the national language itself, and the specific symbols and symbolic values, which are, to be sure, historical in the sense that they evolve over time, are peculiar to the national being—in this case, the Portuguese. Ribeiro suggests that only those who share in this substratum can successfully understand the national "language"—especially its use in "aesthetic" production (*Arte* 138–41). He also makes this symbolic realm the linking point between national thought and the so-called glorious past of Portugal: key events register in important ways in the national symbolic, thus both giving it a specific shape and providing symbolizations for specific characteristics and values.

Ribeiro's version of Portuguese history has the country lose touch with its own uniqueness in the sixteenth century and begin to glimpse it again only in the various canonized traditionalistic figures of the nineteenth and twentieth centuries. (He thus replicates in a different mode the glory–fall–potential rebirth narrative paradigm that underlies much of modern Portuguese historiography [Sousa, *Rediscoverers*].) And, in a statement that is important for this study, he goes on to suggest that Portuguese education needs to "return" to a grounding in "Portuguese philosophy" and that philosophy per se—presumably as he defines it—should be made a part of the curriculum (*Arte* 239–42).

As regards "aesthetic" language usage: "We must read the images, intuit the meaning of each [symbol], [and] interpret the successive and simultaneous composition of them all according to the hermeneutic rules taught us by aesthetics" (227). "Aesthetics," in this case, clearly refers to the second usage described above, with the national-traditionalistic grounding that Ribeiro attributes to it, and equally clearly it has as one of its functions the constitution of a set of "national" hermeneutic rules—as a part of what can be understood in schematic terms as a "nationalist" literary institutionality.

What we can now call Ribeiro's "hermeneutic localism" can be seen to be of a piece with the positions of many supporters, official and unofficial, of the fascist regime. It clearly finds echo in *Estado Novo* theory and practice of interpretation of cultural products. To be sure, outright disagreements are to be found, but the basic tenets of the *traditionalistic position* (my term) are fairly well shared, and Ribeiro's position as outlined above touches most of the shared bases.

The great logical problem with the traditionalist argument—one that can be seen to underlie many of its specific rhetorical and conceptual difficulties—can be gleaned from the foregoing and expressed as follows: If the traditionalistic outlook is correct in its own terms, why does it need to be argued at all? That is, if nationalities are uniform in their symbolic bases, each with its own unique characteristics, and understanding is uniformly grounded in those characteristics, then the system would seem to be perfect and, among the effects of that perfection, would not require such publicity as Ribeiro and the others engage in. Indeed, were their outlook to be taken literally there would seem to be no epistemological free space from which actually to be able even to think the arguments that they put forward. There is, then, a need to account for a significant quotient of play within the system seen in its own terms. But such an accounting would, paradoxically, contradict the very argument for the system.

This sort of paradox is repeatedly observable in instances of state or state-supportive language. A defensive tone pervades fascist political discourse virtually since its inception (though that tone becomes increasingly magnified—to the point of seeming paranoia—in the decades after World War II), and much of it is traceable to this root paradox. Oliveira Salazar himself, for example, was quite capable of saying in effect that only "true Portuguese" were valuable, thus implicitly admitting that there were "other" Portuguese who did not share, much less act out, the prescribed view of nationality.[3] And Quadros, of all these thinkers the one who cast the widest net, was nonetheless regularly capable of characterizing those whose views differed from his as "those who are ignorant of them [i.e., the "advances" represented by "Portuguese philosophy"] or … who do not wish to recognize or accept them."[4] If Ribeiro's argument were to be taken at face value, there would be no space from which to conceive such an unwillingness.

As regards literary institutionality, in its argument for an authoritarian-Catholic state, the *Estado Novo* was dually invested in the entire matter of the autonomous sphere of art inherited from the past one-hundred-plus years of Portuguese institutional practice. The avowedly anti-liberal "organic" state model that it theorized—probably inherited quite directly from the Action Française[5]—with small-scale municipal units and professional corporations existing in a loose but direct relationship to a central authority really had no place in it for an institutional sphere in which creative and critical writings circulated according to the laws of that sphere itself—i.e., according to its autonomy—and in so doing functioned as what have been referred to above as shapers of the individual's relationship to the social-symbolic realm and therefore of her or his own self-concept. Presumably, that relationship—one of the arenas of the (re-)creation of individual subjecthood—was to be articulated, within the *Estado Novo*'s enforced "medieval" polity (Monteiro and Costa Pinto 213), only by family and local interactions and/or interactions with the institutions of state and church. Indeed, looked at from this vantage point, the efforts of Ribeiro and the several others mentioned here as regards location of the concepts of nationality and national history represent nothing more than a thinly veiled attempt to do away in practice with the inherited "liberal" sphere of literary institutionality. The reverse pole of the paradox, of course, is that their effort to do so was usually carried out precisely within that sphere whose abolition was the effort's objective. Indeed, it can be argued that the entire state structure engaged in a variety of this conflicted practice as regards literary institutionality—as opposed to other areas of circulation of ideas, in which the state openly admitted no access save its own.[6]

On a practical level, maintenance of the sphere of literary institutionality in a modified, controlled version (censorship was practiced, which served to focus subjects of discussion and to narrow allowable terminology) held significant advantages for the *Estado Novo* and its ideologues. First, they could claim that it was not their purpose to seek to crush individual expression by directly enforcing uniformity in concept; they could indeed point to something that looked like a free exchange of ideas. This was especially important in the post-war West, when Portugal, after starting off as an Axis collaborator, ended up a charter member of NATO (1949). Second, both by means of direct state intervention in the sphere (through its own publications as well as the personal and/or financial penalties heaped upon publishers who ran afoul of censorship) and by means of financial support of sympathetic individuals and/or initiatives within the sphere, it exercised considerable control over the actual shape of the "free exchange of ideas." Third, this relatively "open" space had great practical uses no matter what the theoretical inconsistencies might have been. In the most basic of senses, it existed as a trap for anyone in opposition, for it provided the space within which they might reveal themselves and thus established the terms within which their products—or even their presence[7]—would be tolerated. Thus the antagonistic maintenance of a para-liberal sphere of literary institutionality contradictory to state logic served as a very sensitive sounding-board through which an entire set of political-intellectual relationships were brokered.

Within this delicate arrangement a number of very particular phenomena are to be observed. In general terms, the gesture of most of the traditionalists was an incorporative one: in differing ways their mode of operation was to find broad terrain that could be presented as designating common ground and, avoiding detailed analysis that might cast doubt on their broad approach, claim that their common ground applied to many actors on the subject in question. Ribeiro's argument outlined above is a virtual paradigm of that strategy. In his rendition, "Portuguese philosophy" is so broad a concept and itself comes grounded in so diffuse a set of premises that it is easily deployed to incorporate cultural products that could be understood from a contrary viewpoint with equal if not greater plausibility. This incorporative action is illustrated within "Pessoa" criticism by the many-year struggle between Jacinto do Prado Coelho, chair professor of modern

Portuguese literature at the University of Lisbon, and the aforementioned António Quadros over interpretation of "Pessoa." As Prado Coelho proceeded, from the late 1940s through the 1960s, to analyze Pessoa's poetic texts according to his preferred *werkimmanent* methodology, Quadros continually attempted—in public print—to bring the results of that analysis into the ambit of his preferred traditionalist critical discourse. Prado Coelho in turn continually attempted to distance himself from that discourse—also in print—precisely in the name of literary criticism as opposed to what, in one instance, he openly labeled, with palpable deprecation, "Portuguese philosophy."[8] What is at stake in the relationship is precisely the former's effort to maintain a literary criticism—and, by logical extension, an autonomous literary institutionality—independent of state and/or state-supportive discourses, while the latter continually tries to "incorporate" such criticism. In this one illustrative case, by the way, Prado Coelho found a kind of stasis: in the editorship of the journal *Colóquio*, whose editorial policy he proclaimed to be "anti-polemical."[9] In general, however, the sphere of literary institutionality that should not have existed provided a very complex space in which debate of a limited, directed sort could take place while simultaneously the state could identify opposition discourses and act with regard to them, in many cases through a logic of incorporation.

This, if it does not amount to the "liquidation" of the sphere of literary institutionality to which Bürger refers, at the very least describes a situation in which that institution exists in a highly fluid, variable, indeed, to use Bürger's term, "precarious," state. In effect, Portugal's equivalent to Nazi Germany's *Entartete Kunst* was to be found in the prison at Caxias and that prison's frequent embrace of culture producers—or, for that matter, anyone else—who fell afoul of state logic (see figure 1).

* * *

Now let us go back to another of Bürger's assertions—namely, that the "effect [of works of art] is decisively determined by the institution within which the works function"—and look at the issues introduced above about fascist Portugal from the viewpoint of the working of literary institutionality.

Portuguese Fascism and Literary Institutionality

Figure 1. Poster of "Greater Portugal." Taken by my wife, Joyce, and myself on an early morning in 1970, this photograph shows a regime propaganda poster affixed to a building wall (see p. 181n6) in downtown Lisbon. The poster itself asserts graphically that "Portugal" includes Angola, Mozambique, and other countries, and therefore is "really" almost as large as all of Western Europe. The chalked commentary ("bullshit") challenges that assertion—and, by implication, the logic in which it is grounded. The key feature for us was not the photo-with-commentary, however, but that we had a collaborator in our picture-taking. An old woman, a stranger to us, voluntarily kept a look-out down the nearby cross-street to be sure no one was in sight and, as soon as we were done shooting, hurried away. (When we returned an hour or so later, the poster had vanished from the wall.)

Chapter One

Bürger's argument, as we have seen, has it that individual works of literature can be understood as effects within, or in relation to, a specific set of systematic, institutional-level rules and expectations for their creation, reception, circulation, and exchange—"commerce" in the sense in which he uses the term. As regards creation and reception, his is in effect a reception-theory argument (he would disagree with that statement) save that he adds the central concept of institution to the production/reception scenario and focuses his work on the area defined by that addition. He thereby both reduces the degree of presupposed normativity necessary for coherence in the uses to which the phenomenologically based reception models coming from Jauss, Iser, and others are put and also explores the linkages to the shape of the actual commerce in art. The addition of the institutional also enables him to examine influences coming from social sectors, including the political/governmental—in Althusserian terms, the obvious institutional features of the "state apparatus" (Althusser 127–86)—for which none of the major strands of reception theory readily account.

One of the weaknesses of Bürger's argument in *Theory of the Avant-Garde*, however, is that it does not devote much detailed work to the sociological dimension that it invokes—most especially, the sites and means of socialization of the aforementioned rules and expectations. In response to criticism on that score, however, he does, in his "Postscript" to the second German edition of *Theory* (Bürger 95–99), mention as obvious vehicles such areas of society as the education system and art/literary criticism, museums, and art/literary histories. In this connection, we can look back on Ribeiro's push to see the Portuguese educational curriculum grounded in "Portuguese philosophy," with its implied hermeneutic rules for application to Portuguese cultural products, as precisely an initiative to capture one of those sites, namely, education, for his traditionalistic outlook. (In terms of actual history, the power of the *Estado Novo* ensured that the capture was successfully made in general terms,[10] though it did not involve the inclusion of "Portuguese philosophy" per se as a curricular item.)

A significant struggle within the area of literary criticism in the Portugal of the 1950s and 1960s puts these several issues on display, highlighting the role of one of the vehicles that Bürger mentions in socializing what I refer to above as "that area of the literary institution … that includes the rules for literary reception." It also profiles the actual stakes involved. The struggle, again, takes place in part over the creation/interpretation of Fernando Pessoa.

Let us look at two exemplary critical pieces. The first is from a mid-1950s article by the aforementioned Jacinto do Prado Coelho, not only chair professor at the University of Lisbon but also, in the 1960s, one of the chief editors of Pessoa's literary remains. The article's title is "Fernando Pessoa's Utopian Nationalism" ("O Nacionalismo Utópico de Fernando Pessoa") (in *A Letra* 271–85). Its argument is less one for a "utopian" nationalism than one for a nationalism that serves as a kind of correlative for personal, cultural, and aesthetic preoccupations attributed to Pessoa: "… Pessoa prefers to invent Portugal shut up in his own ivory tower" (274). That is, for Prado Coelho an undercutting subjective side, which he links to a "European aesthetic restlessness" (272) on Pessoa's part and to an ironic outlook (278), is dominant in that poet's use of nationalistic discourse:

> [I]t is by placing his eyes on the future, on a subjective, mythic Portugal, that Pessoa defines Portuguese art; to define he doesn't need to observe, just to dream. Doesn't this portrait of Portugal look like a self-portrait, the image of the uprooted, divided, dispersed poet capable of defending with equal conviction (or lack thereof) the ideas of [the poetic heteronym] Fernando Pessoa "himself" and the opposed ideas of [another of Pessoa's poetic heteronyms] Álvaro de Campos? (279)

The other article comes from the late 1960s and was written by Prado Coelho's approximate contemporary, the aforementioned Amândio César—journalist, Technical School teacher in Lisbon, and, in the 1950s and 1960s, a prolific creative writer, essayist, and cultural commentator and, as has been noted, frequent contributor to the *Diário de Notícias*'s "Paragraphs on Overseas Literature." His general critical orientation can best be signaled by reference to the publication in which this particular article appeared: while publication site does not betoken political orientation in some determinate way, *Gil Vicente* (1925–1974) was in fact a right-wing publication connected, in its origins, to the Portuguese Integralist movement. In the 1960s, César appeared in its pages with some regularity, and his work is quite consonant with its editorial directions.

In "Fernando Pessoa, Poet of *Mensagem*" ("Fernando Pessoa, Poeta de *Mensagem*"), César's way of dealing with the combination of nationalistic and "subjective" discourses in Pessoa's book of poetry is quite clear:

> You cannot say that Pessoa was a political-party poet, though personally, as a man, he may have followed a certain doctrinaire line. But when he sang Portugal he was simply a Portuguese feeling within himself the past that was the soil in which he imagined that the tree that he desired, or dreamed of, as great with future or futuration would grow. (155)

And he ends up characterizing the structure of the book as the "mystic body [of the nation]" (156), observing that "the doctrinal body of *Mensagem* can be profoundly felt by us who are there as the People" (156).

Both Prado Coelho and César ultimately base their reception on an allegorical arrangement (though in both cases the issue is more complex than that bald statement suggests). For his part, Prado Coelho sees the "subjective" side as dominant and the national-historical discourses as dependent on it, while César sees a pulling-together of the two sets of items in what he calls "tension," but a pulling-together that in effect subordinates the subjective side to the nationalistic one through use of specific tactics that, as we move on, will presently come to the fore.

For Prado Coelho, Pessoa is "European" because he is ever restless, ever "ironic" about his own production, and/or about language itself. Ultimately, for him, Pessoa is the European high modernist, for whom art is the organizing principle for life. (That view would come to dominate the classical critical literature on Pessoa.) That attitude, in the context of the political stakes of literary critical modes, paints Prado Coelho as, in a broad sense, a liberal—in institutional terms if not in political ones. By contrast, César argues that *Mensagem* combines the sense of the Portuguese lyric-nationalist writers of the turn of the twentieth century with a complexity of vision that supersedes those prior writers' simple vision without destroying the nationalistic element that, to his mind, they have in common. To César's argumentation comes linked that of António Quadros, which asserts that Pessoa in effect reads Portuguese nationality within himself and engages in a cultural-spiritual "mission" made possible by his own embodiment of the nationality (311–22). The clash of outlooks here described can be carried much farther, and there are many more points antagonistically in common, so to speak.

If we take into account such statements as Prado Coelho's that "Pessoa's portrait of Portugal looks like a self-portrait" or that "it is by [Pessoa's] placing [of] his eyes on the future, on a subjective, mythic Portugal that [he] defines Portuguese art" and think of them as initiating an explanatory regress from the work in question to hermeneutic rules—to, then, the sphere of literary institutionality—we see, first, an emphasis on issues of artistic subjectivity. Quite apart from the specific issues of reading immediately at hand, the reader is being instructed to see his or her task as involving understanding of such issues as the complex of interrelationships among a producer, the artistic medium involved, and some sort of referential gesture. That understanding is to come in a one-to-one relationship between producer and receiver. No language-level elements intervene between the two save those of "art" and of a transparent natural language (one therefore conceived very differently from the traditionalists' "language"). The reader is being told that he/she can learn to work with the specific structures of both of those elements. (Or, more likely, the reader is having such instruction, received multiple times before, here reinforced.) Reception is thus directed: the reader is being told or reminded through that regress how the task and structure of reading such texts is constituted, namely, that they involve the "meeting" of an individually produced text and a reader whose principal tools are transparent linguistic and abstract analytical ones. Such passages, then, present the reader with hermeneutic rules for *Mensagem* in particular and also the general hermeneutic rules for literary (here, poetry) reading as a mode of activity.

In the other of our paired examples we encounter César's "mystic body" metaphor—one clearly drawn from Catholic symbology and equally clearly indicative of a form of transubstantial identity between poet and nation. Moreover, that identity "can be profoundly felt by us … ," with the "us" referring to a presupposed community pre-united by Portuguese nationality. In effect, then, reading has as its ground that same transubstantial identity between reader and author/text. César thus propounds hermeneutic rules grounded in a preexisting, nationalistic commonality. (This is what I meant earlier when I said that César's reading allegory involved some specific tactics: he actually takes one of the terms in "tension," namely, nationalism, and makes it the arbiter of the allegorical relationship as well.) As his diction suggests, for him reception is a matter of a "feeling" (Ribeiro used the term *intuition*) that precedes—and likely therefore eliminates—complex analytical reading processes, a feeling originating in the message's articulation of the national-ethical element presumed to ground the reader-text encounter itself. Seen as a regress to the sphere of institutionality, such a view argues for a very different institutionally mandated reception scenario, one in which, first of all, *Mensagem* is a highly privileged kind of text (Prado Coelho is pointedly responding to this sort of reading of *Mensagem* in his article). It is a text in which the phenomenology of reception has a quite specific—and nationally idiosyncratic—nature. This arrangement clearly does not require the presence of an autonomous sphere of literary institutionality constituted of values and rules in para-economic circulation. Indeed, it would be undercut by that presence.

A number of roughly parallel instances could be noted of the traditionalists' argument that a national-ethical element grounds hermeneutic practice. A classic example comes in relation to the "Exposition of the Portuguese World," put on by the *Estado Novo* in Lisbon in 1940. It is reported that in the section of the exposition dealing with Portuguese history (this is not to say that it was otherwise in other sections) a clear, consistent effort was made to have visitors "feel" history rather than look at it intellectually. The analogy with Ribeiro's scholastically conceived "intuition" and César's description of Pessoa's "Portuguese feeling" is clear. The documents produced by Exposition organizers—generally post-factum—show as much. One such document, from after the Exposition, actually summarizes that approach: "At the Exposition of the Portuguese World [historical] documents were not read, they were only felt … [T]he eyes comprehended everything just by looking" ["Na Exposição do Mundo Português não se leram documentos; sentiram-se apenas … [T]udo os olhos entenderam só de olhá-los"] (Ramos do Ó 181). That strategy, of course, could represent a calculated response to low public literacy rates, but it also fits perfectly into *Estado Novo* dictates in the area of hermeneutics. Indeed, the Director of the Exposition, Augusto de Castro, says as much by proclaiming that the Exposition, thus strategized, was "the celebration of Portugal's encounter with itself" ["a festa do encontro de Portugal consigo próprio"] (179). It was a self-encounter, then, structured to avoid analysis, not to mention the possible conceiving of critique.[11]

In the Prado Coelho–César contrast and the roughly parallel instance of the hermeneutic presumptions in the 1940 Exposition, we see how the practical rhetoric of such endeavors as literary-critical writing and the representation of cultural history is, in my terminology, "written as well in the institutional sphere." The phrase is one of my own coining, which, at the current moment in writing this book, I need in order to think about issues involved with the interpenetration of discourse and institutionality. I shall use it throughout the coming pages. In the use I shall make of it, it draws upon very simple and familiar elements—indeed, ones so familiar that they are implicit in much critical work without being given the codification that I seek to give them here.

The concept "writing as well in the institutional sphere" can be explained in several ways; I shall try one that has the value of economy. Relying on the concept of social "sphere" already introduced and grounding myself loosely in the Marxist concept of the reproduction of the conditions of production (the *locus classicus* being the essay on Feuerbach in *The German Ideology* [Marx and Engels 3–78]), I understand "writing as well in the institutional sphere" to say, in the dimensions that concern us in this book, that production is always enabled/authorized by existing social structure, be it material or superstructural. Cultural production—whether it be the creation of a cultural product or the performance of the reception of that product—thus comes grounded in socially based authorizing rules and procedures. "Writing as well in the institutional sphere" signals several matters in this regard. Let me mention three. First is the basic fact that a work of literature comes grounded in such authorizing conditions—in phenomenological terms, in its received "horizon." (While it conceives of itself in other terms, Aristotle's *Poetics* is constructed upon that position, as are all neo-Aristotelian critical modes, much stylistic criticism, Anglo-American New Criticism, and many other critical modalities.) Second, that work's self-deployment in its effort to communicate with the potential receiver—who is presumed to bear the reception side of that same received horizon—manifests that grounding. That is, as we read it, a literary text perforce tells us readers what terms it wants us to meet it on, presuming that we are competent within the current horizon of literary-hermeneutical expectations (which is historical and therefore ever evolving; moreover, in a given situation, there may be competing and perhaps even overlapping subsets of rules within a given horizon). While we can say that all literary writing is, from beginning to end, "written as well in the institutional sphere" in the sense that it necessarily exists in an authorizing relationship to a current horizon, a work can express such grounding in recognizable ways—through more-or-less-overt reference to one or more of the enabling conditions (I have previously labeled some of those enabling conditions "hermeneutic rules"). It is such overt reference that I usually refer to as "writing as well in the institutional sphere," and in those cases the phrase can reasonably be shortened to "writing in the institutional sphere" as long as we bear in mind that it is necessarily always one of two simultaneous "writings," the other being the authorized linear writing, the written or spoken "cues" that we receive as we receive a text. (Actually, one can point to more than just two simultaneous "writings" in what we receive; the point, however, is not crucial for what follows.) Practically speaking, then, the concept "writing in the institutional sphere" usually designates a passage, a figure, a formula within a text where such reference is patent, that textual feature, then, initiating what I have been calling a "regress" to the "institutional sphere"—"regress" because the enabling conditions precede the reception relying upon them. In practical terms, a given passage in a work of literature can refer us more or less openly to the rule or rules that govern our "commerce" with it. In simple terms: "You're supposed to read me (and other works like me) this way, and here is why." Third: we can read these messages conveyed to us by the text if we maintain awareness of that task as we read.

Approached with an eye to this issue, such discourses as criticism, education theory and methodology, and some areas of public policy discourse can be read, in detail, as overt, ready-made institutional-sphere operators. The comments made by the organizers of the 1940 Exposition fit roughly into the last of those categories, while the hermeneutic rules simultaneously relied upon and promulgated by such as Prado Coelho and César illuminate regresses within the area of literary criticism, albeit an area conceived of by the two in wholly conflicting ways. In the area of literature, many "scenes of reading" can be understood as initiating regresses to the "institutional sphere." By the term *scene of reading* I refer principally to passages that New-Critical exegesis used to refer to as loci that suggested modes of literary reading, usually the reading of the work in which they appear. More recent use of the term involves psychoanalytic reading, following the lead of such as Mary Jacobus. The "scenes of reading" singled out by Jacobus in *Psychoanalysis and the Scene of Reading* are totally open to analysis as "writing as well in the institutional sphere." So too are *artes poeticae*, literary manifestos, and the like.

The ample recourse I shall have to the concept of "writing in the institutional sphere" in the following pages will both exemplify the term and add further dimensions of meaning to it.

* * *

Now in the institutional-sphere struggle in *Estado-Novo* Portugal, political power was on the side of the traditionalist outlook—literally to the death. As we have seen, the *Estado Novo* cultivated and propagated the hyper-nation: a set of institutional-sphere practices ranging from control over the ability to put language into the public domain, on the one hand, to the attempt to govern how experience would be interpreted, on another, down to the regulation of how literature should be read—all grounded in the nationality in roughly the ways we have seen illustrated. As is made clear in the language and outlook of exponents of the "traditionalist position" outlined in the preceding pages, those practices were articulated and justified by continual reference to a specific version of Portuguese history and status as a colonial power. The history, generally referred to in critical circles today as "the monumental historical narrative" or one of a number of varieties of such phraseology (e.g., Costa Pinto, "Twentieth-Century Portugal" 35–36; Monteiro and Costa Pinto 207, 213–14), regularly included periodization much like that proposed by Ribeiro (p. 22, above). It also included highly codified explanatory discourses about figures of the medieval and early modern periods and the deeds attributed to them. The historian António Costa Pinto summarizes succinctly: "… [under the *Estado Novo*] the official version of Portuguese history was rigidly codified. History was revised and relative pluralism eliminated" ("Twentieth-Century Portugal" 35). Motifs that recur in the *Estado-Novo* historical narratives include the proposition that Portugal was founded by divine act and that its "monumental" past is all the more remarkable given the smallness of the country—with, all but needless to say, the former proposition being presented as explanatory of the latter.

This "national" mythology is, of course, specific to Portugal only because of its (considerable) peculiarities—despite claims of uniqueness on the part of Portuguese nationalist thinkers (cf. the epigraph to this chapter). Like European nationalisms in general (including those produced in the European-colonized Western Hemisphere), its roots lie in the late eighteenth and early nineteenth centuries, though—again like the others—it claims much greater antiquity for itself. Like the others it has functioned as an effective socio-cultural agglutinating force for post-Absolutist society in both the cultural and the economic spheres. It has done so through the construction of supposed social commonalities—typically a uniformly shared history and/or an ethnic/racial commonality. Most importantly for present purposes, like the others it involves a set of discourses that can only be termed "ideological," since they have no verifiable basis beyond their own, often admirably creative, assertions.[12] (Henceforth, when I repeat the terms *nation, national,* and *nationality,* I wish it understood that I am naming a category within my object of study, not an item from within my own analytical discourse.)

Now I am not claiming much coherence for Portuguese fascist nationalist thought; pressed at all, it falls into a jumble of internal contradictions, only some of which have we seen in the preceding pages. Nor am I claiming high operative value for it either: it is doubtful that the average Portuguese either behaved according to it or even accepted it, especially by the 1960s (Sousa Santos 43). But it did hold sway politically and grounded state policy, particularly in the areas of education and publishing. Hence its most powerful function: it served quite successfully to limit the possible links that might be fashioned by Portuguese between day-to-day experience and the nationality about which they frequently heard: in effect, it had success as a cultural regulator just because of its social power, albeit in many social spheres a power more subtly wielded than the label "fascist" is wont to signal.

The foregoing pages suggest not only some of the issues at stake within the hyper-nation that was fascist Portugal but also ways of understanding them in some of the key areas that comprise literary institutionality: the precariousness of the autonomous sphere of art, the complex relationship between literary texts and features of literary institutionality, and particularly the critical promulgation/enforcement of institutional-level hermeneutic rules that involved a reception practice in which reception was asserted to have a "national" ground, thus was open only to Portuguese on the basis of a kind of identification with that ground, and therefore not only did not require a strong analytical dimension but in fact functioned more nearly optimally without one.

I shall now, having recourse to this brief historical précis and these critical concepts and terms, return to pursuit of the smile question.

* * *

José Saramago was born on November 16, 1922 in the village of Azinhaga, in the province of Ribatejo, in central Portugal. He was moved to Lisbon as a youth and was educated there. Born to a family of scant means—in effect, a peasant family seeking to better itself by moving to the capital—he was the recipient of technical training as a machinist and began productive life in the mechanical trades. He later went into public service and from there into journalism and publishing. In 1969 he joined the Portuguese Communist Party, which had been outlawed by the fascist state; he remained a member for the rest of his life. In the early 1970s he was an editor and political columnist of the *Diário de Lisboa*. After the Revolution of April 1974 that overthrew the *Estado Novo* he was the adjunct director of the Lisbon *Diário de Notícias*—the aforementioned unofficial regime organ—being dismissed from that position upon the anti-left uprising within the military in November 1975. From early in his life, he wrote literature. His first work, the novel *Terra do Pecado* ("Land of Sin") was published in 1947. From the second half of the 1960s on, he produced poetry, novels, short stories, and theater in earnest. After his dismissal from the *Diário de Notícias,* he turned full-time to writing. The novel *Memorial do Convento*, in 1982, brought him international recognition, which was increased by *O Ano da Morte de Ricardo Reis*, in 1984. A large number of novels and other works followed. In 1998 he received the Nobel Prize for Literature, the first recipient of that prize from the Portuguese-speaking world. Saramago died in 2010 at age 87.

Chapter Two

Baltasar and Blimunda
The Readership Pact and the Release of Pleasure

> Among the various kinds of internal inhibition or suppression there is one which ... is given the name of "repression" and is recognized by its function of preventing the impulses subjected to it, and their derivatives, from becoming conscious. Tendentious jokes ... are able to release pleasure even from sources that have undergone repression.
>
> —Sigmund Freud
> *Jokes and Their Relation to the Unconscious*

Given that I have identified this project on the ground of personal anecdote about reading (though, as I have indicated, other readers' reactions echo my own), it seems fitting that I launch my exploration at that point. In this chapter I shall therefore be using my own readerly experience with *Baltasar and Blimunda* as the starting point for the development of a phenomenology of reading for the novel. Please recall that as the basis for that development I shall be inventorying, in phenomenological reduction, features of my own reception, a process that fits roughly within the parameters that Iser (*The Act of Reading*) creates for that combination of cultural competency and textual activity that is his "reader." But recall as well that I shall be moving in and out of that position as I explore, and reason from, specifics that arise as I seek to cast some of its results in a light that will further my smile pursuit. When alluding to my own readerly reactions I shall use first-person singular pronominals. I count on the reader of these pages to differentiate such instances from ones—this paragraph is full of them—in which I make use of an authorial-editorial "I."

Chapter Two

* * *

I do not recall a specific passage that first elicited my smile. More likely, they were "passages" in the plural, for the effects that Saramago's novels create usually come through accumulation of many touches. I do, however, recall that, in reading, I was experiencing a curious sense of joy and feeling of liberation that clearly had something to do with the expectations that I brought with me to my encounter with the text and with the text's particular and unusual way of articulating with those expectations. That experience continued on through my reading of the novel and, indeed, in modified forms, characterized as well my reading of the author's two subsequent "historical" texts. Let me, to begin, go to that same starting-place: *Baltasar and Blimunda*'s first two small chapters—important but hardly crucial sections within the overall novel structure, and therefore in a sense, chance selections.

Baltasar and Blimunda begins with an "inside" narrative précis of the two-year-old marriage of King John V of Portugal and Maria Anna Josepha of Austria as regards the crucial topic of production of an heir to the Portuguese throne. The represented year is 1711. The précis is rendered by a narrative voice that, from the outset, includes what might be termed a historical-anthropological dimension in its outlook—i.e., it analyzes, in front of me the reader, the cultural practices of the royal palace in early-eighteenth-century Lisbon almost as though it were carrying out an ethnographic study. Simultaneously, through its choices in diction and rhetoric, it emits side observations and innuendoes about its object of analysis that I can only receive as sarcastic and irreverent. For example, on the novel's very first page—beginning, in fact, with its second sentence—I receive the following narrative remark on the issue of issue:

> Already there are rumors ... that the Queen may be barren... The thought that the problem might lie with the King is not even to be entertained, first because infertility is a malady that befalls not men but only women, who are often disowned as a consequence; and second because there is material proof, should any be required, in the legion of bastards sprung from the royal seed who are filling the realm—a process that, to say the least, continues on unabated.
>
> [Já se murmura na corte ... que a rainha, provavelmente, tem a madre seca ... Que caiba a culpa ao rei, nem pensar, porque

a esterilidade não é mal dos homens, das mulheres sim, por isso são repudiadas tantas vezes, e segundo, material prova, se necessária ela fosse, porque abundam no reino bastardos da real semente e ainda agora a procissão vai na praça. (*Memorial do Convento* 11)]

I note that the narrative voice thus immediately establishes an overt practice of simultaneously representing, analyzing, and undercutting the symbolic of the time. Analyzing in such authoritative-sounding phrases in discernment of period convictions as "infertility is a malady that befalls not men but only women, who are often disowned as a consequence." Undercutting in such phrasing as "the thought that the problem might lie with the King is not even to be entertained." The Portuguese phraseology of this second utterance—which is roughly identical in rhetorical terms to my translation—is actually common in daily speech, but its use in this application is much more powerful than is the case in daily usage. A kind of litotes, it names a thought in the very process of declaring its interdiction, thereby in this case also naming a social figure—the absolute monarch—powerful enough to be the subject of such interdiction. It thus brings the specific interdiction to the light of day. And then—too late—it rhetorically reestablishes that interdiction in what comes off as a mock gesture. The narrator thus in effect winks to me—with a not terribly well disguised wink—intimating that the king is hidden behind a social convention that is at one and the same time socially powerful and highly permeable. That rhetorical gesture leads me through a series of actions and reactions that call up in me, among other matters, both my current and my personal-historical relations to authority figures and to social power—especially any social power presuming to tell me what I must think and how I may carry out analysis of my social environment. It also suggests that I should be aware of the option of looking behind appearances—in general and perhaps specifically in (this) reading. The tone, however, is light-hearted, and I make due note of that tone and cast this reception inventory in a similar mode. I thereby, at the text's invitation, invest a personal quotient in my reading, thus effectively giving over aspects of my subjectivity to the meaning-making of the reading process. In effect, read with an eye to these issues, the passage both directs and thematizes my role more or less as theorized by such as Iser. Rhetorical/readerly gestures like this one recur literally hundreds

Chapter Two

of times throughout the three novels, and their involvement of me through reception follows basically this pattern.

A longer passage that comes shortly after the one reproduced above continues aspects of its lead. It deals with the regular, twice-weekly royal love-making that fervently—and thus far unsuccessfully—seeks to produce offspring:

> [The King's] footmen have helped him to undress and have garbed him in the appropriate ceremonial robes. Each garment has been passed from hand to hand with as much reverence as if it were a holy relic that was used to bless some virgin. The ceremony is enacted in the presence of sundry footmen and pages; one opens the wardrobe, another draws back the curtains; one raises the candelabra, while another regulates the flames. Two footmen stand to attention, and two more follow suit, while several others hover in the background with no apparent duties to fulfill. At long last, thanks to their combined labors, the King is ready. ... At any moment now, Dom João V will be heading for the Queen's bedchamber. The vessel is waiting to be filled. (*Baltasar* 3)

> [Despiram-no os camaristas, vestiram-no com o trajo da função e do estilo, passadas as roupas de mão em mão tão reverentemente como relíquias de santas que tivessem trespassado donzelas, e isto se passa na presença de outros criados e pajens, este que abre o gavetão, aquele que afasta a cortina, um que levanta a luz, outro que lhe modera o brilho, dois que não se movem, dois que imitam estes, mais uns tantos que não se sabe o que fazem nem porque estão. Enfim, de tanto se esforçarem todos ficou preparado el-rei ... já não tarda um minuto que D. João V se encaminhe ao quarto da rainha. O cântaro está à espera da fonte. (*Memorial do Convento* 13)]

I read the likening of the king's robes to a "holy relic" as continuing, in the one term, the mix of symbolic-anthropological analysis and undercutting light sarcasm in which I am asked to react in reception. The references to the "labors"—or, implicitly, lack thereof—of the king's multiple attendants extends the sarcastic element, and the last sentence refers back to an ethnographic-sounding development carried out over the pages of this first chapter that attributes to the characters and to the time period the attitude, in continuation of the ongoing exposition of the symbolic-level misogyny apparently being attributed to eighteenth-century Portugal, that "... a woman is essentially a vessel made to be filled" ["... sendo a mulher, naturalmente, vaso de receber"] (1 [11]). Moreover, it imputes that attitude to the king as he undertakes preparations for this particular installment of the semi-weekly encounter and, in continuing through its rhetoric to try to locate me in the manner we have seen, invites me to adopt a skeptical if not critical position toward that attitude and the practices deriving from it (cf. Piaia).

The narrative development will proceed to the following passage, which marks the end of the royal assignation:

> It is Dona Maria Ana who tugs the bellpull, whereupon the King's footmen enter from one side and the Queen's ladies-in-waiting from the other. Various odors hover in the air and one of them is unmistakable; without its presence the long-awaited miracle could not possibly take place. Besides, the much-quoted immaculate conception of the Virgin Mary occurred but once so that the world might know that Almighty God, when He so chooses, has no need of men, though He cannot dispense with women. (*Baltasar* 7)

> [É D. Maria Ana quem puxa o cordão da sineta, entram de um lado os camaristas do rei, do outro as damas, pairam cheiros diversos na atmosfera pesada, um deles que facilmente identificam, que sem o que a isto cheira não são possíveis milagres como o que desta vez se espera, porque a outra, e tão falada, incorpórea fecundação, foi uma vez sem exemplo, só para que se ficasse a saber que Deus, quando quer, não precisa de homens, embora não possa dispensar-se de mulheres. (*Memorial do Convento* 17)]

In these early passages, then, I the reader, consciously or not, see the narration/narrator carrying out several operations simultaneously. Principally, as we have already observed, he (I shall justify the gender attribution later) manages to sound both sarcastic and historically and ethnographically authoritative at the same time. As regards the authoritative dimension, he speaks quite assuredly as he carries out a symbolic-level analysis of period customs and practices in the process of narrating happenings in which they are embodied. I am therefore given reason to suspect that that authority finds its ultimate ground in historical investigation—i.e., that he is analyzing the fruits of research into

Chapter Two

early-eighteenth-century Portugal and specifically into some of the events and personalities depicted in the novel. And I read under that conviction, with an eye to its full validation in the novel's coming pages.

If I do some parallel digging on the time period (admittedly, in that act exceeding my bounds as either Iserian reader or reader of my own reception and instead becoming a researcher), I find that I have read the signals correctly: a great deal of research is poured, both directly and indirectly, into the pages of *Baltasar and Blimunda*. One of the most striking ways in which that is done involves the inclusion of virtual parallel passages to period documents. While the bedroom scene between the king and queen does not contain any such parallels, such later scenes as the sanctification and the consecration of the Mafra convent closely echo parts of the accumulated literature about the construction project that produced Mafra, much of it harkening back to the nineteenth-century text of Joaquim da Conceição Gomes, though other identifiable sources are involved as well. Indeed, if we consider only Gomes and *Baltasar and Blimunda*, we can see that a number of extended passages in the novel are directly patterned on its antecedent, and specific phrases are all but identical. For example, where, in a part of the consecration scene, Gomes reads:

> No lado esquerdo do cruzeiro armou-se um côro para os músicos, todo guarnecido de damasco carmesim; e havia-se ahi collocado um orgão; proximo do côro fôra estabelecida uma bancada para os conegos da patriarchal. (Gomes 72)

Memorial reads:

> ... à esquerda do cruzeiro armou-se um coro para os músicos, forrado de damasco carmesim, com um órgão que tocará nas ocasiões próprias, e ali estão também, em bancada reservada, os cónegos da patriarcal ... (135)

translatable as:

> To the left of the crucifix an enclosure has been erected for the musicians, draped with crimson damask, and complete with an organ that will be played at the appropriate moments. The canons of the diocese will sit in specially reserved seats ... (*Baltasar* 119)

Clearly, in this case the English comes only as an explanatory gloss of the Portuguese. What is important is comparison of the two Portuguese texts: Saramago is quite deliberately putting the Gomes text into his own. In effect, the hints in the text—principally, just its authoritative tone—have led me to discover that documentary texture has figuratively been poured onto the page, but had I not done the research necessary to discover that fact the hints would still support my readerly conviction that something like that is indeed what is happening. This importation of language from the historical record, language related to the period in question, is a consistent practice, albeit in different realizations, in all three of Saramago's historical novels, as we shall have the opportunity to see.

Simultaneously—for example, in the sarcastic picking-up of the conviction that "woman is essentially a vessel made to be filled"—the narrator ironizes some of the results both of the historical research he is representing and also of the "anthropological" analysis he is in the process of carrying out. Indeed, the narration is set up in such a way that not only do I receive, for example, the aforestated conviction about women as analysis of the symbolic attributed to the time but I also simultaneously receive it as a statement that raises questions about aspects of that symbolic. I am thus presented with a structural irony to unravel: the first reception—namely, the one made historico-anthropologically in establishment and analysis of the characters and their era—is being rejected as inadequate, and that rejection is presented with a touch of humor. I am thus pushed, in order to read successfully, to create a second analytical discourse that comprises the anthropological outlook (which—unless I have recourse to such as my parallel digging—I have to take on faith, comes grounded in responsible research) and a strong critical dimension: one that interrogates the results of that first, transparently anthropological impulse. This is not to say that the creation of such a discourse is my only possible response; it is, however, obviously the response the text seeks to impress upon me, and it is one I accept. As regards the particular matter at hand, this set of practices is capped by the narrative observation—in virtually the deconstructive pointing-out of a constitutive aporia in the eighteenth-century symbolic—that God has no need of man but apparently cannot dispense with woman. That claim, in my reading, sets up an ironic dissonance with the represented symbolic of the time that reduces woman to "essentially a vessel made to be filled" by man. At very least, it is being hinted that something has been overlooked: in a sense that is very important for the symbolic itself, the presumably empty or inconsequential "vessel" is more important than the (self-)designated agent of the "filling." I am virtually required to deal with that aporia if I am to successfully carry out my role as reader. The aporia is also an example of one form of a "constitutive blank" (Iser, *Act* 167), the presence of which in the text necessarily enlists my reception activity, which in turn enlists and utilizes my subjectivity (see Chapter 1, p. 17).

Several other matters attract my readerly focus as I seek to orient myself within the novel's first chapter. One prominent matter has to do with the constitution of the narrative voice and narrative position. In those passages the narrator presents himself to me with attributes of ethnographer, ironist, and irreverent commentator. In very simple terms, for example, while it is not unprecedented, it is unusual and therefore shocking to see the lives of Portuguese kings and queens discussed, in print, in such terms as appear in *Baltasar and Blimunda*—and especially in this tone of voice. Traditionally, in serious writing in Portuguese—especially when traditionalism rules the day, as under the *Estado Novo*—the facts about such as a royal marriage and similar "inside" issues, especially any that might be unflattering, may be given in dry, historical discourse but not have fun poked at them, much less become the subject of comic speculation. The interdictions broken before my eyes in the first small passage reproduced above are, then, two. First, the period taboo against imagining that the male of the species—not to mention the King of Portugal!—might ever be infertile. Second, the taboo, more or less contemporary to my reading, against treatment in this manner of the sex lives of Portuguese sovereigns within any literature designed to be taken seriously. Moreover, the two are complexly linked: the first raises questions, especially if we locate my reading in the post-revolutionary period, about the inherited "monumental" version of Portuguese history; the second, of course, is a general version that comprises the first as well as others and is equally applicable to 1711 and the 1982 date of this novel's first public reading. I thus begin to identify a complex transtemporality at work within the revelation of the interdictory structure.

It is of interest as well to note that the object of this scrutiny, King John V, was in the post-revolutionary period one of the points around which struggle for (re-)interpretation of Portuguese history took place. John V had been treated quite kindly in the monumental version: as a provident monarch whose reign marked a regeneration of Portugal's standing amongst European countries. After the revolution, revisionists saw him as absolutistic, self-indulgent, lavish, and uncaring of the populace (Oliveira Marques 569–70; Frier, "Padre"). His representation in *Baltasar and Blimunda* participates in that struggle and, again, implicitly urges me to do so as well—presumably from some revisionist position.

A second narrative dimension introduced at the outset of *Baltasar and Blimunda* is related to that transtemporality: it is narrative pan-historicity. In a passage that comes between the preceding two reproduced from the first chapter, as the king is preparing to depart for the queen's bedchamber and their encounter of this night, Nuno da Cunha, an influential bishop and head of the Inquisition, and an elderly Franciscan friar named António de São José come to speak to him. The narrator breezily remarks:

> Before he [Nuno da Cunha] approaches the King to deliver his news, there is an elaborate ritual to be observed with reverences and salutations, pauses and retreats. These constitute the necessary protocol when approaching the monarch. We shall treat these formalities as having been duly observed, given the urgency of the bishop's visit and the nervous tremors of the elderly friar. (*Baltasar* 3–4)
>
> [Entre passar adiante e dizer o recado há vénias complicadas, floreios de aproximação, pausas e recuos, que são as fórmulas de acesso à vizinhança do rei, e a tudo isto teremos de dar por feito e explicado, vista a pressa que traz o bispo e considerando o tremor inspirado do frade. (*Memorial do Convento* 13)]

Here, as regularly in the text, the narrator points himself out as a narrative focus alien to the represented world of the text. That is, the narrator presents himself not as some technical voice inherent in the historical horizon of the narration, as is the case in the conventional historical novel, but as a historically situated locus of narrative production: he exists in the present—historically, the time of the publication of *Baltasar and Blimunda* and functionally in the time of its production by, and communication with,

47

Chapter Two

me—but is capable of imaginatively penetrating the fictional world he is rendering in representation of a Portugal of nearly three centuries earlier. He is, for example, quite ready to allude to the 1974 Revolution that overthrew the *Estado Novo*—such allusion is made in one way or another in all three historical novels, thus becoming a key touchpoint in narrator-reader communication. In *Baltasar and Blimunda* the allusion is one made to carnations that "one day" will be put into "the barrels of rifles" (139 [156])—a gesture that came to symbolize the 1974 "Carnation Revolution." This pan-historicity, which is realized in a number of complex ways in Saramago's writings, is doubtless one overt marker of the phenomenon that Eduardo Lourenço points to when he observes, in a gnomic phrase, that Saramago's historical works "represent the opportunity to revisit the present" (E. Lourenço, *Nau* 100 [*Little Lusitanian House* 124]).

That passing allusion to 1974 and others like it clearly presume an ideal reader who is a contemporary Portuguese—who therefore understands that he or she is living in a moment shortly after that rupture in the history of the country that is being alluded to. Hence another dimension of the (historical) ethnographer and one that complicates it considerably—because, seen in the simplest of terms, it produces what can only be called anachronism. For example, in such passages as those reproduced and alluded to above, in which the attitude that "woman is essentially a vessel made to be filled" is ironized, that irony appears to take on a retroactive dimension that would seem to say "we here in the late twentieth century can look askance upon the attitudes of the early-eighteenth." (This anachronistic effect has much more about it, however, as we shall soon see.)

Narrator deployment is a highly distinctive feature of these first pages and—as I learn in moving on—will remain so throughout the novel. For example, in contrast to taking up a constant point of view, as is the conventional arrangement today deriving from the para-scientific practice of the nineteenth-century-style novel, the narrator changes position frequently, sometimes rapidly; witness his discussion with me in the passage immediately above, about how he is going to vary his narrative procedure on this occasion—comically alleging that he is doing so because of the characters' haste. The narrator of *Baltasar and Blimunda* can be all-knowing at one moment, declare his ignorance at another, seemingly be impersonal at the next, address me immediately thereafter, and so on. And from passage to passage he can locate himself very differently within or in relation to the represented world of eighteenth-century Portugal (cf. A. Lourenço 75–77; also, re "historiographical metafiction," see Hutcheon 11). The changes in point of view are often abrupt, thereby calling my attention to themselves. Sometimes such change is even discussed openly. The following passage, from toward the end of the novel, after Baltasar and Blimunda have been separated and Blimunda vainly searches for her lover, involves just such a discussion pushed to the point of philosophy:

> [T]here is neither shepherd nor flock but only a deep silence as Blimunda comes to a halt, only a deep solitude as she looks around her. Monte Junto is so close she has the impression that she need only stretch a hand to touch those foothills, like a woman on her knees who is stretching out an arm to touch her lover's hips. Blimunda was clearly incapable of such subtle thoughts; therefore, we are perhaps not inside these people and cannot tell what they are thinking. All we are doing is putting our own thoughts into the heads of others and then saying: Blimunda thinks, or Baltasar thought. Perhaps we have also imagined them with our own sensations, just as when Blimunda touches her lover's hips and imagines that he has touched hers. (*Baltasar* 315–16)

> [Não há pastor nem rebanho, apenas um profundo silêncio quando Blimunda pára, uma solidão profunda quando olha em redor. O Monte Junto está tão perto que parece bastar estender a mão para lhe chegar aos contrafortes, como uma mulher de joelhos que estende o braço e toca as ancas do seu homem. Não é possível que Blimunda tenha pensado esta subtileza, e daí, quem sabe, nós não estamos dentro das pessoas, sabemos lá o que elas pensam, andamos é a espalhar os nossos próprios pensamentos pelas cabeças alheias e depois dizemos, Blimunda pensa, Baltasar pensou, e talvez lhes tivéssemos imaginado as nossas próprias sensações, por exemplo, esta de Blimunda nas suas ancas, como se lhes tivesse tocado o seu homem. (*Memorial do Convento* 341–42)

The implications of this brief meditation reach to the point of bringing up the transferential entailments of narration—and of reading—not to mention basic issues of epistemology. Also,

Chapter Two

the meditation's impact serves to keep me from undertaking a hermeneutical practice based on strong identification with the characters, an effect created at the novel's outset and, as here, reinforced throughout. But the passage's most obvious effect is to raise for me the question of the constitution of the narrative point of view—in this novel and in general—specifically as regards the limits of knowledge. This meditation does not, however, keep the narrator from soon returning, without explanation, to the very omniscience that he is questioning in the passage. Other attributes of the narrative voice, as well as other entire dimensions of narrative deployment, are added to the mix as the novel moves on. (I should point out that most of the foregoing does not constitute innovative reading on my part. Indeed it reiterates bedrock literary criticism of Saramago's work [e.g., Frier, *Novels* 31–43]—albeit doing so within an analytical context and for analytical purposes that differ from standard literary-critical ones.)

Finally, there is another factor that accompanies these narrative phenomena: as we have already seen, I, as reader, am in multiple ways involved in them. For the moment, we shall look at what we can call the "transactional" aspect of that involvement—understood as the dynamic interplay between narrator seen as the locus of rule-providing and me, the reader of literature socialized as such, attempting to make meaning of this particular novel text. In the passage reproduced above about the highly ritualized ceremony attendant upon approach to the king (p. 47), I am both addressee of the narrative remarks about that ceremony and perhaps part of the "we" along with the narrator. I am thus narratively endowed with the same pan-historical space that he arrogates to himself. I am invited, by the force of the deployment of the text and my participation in making its meaning, to share, according to the dictates of the invitation, all the various features in the narrator's self-positioning with regard to Portuguese history, both intellectual and perspectival, that we have seen thus far (save, of course, that of ethnographer, for which function, as we have also seen, I am constrained to accept what I am told, persuaded by textual hints of reliability). For example, when the interdiction against thinking that it might be the king who is infertile is exploded rhetorically in the third sentence, I am asked by the narrator to share in that irreverent debunking and to examine my own analytical position in the light of it, and I am, in subsequent, similar rhetorical gestures, virtually shown how to look at an event or a document from multiple angles, how to seek opportunities to understand and to carry out similar analytically based irreverence on my own part. In effect, I am invited to look upon Portuguese history with an attitude similar to the narrator's, and a part of that invitation is the implicit call to share the narrator's breezy, irreverent, and structurally ironic attitude toward that history (for a critical analysis that parallels my "reception/reading," see Arnaut and also her references).

Now to return to my incipient reading of my own reception of the novel's first pages. Coupled with the focus in the first chapter on the sexual practices of the king and queen, as well as the issue of issue, is a connection to the traditional Catholicism of the time. The aged Franciscan friar who has come to see the king is regarded as a visionary. He says that if the king will agree to build a convent for the Franciscan Order in the hill village of Mafra (roughly twenty-five kilometers north of Lisbon), he can guarantee that the queen will bear a son. In his concern to have a legitimate heir, the king agrees. One of the principal plot lines of the novel—and one that gives it its title in the original Portuguese—involves the consequent building of the monastery, church, and national palace of Mafra.

The second chapter deals principally with incidents of theft involving Lisbon churches and clerics. It then moves back to deal with the matter of the king's pledge and its historical fulfillment in the building of Mafra. At the end of the chapter are the following lines:

> [B]ecause the Franciscans are so well endowed with means to change, overturn, or hasten the natural order of things, even the recalcitrant womb of the Queen must respond to the solemn injunction of a miracle. All the more so since the Franciscan Order has been petitioning for a convent in Mafra since the year sixteen twenty-four... . [S]ix years ago, in seventeen hundred and five, ... the Royal Court of Appeal turned down the petition ... [B]ut now [the court judges] will have to hold their tongues ... , for Frei António de São José has promised that once the friars have their convent there will be an heir to the throne. A pledge has been made, the Queen will give birth, and the Franciscan Order will gather the palm of victory, just as it has gathered so many palms of martyrdom. A hundred years of waiting is no great sacrifice for those who count on living

Chapter Two

> for all eternity. ... [I]t would be folly to suggest that because of secrets divulged in the confessional the friars knew of the Queen's pregnancy even before the Queen herself knew and could confide in the King. Just as it would be wrong to suggest that Dona Maria Ana, because she was such a pious lady, agreed to remain silent until the appearance of God's chosen messenger, the virtuous Frei António. ... There is nothing to add to what has already been said. So let not Franciscans be impugned, unless they should become involved in other equally dubious intrigues. (*Baltasar* 15–16)

> [(S)endo tão favorecidos os franciscanos de meios para alterarem, inverterem ou acelerarem a ordem natural das coisas, até a matriz renitente da rainha obedecerá à fulminante injunção do milagre. Tanto mais que convento em Mafra o anda a querer a ordem de São Francisco desde mil seiscentos e vinte e quatro ... (A)penas há seis anos ... , em mil setecentos e cinco, deu parecer desfavorável o Desembargo do Paço a nova petição ... [M]as agora [os desembargadores] vão ter de engolir a língua ... , que já disse frei António de S. José que convento havendo, haverá sucessão. A promessa está feita, a rainha parirá, a ordem franciscana colherá a palma da vitória, ela que do martírio tantas colheu. Cem anos à espera não será excessiva mortificação para quem conta viver a eternidade. ... Agora não se vá dizer que, por segredos de confissão divulgados, souberam os arrábidos que a rainha estava grávida antes mesmo que ela o participasse ao rei. Agora não se vá dizer que D. Maria Ana, por ser tão piedosa senhora, concordou calar-se o tempo bastante para aparecer com o chamariz da promessa o escolhido e virtuoso frei António ... Não se diga mais do que ficou dito. Saiam então absolvidos os franciscanos desta suspeita, se nunca se acharam noutras igualmente duvidosas. (*Memorial do Convento* 25–26)]

The first part of the passage again involves implicit assurance from the narrative voice that research has been done on the entire history of the Franciscan petitions to build in Mafra. Also, narrative sarcasm and irreverence for officialdom clearly abound in the passage—a phenomenon that widens the range of issues to which I am asked to apply them—and, as before, invite me to join in. They have by this early point come to characterize the narrative voice in *Baltasar and Blimunda* and will be continuously elaborated upon throughout the remaining 300-plus pages of the novel. Here they are fortified by the actual suggestion that there might well be a better, less "mystical" explanation for the timing of the queen's pregnancy in relationship to Frei António's "inspired" prediction and the resulting royal pledge to build Mafra. One possible explanation involves, in opposition to Church guarantees, violation of the sanctity of the confessional! A similar combination of narrative elements occurs several other times in the novel, adding a dimension of critique to the ongoing tone of irreverence.

The above passage also involves a different version of the structural irony that I observed in the first chapter. The suggestion of collusion about the news of the queen's pregnancy forces me to ironize especially the adjective *virtuous* applied to Frei António de São José in precisely the same way that I previously ironized period beliefs about the place of woman, save that the touch of what I have provisionally labeled "anachronism" present in the former case is absent here. The result of the ironization is that I come to see *virtuous* being used simultaneously to convey the accepted concepts of the time and to cast doubt upon their explanatory accuracy. As a result I am given reason to wonder about one particular aspect of that explanation: the narrator's apparent explanation of Frei António's "nervous tremors" ("inspired trembling" in the Portuguese original). Is he trembling out of visionary inspiration, as seems to be being stated, or, as is in the same breath slyly suggested for my readerly consideration, is he trembling out of nervousness because of the uncomfortable position in which he finds himself? Could he be having difficulty because he knows he will be representing falsely to the king? What would nervousness thus understood have to say about "virtue?" I receive no answers to such implicit questions. Saramago novels often suggest questions, or rehearse multiple explanations, and then provide no answers (cf. Hutcheon x), thereby putting pressure on me to find my way through the challenge presented and/or to accept the position that definitive explanations are not always possible and/or to raise the question of the nature of explanation itself. In this case—typically—no more is made of the question.

In more general terms, the suggestion of alternative explanations provides an ironic end to the second chapter, especially since the chapter begins with the proclamation—albeit one already readable as sarcastic—that "the nation has ... been well served by miracles" (9 [19]). The cumulative force of the chapter, as it moves from "miracles" in general to the "miracle" of Frei António's supposed vision, is to ironize retroactively the various

53

national-historical instances traditionally characterized by use of the word *miracle* and to do so in the same way that *virtuous* is ironized. One explanatory narrative glossing the basic semantics of *miracle* (other, related terms from the passage reproduced above might be given in its stead, such as "God's chosen messenger") upholds the "official" version of the queen's pregnancy and the subsequent birth of the heir to the throne as divinely ordained and divinely revealed. Another, opposing narrative would see *miracle* as a term, characteristic of the explanatory discourses within the symbolic of the theocentric culture of the time, that is being used to explain otherwise inexplicable phenomena. Here, I find myself deciding, "inexplicable" would refer to phenomena whose actual explanation has been concealed for political reasons.

In the light of the chapter's first words, doubt is thus cast on other key "Portuguese miracles." The two likely to come to the Portuguese reader's mind are Christ's appearance to King Afonso Henriques before the battle of Ourique in 1139—source of a considerable portion of the *Estado Novo* traditionalists' image of Portugal as a divinely founded nation (cf. Chapter 1, p. 35) and of much of the Christological iconography involved in Portuguese self-representation down through the centuries—and the appearances of the Virgin Mary to three peasant children at Fátima in 1917. The Fátima "miracle" was regularly put to propaganda use by the fascist regime, and its debunking was a task taken up by several writers after that regime was overthrown in 1974. Saramago makes innuendoes about Fátima in *The Year of the Death of Ricardo Reis*. And he tackles the Ourique "miracle," tangentially, in *History of the Siege of Lisbon* (*History* 1996 124–31 [*História* 142–49]).

Once again, I as reader in the process of constructing the text while being constructed by it, in part as a reflex of the narrator's fluid self-positioning, am implicated in these modulations (this is not to say that all readers operate identically within that constructed locus). That is, I am urged, as a part of my very task as reader—in this case, as part of my successfully making meaning of the texture of this novel—to take on and deal with the contradictory set of interpretive possibilities that the narrator presents, often in humorous tone. I am thus forcefully invited also to look askance—or, at a minimum, to look analytically—upon some of the key received bases of the so-called nationality. It is hard to imagine a thoroughgoing reading of the novel that does not entertain that invitation in some manner, even if to reject it on some ground or other and go on reading against the grain.

What can be concluded as a set of basic hermeneutic principles from what *Baltasar and Blimunda* itself tells me thus far through my articulation with it? Let me list a few summary points and elaborate upon them in ways that go beyond what the preceding passages have demonstrated but not so far as to introduce concepts not previously prepared for. (Because of the intricate relationships amongst points, there is some repetition.)

1. I soon understand that the basis of the novel's narration is provided by the combination of two discourses. The first is grounded in a simple historical code apparently descriptive of the characters and the basic concepts of the time, in conjunction with an anthropological discourse that analyzes the socio-symbolic dimensions of those concepts up to certain limits (generally, those imposed by traditional history-writing). The second takes up that historico-anthropological discourse and subjects it to something like a critical analysis, albeit one carried out with a jocose tone. The two mutually imbricated discourses are set forth simultaneously.

2. It shortly becomes clear to me that the gap between the two discourses constitutes the mechanism for an ironizing in which the second discourse continually ironizes the first. Because of the anthropological register of the narrative language, that ironizing at times approaches the status of classical deconstruction, in which a constitutive aspect of the symbolic structure being analyzed is shown to represent an arbitrary choice dependent upon its rhetorical opposite(s) for its very existence. The ironizing serves to send me hunting for those rhetorical opposites—I, in order to negotiate the text successfully, begin to create and expand that second discourse as I read. The overall result of my participation in the ironizing is to cause me, at a minimum, to be suspicious of the first discourse— even though it continues to provide the discursive basis of the narrative—and to constitute the second as more powerful (cf. Piaia). This ironic undercutting of one discourse in favor of the other is sometimes fortified by an anachronistic outlook apparently dismissive of the practices of the represented era (though the full dimensions of this effect have not yet been explored).

3. Through this mechanism I am continually recruited to the side of the second discourse as I read. Indeed, the text clearly wishes me to read from that viewpoint. It must be emphasized, though, that actual reader responses may involve many reactions, including rejection of that recruitment and the adoption of reading strategies completely other to it.

4. The reader-narrator link is thus a complex one in which I am repeatedly invited—when not constrained in one way or another—as a constituent part of the reception itself, to follow the narrator along in his irreverence toward received verities. The principal vehicle that seeks to establish this link has been pointed to in general terms in 3, above. Its presentation there can be elaborated upon as follows: the narrator repeatedly addresses me, implicitly when not explicitly, in the foreground of the narration, as a fellow Portuguese of the late twentieth century, and that address often comes—again, implicitly when not explicitly—in relationship to the structural irony outlined in 2, above. As we have seen, the narrator-centered "second discourse" outlined in 1, above, is shared with me, and in that sharing I am asked to follow the narrator's lead and to look back as well upon the country's historical legacy. That "look back" is a very specific one: it involves what are, structurally speaking, a set of private jokes and other private communications in criticism of the presumed verities within the received version of that legacy (cf. Frier, *Novels* 10). The "private" aspect of the sharing is an additional basis of my potential recruitment to the narrator's general positioning. This entire set of functions—and others yet to be identified—constitute what I call the "readership pact" between narrator and reader. (Several critics refer to aspects of this pact, and Piero Ceccucci ("Paródia") characterizes it in terms compatible with those here, albeit without dealing with its structural effects within the novels; see Ceccucci and also his references.)

5. The received historical legacy is sometimes set forth textually through inclusion of, or allusion to, documents from the country's past related to the matters at hand.

6. Another aspect of the narrative's effort to construct its own reception is its continual refusal to allow me to engage in a reception in which I identify with the characters. That refusal implicitly acknowledges that such an identificatory reading is one I might otherwise wish to choose. It also represents an aspect of my recruitment to an irreverent and/or critical stance in reading.

It is through this set of narrative relationships that the sprawling plot of *Baltasar and Blimunda* is set out. While it is not my goal to summarize plot, much less interpret the novel, the coherence of the rest of this chapter demands that I set out basic plot lineaments. The novel includes the depiction of the vast planning, siting, grading, and building project that, over more than fifteen years, produced the palace-convent complex of Mafra. But that plot element crosses another: one involving Padre Bartolomeu Lourenço de Gusmão and his desire to create a machine upon which human beings can fly. Just as the construction of Mafra is historical, so too Lourenço is a historical figure, and his investment in the possibility of human flight is equally historical. Indeed, in point of historical fact, he is considered an early pioneer in lighter-than-air flight, having built flying machines that were given several successful public tests. In *Baltasar and Blimunda*, however, the priest, using what can only be termed—oxymoronically—Scholastic mechanics, is actually able to create a totally functional machine, called the *passarola* ("big bird"). Both the word and its application to Padre Lourenço's experimental aircraft are historical—but the machine depicted in the novel has little to do with its several historical counterparts. In the novel, Lourenço, Baltasar, and Blimunda fly in the *passarola*. Virtually predictably as well, the peripatetic narrator takes on semi-character status and has a turn upon it. In what can be thought of as an anticipation of cinematography (if we locate ourselves in the represented year of 1711), he narrates one passage from aboard the *passarola* as it flies above the Portuguese countryside (217–18 [241–42]). Those two large historically based pieces of the plot are held together by the story of the chance meeting, intimate relationship, and eventual separation of the aforementioned fictitious lower-class Portuguese couple Baltasar and Blimunda. They assist Padre Lourenço and also work in the construction of Mafra. Blimunda is particularly important as both she and her mother possess what are characterized as supernatural abilities of sorts—though, just as in the case of António de São José's "trembling" and other phenomena represented in the text, I might ask myself if that characterization is not the product of the narrator's irreverent use of an eighteenth-century explanatory system. Be that as it may, as a result of those abilities, Baltasar and Blimunda both fall afoul of the (ethnographically described) Inquisition. Blimunda's supernatural abilities include the ability

Chapter Two

to see inside people and things—which was historically one of the kinds of "sorcery" identified and punished by the Inquisition (cf. Mello e Souza 348). Just as he does in the case of Padre Lourenço's successful "Scholastic" flying machine, in a gesture that comically accepts the explanatory system of eighteenth-century Portugal, the narrator presumes that Blimunda's abilities are true ones. For example, her ability to capture human wills is crucial to the success of the *passarola*, buoyed as it is by containers of captured wills. Those same abilities enable Blimunda to "look inside" the theocentric symbolic construct of the era through a series of meditations. (She, of course, does not think of them in that manner.) Baltasar and Blimunda are separated at novel's end through a combination of the forces of the aeronautic experimentation and the acts of the Inquisition. Blimunda spends many years searching for the lost Baltasar, only to reunite with him from afar as he is being put to death in a public *auto-da-fé*.

* * *

Save for the fluid, pan-historical scope that the narrator arrogates to himself, the resulting touch of what appears to be anachronism, and the presence of a set of truly impossible happenings, the foregoing hermeneutical précis and plot summary would not seem to distinguish *Baltasar and Blimunda* or my reading tasks for it significantly from those applying to a traditional novel in which structural and perhaps also verbal irony constitute a central feature—the realist novels of a Flaubert or of an Eça de Queirós, for example. Whence, then, my smile?

It derives at least in part, I discover, from two elements that can be approached only now that the preceding groundwork has been laid. The first can be articulated by reference to such novelists as the aforementioned. As I analyze my smile quest for myself at this stage in my reading, I conclude that what distinguishes *Baltasar and Blimunda* from the practice of Flaubert and Eça de Queirós is that in it I am not being interpellated, in the classical Althusserian sense of the term (Althusser 173–83), by the "second discourse." Or at least not in the same ways that Flaubert's texts or Eça de Queirós's seek to interpellate me. As I read *Baltasar and Blimunda*, as opposed, for example, to *Madame Bovary* or *Cousin Basil*, it does not ask me to interpret history through the lens that the second discourse holds out, with the implicit proposition that its analysis is *the* correct one as opposed to the discourse being debunked. To be sure, *Baltasar and Blimunda* orients me forcefully to the "second discourse" and provides a platform for me to become suspicious about received traditional explanations, if not to reject them outright, and to engage in a reading that looks for the underside of assertions and also eschews facile "identification." But there is no cohesive alternative explanation attached to that "second discourse" seeking to establish its own authority. That discourse is not grounded in an obvious substantive masternarrative like the liberal one underpinning the irony in the works of the two novelists I here use as foils. It does, to be sure, come with explanatory language attached, and that language has implications of various sorts that it will be important for me to be aware of. But no modern-style *grands récits*. On its surface this novel does something quite different: it asks me, if not to suspend judgment, at least not to leap to the expectable conclusions. In sum, I am not being recruited to the viewpoint of some sort of critical symbolic anthropology; I am merely being shown it as an analytical tool, likely one analytical tool of many possible, with which to look critically at various aspects of the Portuguese cultural legacy as they present themselves—presumably, outside *Baltasar and Blimunda* as well as within it. As we have now seen amply demonstrated, the narrative voice itself models the "look" at that legacy in multiple ways and comes at it from differing narrative/explanatory positions, thereby actually discouraging the creation of a counter-narrative fashioned in the same manner as the stabilized grand narratives of modernity, or the specifically Portuguese "monumental history," which, structurally and functionally, was just one variety of grand narrative so created. Indeed, the absence of a defined project within the text to create a counter-narrative that reaches much beyond the rhetorical eliminates any means of creating a systemic limit to the analytical possibilities that I might take up as I read, thus encouraging me to entertain critical approaches from many angles.

What emerges from these elements complexifies the narrator-reader pact identified above. The narrator, aided by the general deployment of the text, continually invites me to accompany him on what amounts to a ransacking of the inherited markers of "Portuguese nationality" as seen from the point of view of the present. By "ransack" I refer to many possible attitudes, all invoking some degree of skepticism about those markers' positioning, traditionally supposed content, and interpretation. I am clearly invited to adopt his facile sarcasm and irony, but often underlying them within his voice is something more: an intense, careful, even suspicious scrutiny, as is modeled in such passages as his treatment of the circumstances of Frei António de São José's "vision" (and, as might by now be expected, many, many others)—and, of course, the invitation to me to exercise similar scrutiny as I read.

The narrator who engages in this pact, in his continuous self-thematization, includes self-personification: he regularly, by implication, invites me to conflate him with the author, José Saramago, including Saramago's public self-presentation, a part of which is his left political stance. Hence my use of gendered pronouns to refer to "him." Because of the constant invitation to identify narrator with author, the idea is fostered in me that "the author, José Saramago, is sharing a story, a joke, an innuendo, with me." I shall henceforth use the term "implied author" to refer to that combination of narrator and allusion to the historical author that relates to me in this complex way. In effect, there is a textualized "José Saramago" in the foreground of *Baltasar and Blimunda* (and, in differing configurations, the other two historical novels as well), and that figure works to hold in place the elaborate relationship with me that I have been examining.

That complex pact between myself as reader and the implied author is cemented by yet another factor, which constitutes the second element I have referred to above in exploration of the constitution of my smile. There is the sense, as the implied author implicitly invites me to accompany him in the ransacking of an area of received national lore, not only that such an operation has something intellectually subversive about it but also that the stakes are high. Here, I think, is the crux of the dynamics that elicited my original smile, at least as far as *Baltasar and Blimunda* is concerned: at the core of the implied author–reader journey into the Portuguese cultural legacy there lies the constitutive admission that such activity has until recently been forbidden on various fronts: political, intellectual, and, most importantly for the activity of novel-reading, hermeneutical. The call that is transmitted to me by and through the implied author–reader pact is not simply "let's ransack together." Instead it is something like: "before, we were dictated to very forcibly about how to understand these matters; now that we are free to do so, let's ransack together." In short, the narrative pact of *Baltasar and Blimunda* implicitly holds out a specific liberatory dimension and derives much of its communicative power from the implicit but insistent invocation of that dimension. In fact, as we have seen, the second and third sentences of the book, reproduced and briefly analyzed at the outset of this chapter, reenact rhetorically a process of pointing out an interdiction and being freed from it that imprints that dimension upon the text. We have already noted as well that varieties of that rhetorical gesture recur throughout the novel, thus extending that sense of overcoming interdiction and perpetuating that imprinting.

As we have also seen, the liberatory gesture there included is constructed in relation to the hermeneutical rules I bring with me to the task of reading, rules fashioned in some considerable part in relation to the practices promulgated by Portuguese fascism and thus to the literary institutionality under fascism capsuled in the preceding chapter of this study. Thus when the implied author remarks on the role of "miracles" in Portuguese history, speaks in an offhand tone about the private life of a highly controversial king, or refers to Portugal as "a nation of thieves" (10 [20]), such remarks are being launched, in my presence and in invitation of my agreement and readerly collaboration, against a hermeneutical tradition that not only foregrounded the opposite analysis and sought to enforce a "rigidly codified" (see p. 35, above) reading of cultural documents consistent with that opposite analysis but also formulated a literary institutionality that made it dangerous to question that outlook, even in the process of reception—to the point of social ostracism, economic hardship, fear for personal safety, loss of liberty, and even loss of life. But most importantly, to the point of self-doubt. As a result, my reading activity is being carried out upon the ground of the invocation and utilization of that immediate institutional history, and the text continually reminds me of that fact.

This connection modifies the "anachronism effect," linked to narrative critique and its pan-historicity, introduced above (and explains my refusal in the earlier pages of this chapter to characterize the mode of critique of, say, gender attitudes attributed to the eighteenth century as simply "anachronistic" and nothing more). We now see that it is not principally the earlier time period itself that is being ironized; it is the received and, under fascism, rigidly codified and rigidly enforced interpretation of those times that is the primary target. In *Baltasar and Blimunda* it is the historical narrative that is being attacked, at the very moment that historical narration is being performed, and the narrative under attack is seen as linked to a specific institutional situation: enforced traditionalist narration/narratability of the nation under the *Estado Novo*. In our case in point, the attitude about woman is not being attributed to the eighteenth century, at least not to it alone. It is being ascribed to the received characterization of the era and/or of the nationality and to the strictly enforced interpretive rules that both produced that characterization and sought to enforce themselves in any and all like hermeneutic situations. In effect, a part of the ironizing of the general proposition about the role of women capsuled in the phrase "woman is essentially a vessel made to be filled" is that that general attitude was embraced by fascism and ascribed positively to the Portuguese cultural heritage and that it was one of a complex of issues similarly fashioned and enforced.

In point of fact, especially early on, the *Estado Novo* proclaimed woman's "return to the hearth" ("regresso ao lar") and to the role of "traditional" motherhood, and it supported that stance by both constitutional language and decree (see Cova and Costa Pinto; also, for an analysis of the complexities of that assignment of place to woman, see A. Ferreira). Other cases similarly analyzable are the presence in Portuguese history of foundational "miracles" such as Ourique, Fátima, and Frei António's "vision." The same can be said for the concepts of "virtue" and "God's chosen messenger" as applied to Frei António and the other items referred to above, as well as the countless additional like items—understood as forms of Iserian "constitutive blanks"—that fill Saramago's historical novels: much more frequently than not, the precise target of critique is the interpretation enforced and/or allowed in the immediate, fascist past as I bear it into my readerly meeting with the implied author figure, a figure who progressively constitutes himself as bearing a similar hermeneutical history.

What Saramago's narration invites me to take on as I read, then, is the literary institutionality that characterized the era before 1974, one that continues to play a strong, though receding, role in Portuguese culture today and certainly did in the post-revolutionary period when *Baltasar and Blimunda* was written, published, and received—by a majority of readers, with enthusiasm.

*　*　*

With this new sense of the stakes involved, let us return to the matter of my smile, now with a different focus: that provided by Freud's *Jokes and Their Relation to the Unconscious*, upon which both the epigraph and the title of this chapter draw. (I should point out that here and henceforth I have occasional recourse to theoretical discourses—psychoanalytic, psychological, and other—largely for their analytical-discursive value. I use them in very basic ways only and would not like that use to be understood as constituting a "reading" of the Saramago texts from the point of view that those discourses set out.)

In his study, Freud tells us that jokes, especially, for our purposes, what he refers to as "tendentious" jokes—i.e., ones having a clear purpose—function in a very complex way. In overview (tailored a bit to the current context), that functioning is as follows. The joke involves three parties: the teller, the object, and the receiver, or the person "in whom the joke's aim of producing pleasure is fulfilled" (Freud 100). The joke material, in effect the tenor of the joke, occupies some interdicted terrain, be it a taboo, a moral stricture, a social prohibition, or what have you (104–05), which is called the "obstacle" (117–18). That terrain is the site of an act of suppression or repression—in the Freudian scheme, the inhibition of circulation/discharge of libidinal energy. In the simplest of senses, a joke creates the effects that it does because it allows the receiver to overcome that obstacle within his or her libidinal economy. It achieves its reaction—let us take the example of my smile and sense of pleasure—because a portion of the libidinal energy that had previously been inhibited in suppression/repression connected with the social-psychological pressure exerted by *Estado Novo* literary institutionality, principally its enforced preference of specific hermeneutical rules for reading, is released when I am given—indeed, guided to—an opportunity to read differently. Some quotient of that previously suppressed/repressed energy is discharged in such expressions as smile and laughter. In this explanation, then, my smile and the pleasure released through my reading represent elements within a complex psychic economy that I have brought with me to reception. Freud adds that this process of joke-telling-and-reception/reaction can represent a "fore-pleasure" (150 ff.) that can itself generate the libidinal energy needed to begin the process over again and overcome other inhibitions or strictures. Applied to a structure such as a novel, that phenomenon describes the basis of an ongoing readership in which my every smile and every experience of pleasure produces the anticipation of subsequent structurally similar experiences and thus provides the libidinal mechanism for their seriatim realization: my reception of the novel as ironic, iconoclastic, and directed to the "national" heritage in these ways builds on itself.

Let us look at a passage from *Baltasar and Blimunda* in this light. The following is drawn from the beginning of a mid-novel chapter:

> People are saying that the realm is badly governed, and that there is no justice. They fail to understand that this is how justice is supposed to be: with her eyes blindfolded, her scales, and her sword. What more could we wish for, when that is all that has been required: that we should be the weavers of the bandage, the inspectors of the weights, the armorers of the sword, regularly repairing its nicks and adjusting the balance? And then that we ask the defendant, once he has won or lost his case, if he is satisfied with the sentence passed upon him. We are not referring here to sentences passed by the Holy Office, for it keeps its eyes wide open, preferring an olive branch to scales and a keen blade to one grown jagged and blunt. Some mistake the olive branch for a gesture of peace, when it is all too clear that it is kindling wood for the impending funeral pyre. Either I stab you or I burn you. Therefore, if one is going to break the law, it is preferable to stab a woman suspected of infidelity than not to honor the faithful who have passed on. It is a question of having protectors who are likely to forgive homicide, and a thousand cruzados to put on the scales, which explains why Justice holds the latter in her outstretched hand. Let blacks and hoodlums be punished so that a good example may be upheld. Let people of rank and wealth be honored, without demanding that they pay their debts, renounce their vengeance or mitigate their hatred ... (*Baltasar* 171–72)

[Dizem que o reino anda mal governado, que nele está de menos a justiça, e não reparam que ela está como deve estar, com sua venda nos olhos, sua balança e sua espada, que mais queríamos nós, era o que faltava, sermos os tecelões da faixa, os aferidores dos pesos e os alfageme s do cutelo, constantemente remendando os buracos, restituindo as quebras, amolando os fios, e enfim perguntando ao justiçado se vai contente com a justiça que se lhe faz, ganhado ou perdido o pleito. Dos julgamentos do Santo Ofício não se fala aqui, que esse tem bem abertos os olhos, em vez de balança um ramo de oliveira, e uma espada afiada onde a outra é romba e com bocas. Há quem julgue que o raminho é oferta de paz, quando está muito patente que se trata do primeiro graveto da futura pilha de lenha, ou te corto, ou te queimo, por isso é que, havendo que faltar à lei, mais vale apunhalar a mulher, por suspeita de infidelidade, que não honrar os fiéis defuntos, a questão é ter padrinhos que desculpem o homicídio e mil cruzados para pôr na balança, nem é para outra coisa que a justiça a leva na mão. Castiguem-se lá os negros e os vilões para que não se perca o valor do exemplo, mas honre-se a gente de bem e bens, não lhe exigindo que pague as dívidas contraídas, que renuncie à vingança, que emende o ódio ... (*Memorial do Convento* 191)]

The passage, one of the many meditations in the voice of the implied author that dot the novel, involves a more direct critique than appears in most of Saramago's work. Indeed, in my reading it approaches the status of outright denunciation, which I find surprising. One of the features contributing to the sense of denunciation is the suspension of definitive time reference in the first three sentences, an effect facilitated by the fact that this passage comes at the very start of a chapter. Thus the meditation can presume generality (i.e., some wide chronological and cultural applicability) as well as applicability both to the represented time of the context (the eighteenth century) and the time of the interaction between myself as reader and the implied author, an interaction that is forcefully maintained in the foreground throughout the novel. It is only with the reference to the "Holy Office" of the Inquisition that unequivocal selection of principal time focus is made. And even though the primary reference thereafter will be one to the eighteenth century, within the logic of *Baltasar and Blimunda* that reference will not be a totalizing one but rather one retaining referentiality to the time of my communication with the implied author as well. I therefore read it as a generalizing reference to Portuguese cultural traditions.

This generalization through urging me to engage in a historical displacement-in-reading is not an uncommon technique in the novel. Indeed, the invitation to me to take some of the libidinal energy generated by the reception of passages from the text involving trauma and inflect it by reference to my own potentially analogous traumatic experiences, which investment serves to increase the overall libidinal energy being invested, is a common reception phenomenon. It must be understood that the act of displacement-in-reading does not eliminate the source of libidinal energy for sole focus on the site of displacement but rather involves an ongoing exchange between the two. (One should note for the sake of clarity that the entire metaphor of "displacement" is somewhat erroneous, since the "source" is actually already in the reader's libidinal economy and the "investment" is actually a "re-investment.") In the case of the novel, the textual area more regularly involved in displacement-in-reading is representation of the church rather than the justice system—though in the case of the above passage the two are not wholly exclusive of one another. It should be emphasized, however, that this allegorical sense— "allegorical" being the rhetorical term, used in these pages for its descriptive value, while "displacement" is the psychoanalytic alternative—has a much more general effect than thoroughgoing rhetorical performance: what is presented is the ongoing suggestion of correspondence, an ongoing invitation made to me to engage in displacement-in-reading.

The dominant tone of the passage is, of course, one of deep cynicism, but it also prominently includes that dark humor that sometimes correlates with cynicism. The object, in the Freudian sense, is justice in Portugal—in the represented eighteenth century, in the present/immediate past of my articulation with the implied author, and, ultimately, throughout time. The concept of, on the one hand, a ruling elite that can buy its own way along and, on the other hand, a harsh "justice" reserved for minoritarian groups and the lower classes is one I take to be generally applicable. The object is developed through a darkly humorous "reading" of the symbolic representation of Justice—blindfold, scale, and sword. The reading locates "us," the implied author and me, in the dark-comic position of tenders of those symbolic appurtenances comically treated as actual physical features: we are weavers of the cloth for the blindfold, sharpeners of the sword, etc. That positioning, of course, follows the statement that it is somewhere "alleged" that the "realm is badly governed, and that there is no justice." If the allegation is accepted, then in our "tending" of justice we put ourselves in the position of upholding, knowingly or not, willingly or not, an unjust situation, and the allusion to collaboration in an unjust polity—presumably that of the *Estado Novo*—is clearly implied. This entire arrangement can be neatly translated into terms of literary institutionality: if "we" read literature as the *Estado Novo* once urged us to, if we in effect occupy the receiver position in the institutional arrangement that it once sought to enforce upon us, then we are the servants of that justice-that-is-injustice ironically presented in the passage.

The presentation is carried out in what amounts to the form of a joke. The implied author in effect tells me a grim tendentious joke about justice in the relevant context(s) and about "our" complicity in it. He thus both calls up the situation in which "we" were forced to live and names the Freudian "object." He then carries his statement to what he proclaims to be another related but different development: the variety of "justice" practiced by the Inquisition. That transition is carried out by extending the technique of "reading" symbolic features as physical and historical ones. Notably, the statement of that transition, in the phrase "we are not referring here to sentences passed by the Holy Office," is the approximate rhetorical parallel of the syntagm "the thought that the problem might lie with the King is not even to be entertained" from the novel's third sentence, analyzed above (p. 41). And it has the same effect as its forerunner in that it breaks an interdiction by naming it while in the process of comically claiming not to question it. In this case, it seems to wish to elicit from me the question "how are we not so referring?" Since the two parts of the meditation are continuous with each other rather than adversative, I have to read the disclaimer as a blatant false protestation, a denial for some reason—presumably duress, the implied author's and my own. Even more, however, I can read it as the sign that, in becoming specific about Portuguese history/mythology and about how it has sought to enforce itself upon "us" through fascist hermeneutics and other institutions, I have entered an interdicted area—in effect, I am confronting the Freudian "obstacle": justice in Portugal, past and present, as fascist institutionality would have had me understand it. That obstacle has to do with what "we" are allowed to say, or even to think, and it comes fraught with a prohibition that has considerable pent-up libidinal investment about it, whether we think of simple obedience to a taboo or the investment involved in keeping quiet, acquiescing, accepting that we can never be sure of anything pertaining to public affairs. And the words "we are not referring here to sentences passed by the Holy Office" represent a verbal marker of what is essentially the crux of this tendentious joke: the litotes, in its false denial, both contradicts the ground of the *Estado Novo* interpretation and simultaneously brings the interdiction to the fore in force, releasing the libidinal energy bound up in maintaining that interdiction, and helping give rise to … my smile.

As is by now abundantly clear, many roughly similar verbal markers dot the novel: the implied doubt about the reason for Frei António's "inspired trembling," albeit set forth with a different dynamic, functions as such a marker; so too does the grim joke that the olive branch, instead of being a token of peace, should be seen as kindling for the Inquisitorial pyre. Indeed, one of the principal ingredients I note in the text as I work my readerly way through it is that it moves from one such marker to the next, each looked forward to after the prior's effects are spent, in the process of Freudian "fore-pleasure." Given that my reading trajectory is one that moves from one release of pleasure to the next in relation to my reception of what are often instances of indifference or brutality by the powers that be, or even of matters of life and death, it is clear that that movement prominently involves an emotional freighting. And that emotionality is always summoned up by a regress to literary institutionality: it always involves my dealing in one way or another with interdictions in the area of interpretation that summon up an accompanying consideration of institutional-sphere constraints. That summoning-up of institutional constraints can be seen as one version of "writing in the institutional sphere" (see Chapter 1, pp. 33–34). In this case the naming of the constraint both points to a regress to the institutional sphere and raises questions about rules operating in that sphere. Thus analysis from the viewpoint of "writing in the institutional sphere" first and foremost pinpoints an institutional-sphere disruption.

As I read along in this vein I come to interpret some characters too—especially the two title characters—as operating as figures written in the institutional sphere. Blimunda in particular—herself a reader figure of sorts reading the social symbolic of the era in a way that raises questions about the fascist-fetched hermeneutical rules through which apprehension of that social symbolic comes down to me—models the actual practice of the violation of such rules. Moreover, she and Baltasar, in their almost unquestioning choice to collaborate with the heretical Padre Lourenço, present me with ongoing figurations of transgression, even active ignoring, of social norms having to do with interpretation of experience. Indeed, for me the fact that the characters find themselves set against the powerful institutional force of the Inquisition represents one of many instances in the novel in which I invoke both the loose allegory previously observed between the Inquisition in the eighteenth century and the *Estado Novo* in the twentieth and also the consequent displacement-in-reading that I am regularly urged to carry out as I receive the novel.

As a consequence of this instance of "writing in the institutional sphere," it is clear that characters' specific actions or words can sometimes function as regresses to that sphere. Characters, then, can come to be seen as markers of regress—in effect they operate both as literary characters within the narrow confines of the represented world of the text-read-to-account-for-plot and at the same time as operators in the institutional sphere. For example, the following meditation on Blimunda's part:

> She attended Holy Mass is if she were in the presence of Almighty God and listened to the sermon without raising her head, overwhelmed—or so it appeared—by all the threats of hell and damnation that rained from the pulpit. Then she went up to the altar to receive the Sacred Host, and she saw …
>
> She sat on the protruding root of an olive tree. From there she could watch the sea merging with the horizon. In the distance there was heavy rain. Blimunda's eyes filled with tears, her shoulders shaking as she began to sob. Baltasar stroked her hair. … He asked her: What did you see in the Sacred Host? …
>
> Blimunda told him: I was hoping to see Christ crucified or resurrected in glory, but all I could see was a dark cloud.
>
> —Forget what you saw.
>
> —Forget it? How can I forget it, if what is inside the Sacred Host is what is inside men, which is ultimately religion? (*Baltasar* 114–15)

> [… esteve no ofício como se a prostrasse a presença de Deus, ouviu o sermão sem levantar a cabeça, esmagada, ao parecer, por todas as ameaças de inferno que caíam do púlpito, e enfim foi receber a sagrada partícula, e viu. Durante todos estes anos, desde que se revelara o dom que possuía, sempre comungara em pecado, com alimento no estômago, e hoje decidira, sem nada dizer a Baltasar, que iria em jejum, não para receber a Deus, mas para o ver, se ele lá estava.

Chapter Two

> Sentou-se na raiz levantada duma oliveira, via-se dali o mar confundido com o horizonte, decerto estaria chovendo com força sobre as águas, então encheram-se de lágrimas os olhos de Blimunda, um grande soluço lhe sacudiu os ombros, e Baltasar tocou-lhe na cabeça, aproximara-se e ela não o ouvira, Que foi que viste na hóstia, afinal não o iludira a ele … E Blimunda disse, Esperava ver Cristo crucificado, ou ressurrecto em glória, e vi nuvem fechada. Não penses mais no que viste, Penso, como não hei-de pensar, se o que está dentro da hóstia é o que está dentro do homem, que é a religião, afinal … (*Memorial do Convento* 130–31)]

What Blimunda's "look inside" finds is that the Host is not the body of Christ transubstantiated; rather, it contains "a dark cloud." Her equating of that cloud first with what she sees inside "men" and then with "religion" presumably suggests—though several interpretive possibilities exist—that the practice of religion is used to replace an inner opaqueness that characterizes "men." In sum, I read Blimunda as confronting a key feature of the symbolic structure of the era and, to her own chagrin, finding it questionable. Written in the institutional sphere, that act—and many others by Blimunda—model for me a questioning of the received hermeneutical rules. In this case, because of the sacramental object being scrutinized, what is questioned is Catholic cultural grounding—upon which, of course, much of *Estado Novo* discourse rested. Indeed, the hermeneutical rules implicitly invoked in this case strongly resemble those we saw established by Amândio César for interpretation of Fernando Pessoa (see Chapter 1, pp. 29–32). As operator in the institutional sphere, then, Blimunda represents a specific figure: a reader who is able to "see" beyond the strictures seeking to govern reception—although, because she is simultaneously a literary character located in the eighteenth century, the object of her scrutiny and the terms in which she and Baltasar interpret her interpretation are provided by those strictures. In the sense that she "sees," she models a version of what the implied author continually seeks to promulgate to me, the reader. What she urges upon me is that in my reception I seek to "see" beyond conventional rule-making without presuming that such rule-making can simply be ignored in my reception activity. Her activity and the results that it produces also urge me not to use Catholic/national "identificatory" processes in reading.

Again here, then, a liberatory chord of sorts is touched. Somehow, it would seem, a reception on my part that is both conscious of its own activity and its implications and also unaccepting of conventional hermeneutical rule-making is freeing. With Blimunda such reception is implicitly presented as little more than commonsensical, as though some basic ability were being loosed and allowed its free rein. The only clearly prescribed enabling step would seem to be acknowledgement of the constructed nature of modes of reception.

* * *

With these matters in mind, we can now close this exploration of the reader/implied author pact and its relation to my smile by adding to the list begun on p. 55 some more of the primary features that constitute that pact. Unlike my practice in listing the first six items, I shall include here features merely introduced in the foregoing pages and develop them as I go.

7. The "private" sharing between implied author and myself involves a shared sense (recall I am not speaking of conscious sense) of the institutional configuration of fascist Portugal, especially in the area of literary hermeneutics but more widely as well. *Baltasar and Blimunda* problematizes the conditions under which it is being read as one of the bases of its articulation with me. That articulation, ever present at the foreground of the narration, represents the principal point of reader–implied author communication. A given reader may, of course, reject the problematization; it is hard, however, to understand how doing so would allow that reader to derive much from *Baltasar and Blimunda*—which may account for the sharp divergence in reception of Saramago novels, especially among Portuguese.

8. That constitutive problematization of its own reception as a part of that reception is in great part grounded in the structure of the seriatim overcoming of interdictions and subsequent sense of release of pleasure and sense of liberation. As a consequence, it is fraught with emotion. The novel, then, asks me to supply it with a significant emotional core, and presents that element in such a way that it seeks to elicit a repetitive liberatory, at times jubilant, tone from me that, while it contrasts with many of the principal plot elements, nonetheless dominates the novel.

Chapter Two

9. Because of the sense, fostered by the text itself, that *Baltasar and Blimunda* is the product of source research and therefore includes the raw "stuff" of the Portuguese cultural legacy being variously interpreted as it is being set forth (this point continues and expands point 5, above), the sense is transmitted to me that I am being located at the point where interpretation is about to be performed, that I am free to interpret that "stuff" anew with no (apparent) limitations. For example, it is argued in the critical literature (Fokkema 299–300, can stand for all who make the argument)—to my mind, mistakenly—that, in its scenes of mass labor and peasant suffering in the creation of Mafra, the author/implicit author gives voice to the forgotten lower-class Portuguese of the past. In my reading I find no coherent code that substantively rescues those figures from their anonymity or redeems their labor; what I receive is largely a focus on the spectacle of the project (cf. Howe). Indeed, if the argument for redemption is to be advanced, I find it better made from the smaller touches the novel contains: the interpersonal relationships, the life of calm that attaches to Baltasar and Blimunda as opposed to the life outside their relationship, and so on. Nevertheless, what the text indeed does is suggest to me that I am free to think in any such terms in that and other areas—while in the recent past such would be a discouraged, if not dangerous, reading to engage in.

10. It is clearly implied that I must make choices: to read *Baltasar and Blimunda* the way it seeks to have itself read is to read it actively—that is, to engage in scrutiny of what it presents as the "stuff" of the Portuguese cultural heritage. This is one clear limitation upon readerly activity: passivity—including acceptance of the *status quo ante*—is not likely to be a successful strategy for reading the novel, just as, it is therefore suggested, it is not a successful strategy in confronting the cultural heritage in general. Thus, as a corollary to this point, the text tells me that the task of reading the novel and the task of confronting the heritage model each other reciprocally.

11. As a consequence of this emphasis on interpretation, it becomes difficult for me to understand what exactly the status is of the words I am reading. Clearly, in one sense they function like the words of any historical novel—that is, they function in the terms of the first discourse described in point 1, above. But simultaneously they are often there on the pages to be doubted; indeed, their successful reading centrally involves their being doubted. Such language therefore also functions as a set of signs of readerly work I am to do at the site that its presence demarcates. It is thus at one and the same time both constitutive and heuristic. Moreover, the relationship between the constitutive and the heuristic describes the elements involved in self-deconstruction: the text presents itself and provides the ingredients for its own deconstruction at the same time (cf. Hutcheon x; Jameson, *Postmodernism* 240–50, albeit indirectly).

12. In a very practical sense, this self-deconstructing text presents itself to me as follows. The implied author José Saramago can be seen to be making the implicit claim that he can take the "stuff," great and small, of Portuguese history and make a narrative out of it. In this sense he stands apart from me, while in other senses he asks me to join him. It is clear, for example, that the details he adds to the source "stuff" that he has researched are speculative or imaginative when not blatantly fanciful, even if they are there only heuristically. This stance can be—and has been—interpreted as needlessly flamboyant in its irreverence, indicative of a disregard for what there is that is historically "solid" in the country's heritage (several personal conversations). It has also been interpreted as indicative of a publicity-seeking that disqualifies Saramago from being a "serious" writer. That attitude lost considerable ground after the 1998 Nobel Prize, but it is certainly still heard.

13. At the same time that the words on the page function as sites of textual self-deconstruction, they frequently invite regress to the institutional sphere. Indeed, one dimension of the text is its continual practice of openly "writing in the institutional sphere" and having the fact of that writing figure in the interaction between me and the implied author. In fact, in this novel that is otherwise highly suspicious of any sort of unproblematic referentiality, one of the most consistent acts of reference is reference to institutional-sphere permissions and constraints, especially the hermeneutic permissions and interdictions promulgated by Portuguese fascism and brought to the novel by both the reader and the implied author as one aspect of a shared institutional history. Not only does narrative rhetoric, in the common sense of the term—i.e., the "verbal markers" referred to above—function as "writing in the institutional sphere"; so too can the words and acts of literary characters. Noteworthy in this regard are Blimunda's visions, which model for me both general interpretation against the grain of received authority and also, by extension, literary reception similarly against the grain, though in the latter case the authority involved amounts to an institutional-level residue. In that dual modeling they suggest the model-building relationship that exists between literary reception and interpretation of experience (see point 10, above). On a general level, they suggest both that all reception is necessarily involved in an articulation with the institutional level and that awareness of that fact can and should be made a part of the act of reception.

14. The stance assumed by the implied author and described in the previous two points can profitably be thought of in terms of "writing in the institutional sphere." In that connection it bespeaks the activity of remodeling. As we have seen in the preceding pages, some of the central expectations within the inherited implied author–reader contract are being reworked in the novel, especially with regard to treatment of Portuguese history but also in wider application. (In *History of the Siege of Lisbon* we shall see the connection with the writing of Portuguese history openly thematized in a way that follows upon this lead.) That reworking is centrally articulated by the figuration of the locus of narration that is the implied author—a showy, digressive, irreverent textualized figure that is in part himself readerly in the sense that he is all the while "reading" Portuguese history, albeit at times fancifully. (That readerly dimension too will be returned to in *History*.) That locus of narration attracts my attention and focuses my reception to a significant extent upon the implied author and his attributes, which I appreciate the more fully the more I engage with the hermeneutical rules upon which those attributes depend. That stance is roughly comparable to, say, Blimunda's: as was the case with that character, the implied author himself has become a figuration within the institutional sphere—one that bespeaks, instantiates, and seeks to inculcate upon me change in what is institutionally acceptable in the area of novel-design/narration, or what I accept to be. In one key dimension this implied author reassumes a central aspect of the lapsed Eça de Queirós authorial stance (see p. 12, above): the novel is again a vehicle for direct public conversation about public issues. Beyond that point, however, significant dissimilarities of tone and procedure begin to accumulate, the primary mainspring of the dissimilarities being Saramago's cultivation of the in-joke almost literally whispered to me as an aside and his ongoing offer to share an overtly skeptical and irreverent stance with me, as opposed to the systematic social analysis, ultimately grounded in political liberalism and the scientism that came with it, that characterizes the work of his predecessor. (This is not to say that Saramago's is the only voice in the post-revolutionary period seeking to remodel the contours of the admissible authorial stance. A list of authors, ones employing quite varying strategies, could easily be assembled and their practice studied comparatively and contrastively. To attempt such a study here, even in abbreviated form, would be, however, to create an excursus tangential to both the local-study aspect of these pages and my pursuit of the smile question.)

15. As regards the texture of *Baltasar and Blimunda*, the emotionality bound into the reading that it seeks to enforce for itself serves to emotionalize the entire text. For example, if one reads with a cold eye, one observes that the characters are not highly developed in a technical sense; indeed, read carefully, they seem more like enigmas to be deciphered than conventional novelistic representations of human beings. The quotient of emotionality released by the overcoming of interdiction and available for investment elsewhere is such, however, that, say, the very relationship between Baltasar and Blimunda can be interpreted as a great love story carried out in the face of cultural obstacles (again, in my reading the key factor is that the life they create for themselves is characterized by a comfortable calm, has almost the sense of sanctuary about it, in contrast to the rush and violence of the life going on around them). An alternative, more emotionalized reading forms the basis of the Italian opera *Blimunda* (1990), based on the novel, written in collaboration by Saramago (libretto) and the well-known Italian composer Azio Corghi (music) (see Ceccucci, *Viaggio,* esp. 81–85). The reinvestment of emotion comes because the obstacle both for the reader and for Baltasar and Blimunda is authoritarian institutionality—in the characters' case, that represented by the combination of the monarchy and the Church/Inquisition. There is, then, a reciprocal modeling going on, and it results in the complex displacement of emotion from the reading process carried out in the face of the memory of institutional constraints, on the one hand, to the characters' life struggles and the precariousness of their relationship in the face of those struggles on the other—and literally back again.

16. The textual urging upon me to engage in an anti-identificatory reception (see point 6, above) is extended: not only am I urged textually not to identify with characters as a principal reception modality but I am similarly enjoined to avoid invoking a Catholic/national ground for my reading. Fascist hermeneutics, by contrast, enjoined me precisely to foreground those factors.

17. I must acknowledge, as someone interrogating his own reception, that the complex readership role and reader–implied author pact, while they are constitutively grounded in experience of fascist practices, are also constitutively grounded in the assurance that those practices are past. Clearly, the novel could not have been written in the manner here described during fascist times—much less published. I must recognize that the fact that fascist hermeneutic interdiction is past is necessary to create the ironic gap in which the pressure of the interdiction can be relieved to the extent necessary to enable the basic joke structure to work seriatim in the novel. While fascist interdiction is "institutionally past," so to speak, it is so recently past that I bring it enough with me to respond to the text's insistent invocation of it—especially if "I" am a mature Portuguese reader of 1982, only eight years after the revolution. One might argue, then, that all of *Baltasar and Blimunda* can be read as a testimony to the state of the hermeneutic dimension of Portuguese literary institutionality at the time of its writing and publication. Exploration of this issue exceeds the scope of my current endeavor, though some further implications of it arise in the ensuing chapters.

18. Finally, if we shift analytical focus to consideration of overall textual deployment, it is clear that *Baltasar and Blimunda* does something quite distinctive in creating its implied author and deploying him as it does. It is equally clear that that creation draws greatly upon opportunities that have presented themselves within the social and institutional situation of post-revolutionary Portugal. To be sure, one can point to instances, from Rabelais, Cervantes, and Sterne down to the present, of all the narrative techniques employed—though *Baltasar and Blimunda*'s full set does not appear in any one prior title of which I am aware. But the strategy of using those features to interpellate the reader on the basis of the immediate hermeneutical past and the hermeneutical possibilities that have arisen as the result of a social rupture, the presence of which too is kept before the reader as a part of the

Baltasar and Blimunda

overall communication, is unique. This entire matter could be analyzed more fully from various angles. One could, for example, study movements, even conflicts in strategy, within the post-revolutionary horizon by comparing a reading of *Baltasar and Blimunda* with works by other contemporary Portuguese authors. Again, that project and others that could be developed in the general area would represent a turning-away from my smile question and thus will not be pursued here.

* * *

Such, in summary, are the rudiments of the reader–implied author pact constructed in *Baltasar and Blimunda*. As must now be clear, that pact enables a great many complexities to be built into the task of reception: ultimately, it allows the language features of a cogent, highly imaginative work to be received by me the reader as operating simultaneously as loci of regress to issues of current literary institutionality and enables a set of complex displacements and transferences of meaning and of emotion between those two areas to be effected through my reception process (not all of those displacements and transferences have been touched on in these pages). Such features, but not they alone, enable my smile.

They also articulate a rather remarkable transference of another sort. Together, what those textual features combine to do is to replace the hermeneutical rules exercised under the *Estado Novo* with at least the offer of ones of the sort articulated through the reader–implied author pact. Seen in terms of institutional-sphere hermeneutics thought of historically, the reading of *Baltasar and Blimunda* can be thought of as nothing more than forced participation in the complex act of that replacement (let us recall that it is not necessarily replacement in kind). It might be observed as well that the flip side of this replacement of hermeneutical rules is the presentation of the authorial principle as what amounts to implied-author-as-performer: in effect the textualized José Saramago takes over dimensions of the performative function of language through self-thematization at the site of the performance. That self-thematization is the principal vehicle through which the reader-side process of "replacement" is effected.

This reader–implied author pact thus created persists, with modifications, in the following two historical novels. I shall touch on it in dealing with them. But by and large the features elucidated in this chapter will have to stand for their correlates in those chapters as well, since my principal purposes there will be other. First, to explore further some of the issues raised by *Baltasar and Blimunda* but heretofore minimally touched upon. Their full analysis has been postponed because the issues involved are more nearly fully articulated in the later novels. Second, to tackle issues only inferentially present in this first novel and further developed in the subsequent titles of the trilogy. In all cases those issues redound upon what has been developed in this chapter as regards readership, further complexifying what we have seen up to now. Is ate eos excepe eum ius corporrovid ute escime con con repra dolupti bla sitatiis as molor magnis consequ aecus, ipicias apelest iorerio. Me quam alique nulpa idelis non rate nim consequi bea simagni hiliae re sit unt alici nisi dolupta is dolo consequi conseque laborpo rionseq uunture rcipsantio estrum que none nos dolorum haruptat.

Equi soluptatur? Git endi cus ne num natium illes as pro doluptasim aceat.

Epercientius dolupta eptatur, ulparumque pel ma sunt a nobit alit arumquiae. Ficimus quis providitat poreri dolorepe et optae accus venimagnatem re ius rerciliae nobitiusdae doluptatur aliquaerum, niminihicto vit omnis doloreh enderum faccaeperum is et fugiatem harumet aut ut eturion ecuptae aut repudip suntio oditatiore dolutas ma nobis doloreh endipsam volut evelleni coruptat earia nis ad maximus doluptatur, num aut quis dunte conetus, sitius que doloressi sus excessimpe dolores quament experatem cum sa veritatet aut et et preptatur modis magnam que erae dolore dolorios molorepudis secatis magnihicil et mint odi velent.

Onsequibus sum inveles tiandae nem que cus alicidebite omnisquas everum et vollis aditem quatur sint volut et, idebiti stibus everuptas in peliquas derum facipsa nienite quam quiduntia que dolupit, te dist volo eaquam rehenda vere esto volum facea que se pla pelibusa di consect enderum reptat.

Voloris volori reperum quias etum qui optatinti tem fugia intem aborepudis cum que nonet que licitaquid que volore pratatq uatur?

Met quatisci conectemos ea quae es nonessincti tem voluptatur magnatur mi, comnime ma volene nos milloreri se vel id et in

Chapter Three

Reading the Labyrinth
Text as Obstacle in *The Year of the Death of Ricardo Reis*

> While Freud's dream Desire was its own satisfaction, Lacan has hypothesized that Desire is the Desire for "something else," even if the Desired object is unnameable. So viewed, Desire testifies to a fundamental human lack, an anxiety or metonymy ... . Desire does not point to self-induced satisfactions, therefore, but to the inherent incompleteness which drives people to seek Real objects in an effort to appease a psychic uneasiness. The Desiring subject genuinely supposes that a Real object ... is its only goal, one capable of affording ultimate satisfaction if attained. ... According to Lacan, the scope of Desire is infinite; it conceals itself behind the choices that people make in their efforts to be happy, as well as in dreams and common discourse.
> —Ellie Ragland-Sullivan
> *Jacques Lacan and the Philosophy of Psychoanalysis*

The implied author–reader pact inaugurated in *Baltasar and Blimunda* is, as we have seen, a particular and complex one. In the light of the preceding chapter and in consonance with Bürger's postulation of the radical historicity of the institution of art, we can say that such textual manifestations of the literary institution as Saramago's novels are the products of a specific moment in the history of Portuguese literary institutionality, a moment when the institution still retained considerable investment in some of the elements of fascism—even if only the social-psychological residue—and also would seem both to be incorporating the potential to evolve away from the fascist legacy and actually doing so. Such creations as Saramago's historical novels must, then, be seen not only as indices of that movement but also as operators effecting it, a set of interventions carrying out symbolic-level operations within the institutional horizon, which operations urge a different institutional configuration and do so in transaction with the reader, bearer of a version of the literary institutionality and therefore site of the (potential) work of reconfiguration.

Our examination of that transaction has revealed that its psychological structuring works in ways that Freud's analysis of the dynamics of the tendentious joke helps illuminate. What it did not shed light on—at least not fully—is the available motivation, in effect, the tenor of the Freudian "obstacle." In reading *Baltasar and Blimunda* I have all along sensed that there is more at stake in my overcoming of that obstacle than the mere experience of an aesthetically based "pleasure" (whatever that term might be supposed to mean). Surely, the novels have as their basis more than a series of "fascist jokes." The persistence of the national in those "jokes" and their involvement of what might preliminarily be called "national memory" proclaims as much. What, then, are the further stakes within the reception horizon that these novels trade upon and how do those stakes figure in the phenomenology of reading that we have seen heretofore?

In what follows, such questions will be approached through a look at reception issues raised by the second in chronological order of the three historical novels, *The Year of the Death of Ricardo Reis*, published in 1984, two years after *Baltasar and Blimunda*. They will also be approached through a look at non-Portuguese reception of Saramago novels by way of illustrative comparison and contrast. For both tasks I shall have supporting recourse to historiography, economics, qualitative and quantitative sociological work, book reviews, and literary criticism of Saramago's works. I should remark that, as a part of this change in focus comes a change in how I thematize "myself" as reader. Because of the growing complexity of the analysis that the texts impose upon me, the "I " that appears in this chapter and in Chapter 4 while sometimes the recapitulation of the phenomenological subject of Chapter 2, will more often than not be a mixture of that subject and the critical investigator. Hereafter, then, use of the "I" will be as much as anything else a rhetorical device designed to signal that my grappling with issues brought up by my reception still lies at the root of the analysis at hand. Conversely, when such is not really the case, or when the "reader" that I discern is primarily either the reader that the text seeks to create or is a product of the demographics of the time, I use such third-person formulations as "the reader," "the Portuguese reader," and various like formulations, as the immediate context dictates. The choice of when to use first or third person is, then, basically a tactical one. My personal experience will, however, be openly used in another manner: to ground some aspects of what is to follow, I draw upon some of my personal and professional contacts with Saramago readers and with students of his work and draw conclusions from those contacts.

* * *

As preliminary groundwork upon which to approach the first of the two foci, namely, readerly reception as a dimension of *The Year of the Death of Ricardo Reis*, let us engage in a thumbnail sketch of the history of the first fifteen years of Portuguese public life after fascism.

With the events of April 25, 1974, and the end of the *Estado Novo*, a number of issues were—clearly—in need of reformulation. The fascist years had involved a government-centered, authoritarian, right-wing Catholic state that had purposefully reorganized the country in a neo-medieval fashion: re-emphasis on regionalism and "local" "peasant" dress (which in the later years of the regime served tourist purposes); support of (and from) a rural large-tract landholding oligarchy, some of it composed of hereditary nobility, whose outlook favored agriculture and low-skilled cottage and domestic industry (this is not to say that the regime did not benefit from a similar relationship with the small urban industrial sector that it inherited from the preceding First Republic); fostering of "paternalistic" social relations within the social structure as well as between the sexes and in family dynamics; de-emphasis of education; low levels of technical training; and traditional religiosity (Costa Pinto, "Twentieth-Century Portugal" 19–40; Rosas 96–101; Brandão de Brito 102–04; Almeida, "Society and Values" 146–61; Monteiro and Costa Pinto 213–17). This arrangement produced a highly stratified society in which the oligarchs lived in great luxury—large homes, lavish possessions, investments through the London or New York stock exchanges—while the workers, in many cases, quite literally peasants (sometimes "neo-peasants"), were kept at a subsistence level. Social mobility, while not impossible, was improbable, at least outside political and Church circles. Moreover, there was little incentive within the system to effect any change, since those who benefited from it would only see their status imperiled by what we call "development." Such industrial development as there was followed what world systems theory would deem typical "semi-peripheral" patterns (Wallerstein, *Modern World System* 100–03, *Politics* 7): it depended on state support and frequently was instituted in relationship to trade with the Portuguese-held colonies in Africa and the East (the formal term was "the Portuguese Economic Area" [Brandão de Brito 106]) or involved "niche development"—i.e., development that took advantage of opportunities presented by crises and resulting shortfalls elsewhere in the world economic system, which development was therefore usually short-lived. Analysts have characterized this system as one in which agriculture remained "detached from" development (108). That statement, read on its surface (which is not how the analysts meant to have it read), is misleading. Agriculture, dominated by the landholding oligarchy, not only existed laterally to development, it also represented an obstacle to it, in at least two, interrelated senses. First, on a policy level, it was the bedrock support of a state that limited development to the bounds of its own vision for the country, which was decidedly ruralistic. Second, unlike classical industrial development, in which the requisite initial capital accumulation comes in substantial part from the agricultural sector, the Portuguese oligarchs by and large invested surplus capital principally in their own life-trajectories and in luxuries rather than in development in general, much less in any sort of industrial development.

The only chronic problem within the system, at least until the 1960s (pressures from without, both economic and political, began to accumulate after World War II) came within the labor market in the area of wages. Lack of balance in that sector had been endemic to Portugal since well before the advent of fascism—which was acceded to in the 1920s and 1930s pointedly to control interest representation in the labor sector (Schmitter 12–16; Schmitter and Lehmbruch 24–25, 31–32.). Under fascism those pressures were controlled by state intervention and also, starting in the 1950s, were alleviated somewhat by large-scale state-fomented emigration to "Africa"—usually Angola—and, in the last years of the regime, by the exportation of emigrant labor to Europe, principally France.

Social peace was ensured, according to regime logic, by corporatism: state creation of supposedly self-regulating vertical economic sectors (Costa Pinto, "Twentieth-Century Portugal" 30–32; Wiarda). The proclaimed idea was to create a body that would be knowledgeable about the issues of a given industry and would thus be able to deal in a non-conflictive way with problems in that sector. The practical effect was to create something like a narrow, isolated, top-down union, the principal role of which was to suppress labor unrest and occult inequities in the sector (Wiarda 113). And the verticalization dissolved broad-based labor unionism—which, if it did not accept the corporatist order, was then explicitly outlawed (Costa Pinto, "Twentieth-Century Portugal" 31).

The installation of corporations was sporadic throughout the *Estado Novo* years, while their actual effectiveness, even by the regime's logic, is debatable. But installation was ongoing: corporations were still being put in place up to the eve of the 1974 Revolution. And in general one can see in the regime, despite undoubted involvement with international capital at the highest levels, an attempt to keep Portugal economically independent as much as possible—by controlling (i.e., depressing) internal markets (most specifically the labor market), exploiting colonies for the benefit of the mother country, and fostering an inward-turned and historically backward-looking culture.

This structural overview, partial and generalized though it is, clearly coordinates with the hermeneutic localism we had occasion to look at in the first chapter of this study, as well as with the post–World-War-II fascist *isolat* in the area of international relations. Indeed, the social and economic profile, the hermeneutics, and the *isolat* combine to specify, albeit in summary terms, some of the major features of the internal workings of the fascist state. The pattern that emerges on all three fronts is that of a localism that is self-protecting and (ideally) self-sufficient. The guarantor of that diplomatic, economic, hermeneutic, and cultural localism was always the state, broker of internal social "peace" (read avoidance of "class conflict," effected according to a vision that presumed that such conflict, rather than a constituent feature of society as in the Marxist theorization that coined the term, was a variable that could be done away with) (Costa Pinto, "Twentieth-Century Portugal" 35). In external relations the *isolat* took the form of what historians today call "Portuguese exceptionalism": the argument that Portuguese culture is unique in ways summarized by the post–World-War-II development of the concept of Lusotropicalism (see Chapter 1 and also the passage from Eduardo Lourenço used as the epigraph to it).

It is fair to say that after the 1974 Revolution, having inherited this very particular social configuration, the new leadership of Portugal was left with a great many basic decisions to make. It was clear that some sort of economic development—under the circumstances, more or less equatable with industrial development—was needed. But in what areas, to what extent, and, especially, according to what sort of economic logic? The Revolution, which began to a great extent as an attack against Portuguese colonialism and the rationale upon which it rested, took a turn to the left in early 1975 and came to espouse popular land-reform, nationalization of key social services, and industrial development along a socialist model (Sousa Santos 44–45). An anti-left coup within the military in late 1975 redirected restructuring toward a Western model, to which, with varying strategies, the country has since adhered—though the argument has been made regarding the changing strategies that they did not so much involve the discarding of one logic for a succeeding one as the incorporation of one on top of the prior in a heterogeneous mix. Indeed, even after the turn to the right in late 1975, the 1976 constitution retained the language and planning imprint of socialism (45–48). In most cases, with the change of direction in 1975, the land tenancy changes of the first year of the Revolution were reversed, and the oligarchs were reinstated—but within a very different state structure.

At the same time that these internal changes were being carried out, the international economic order was also in the process of change. The welfare state model to which Portugal's planners initially turned was entering eclipse elsewhere. Transnational capital and geographically rather than nationally defined trade organizations were on the rise. The speed and flexibility of communications had internationalized commerce. With those fundamental changes have come the now well known questions about the viability in today's world of the very concept of nation-state-based economic regulation and consequently of the limits of nation-state ability to "govern" in many areas of social functioning. Indeed, the status—even the value, political or analytical—of the nation-state itself has increasingly fallen under question in this regard. Such factors complicated the issue of development for post-revolutionary Portugal.

In terms of day-to-day sociability, the restructuring process itself had a number of effects. Principal among them was the simple fact of consciousness-raising. A populace that was still strongly marked by peasant practices and accustomed to an authoritarian state that purposely depoliticized it (Costa Pinto, "Twentieth-Century Portugal" 34–37)—in many senses, then, in the main a pre-Enlightenment, if not pre-modern, populace—was suddenly made aware of the kinds of decisions that could, and had to, be made. Moreover, it was told that those decisions were being made in its name and was in some cases interacted with by the decision-makers in the process of that decision-making. To be sure, the bulk of the populace was either marginalized from the process as before or was unable to negotiate the leap—cultural and, in many cases, purely logistic—necessary to participate in it. But a portion was not, and many of those who were unable to accompany events were nonetheless aware that they were taking place and grasped something of their relationship to themselves. In short, a populace previously kept unaware of such matters was brought into them to one degree or another.

In the 1970s and 1980s this consciousness-raising was accompanied by a number of events, both internal and international. Internationally, the appearance of foreign investment capital—de-emphasized by the fascist regime—and loan agreements with the International Monetary Fund (in 1977 and 1983). Internally, the "return" of between one-half and one million émigrés and/or their offspring from a now-decolonized Africa, rapid urbanization, the equally rapid growth of an urban, functionally lower-middle- and middle-class ideology, and a near-tripling of the percentage of women in the workforce (depending on exactly how one understands the concept of workforce, Portugal suddenly went from having one of the lowest percentages in Europe to one of the highest).

The national project of the late 1970s, generally one along the lines of the typical Western welfare state, proved untenable, politically if not socially. In the 1980s a kind of neo-liberal free-market logic began to emerge, albeit one brokered by the state, if that is not a contradiction. The fact is, however, that there came to exist a major disjuncture between that prescribed state role as social regulator and the power, or political inclination, it had to carry out that role. That gap between institutional framework and political practice has been dubbed "the parallel state" (Sousa Santos 45–48). In that situation the state increasingly took on, in at times an almost apologetic tone, the role of mediator between its own prescribed but abandoned obligations in a given area of social regulation (to enforce prior agreements, to provide for social welfare, etc.) and, usually, the private enterprise that was operating in a different way in that same area.

Virgínia Ferreira, among others, has observed that in the 1980s, as a result of this complex situation, the Portuguese populace was still characterized by a Europe- and world-oriented elite existing alongside struggling masses (V. Ferreira 180). Those masses, however, were now almost equally urban and rural and, in contrast to the fascist "medievalizing" practice of endeavoring to keep the common people centered on family, municipality, and nationality, were involved in what one pollster investigating social values labels "a mild individualism" (Almeida, "Society and Values" 157). Also, the Portuguese rejected authoritarianism in favor of some variety of participatory democracy. As has been observed by many, however, and verified in polling and other data collection, that populace simultaneously tended to distance itself from the actual practices of the developing liberal democracy at hand and was willing to express that disaffection. To that observation it can be added that the populace was wary of formal social participation in general and was suspicious of any overarching systemic construct, any of the traditional *grands récits* of contemporary Western culture, political or religious. That attitude has produced—or at least correlates with—a tolerance of divergent viewpoints in both areas. The populace, in the place of the now-suspect articles of belief, came to rely instead upon an increased and increasingly flexible use of one's own individual judgment in making life decisions (Almeida, "Evoluções" 67–70). That attitude surely correlates, complexly, with the facts first that under the "parallel state" economic and social realities were often specific to a given place, time, social locus, and set of circumstances rather than easily susceptible of analysis according to a logic grounded in general principles and, second, that a large portion of economic activity was taking place within an "unofficial" economy (Sousa Santos 54 ff.). In a case illustrative of all of these points at once, Sousa Santos tells of one instance in which, the state having failed to enforce labor contracts, workers in a large number of factories labored without pay for a several-month period, afraid not to show up for work lest their jobs be given to others as a result (47). Correlatively, this populace conceived of concepts as quantities to be selected from, manipulated, combined, and worked with to produce bases for action concerning immediate problems rather than as receptacles of conviction (Almeida, "Society and Values" 159–61) and was suspicious of looking to the general future as an area of promise. Instead it preferred to concentrate on short-term control of present or immediately future realities. Social scientist João Ferreira de Almeida, in his highly influential pioneering attitudes studies of the late 1980s and early 1990s, goes even farther and refers to that attitude, which often leads to an individualized combination of religious and political concepts that, in terms of logic or cultural history, do not fit together at all, as "the craftsmanship of ideas" ("Society and Values" 160).

I would add that on the political front this attitude cannot be characterized—as it often is—as simple apathy, for it is clear that the populace was by and large aware of the alternatives it had before it and how they might play out and was attentive to political developments. The attitude was (and continues today to be) rather a disaffection from a process seen as inconsistent or unreliable. Thus the Portuguese Communists, who were the political-intellectual leaders during the first several years of the national restructuring, are correct, at least in their own terms: there is a sense in which the potential that the revolution was seen to possess was not (fully) realized. Especially in the 1980s that sense produced pervasive disaffection and the seeking of alternative, less public ways of achieving personal security (158–59).

* * *

Of the myriad aspects of Portuguese life that one must examine "before and after" the 1974 Revolution in order to get a coherent picture of the post-revolutionary moment, one that will interest us here is Saramago's Portuguese readership—or, really, *available*

Portuguese readership. As a preliminary to examining that issue, it is worth observing that, even pre-Nobel, Saramago's novels literally recast expectations in Portuguese publishing. In a country that would previously publish novels in single print runs of 2,000–3,000 copies at most, starting with the public reception of *Baltasar and Blimunda*, Saramago titles have been printed in runs of tens of thousands and reprinted multiple times. Hence the role that his novel production plays in the history of the market aspect of Portuguese literary culture—and hence too the reception scale to which the next few pages implicitly refer.

If we take 1974 as the pivot point for periodization—a strategy both obvious and supported by the fact of allusion to the revolution within the reader–implied author pact in *Baltasar and Blimunda* (and, for that matter in its two subsequent "historical" partners as well)—the principal readership constituencies for Saramago novels at the time of their publication can, in the first instance, be thought of simply as follows: readers who experienced fascism fully—roughly, those who reached intellectual maturity before 1974—and those who reached intellectual maturity afterward. Let us refer to the former as generation A and the latter as generation B. A second, more complicated criterion must be brought to bear as well, namely, social status. That criterion inflects both generation A and generation B, albeit in somewhat different ways. For generation A, simplifying considerably, we can designate two groups. Group A1: individuals old enough to recall fascism who, necessarily, lived through the revolution and subsequent national restructuring as well; for simple reasons of literacy and economic ability to access written materials in fascist times, these readers, save for the rare anomaly, would have to be lower-middle class and above. Group A2: in effect, a subset of A1, namely, members of the intelligentsia with the same demographic profile as group A1. In my limited experience, dislike of what Saramago was doing with the novel form—and it was often strong, outspoken dislike—was most frequently found in the upper social levels of A1 and quite strongly in A2. From what we have seen in the prior chapter, we can safely conclude that groups A1 and A2 constitute the historical referent for *Baltasar and Blimunda*'s "implied" readership seen in Iserian terms—i.e., the readership that the text simultaneously presupposes and seeks to create through interaction with actual readers (Iser, *Implied Reader*).

Reading the Labyrinth

For generation B, also two groups, though matters grow more complex. Group B1: Portuguese who reached intellectual maturity at the end of the 1970s or during the course of the 1980s, still lower-middle class and above; many of them from the newly urban, growing professional and business sectors of post-revolutionary Portuguese society, or living abroad for professional reasons (Portugal has experienced a considerable "brain drain" since the revolution); both male and female (for historical reasons mentioned above [p. 62], groups A1 and A2 were overwhelmingly male). Both increased access to education[1] and slightly improved economic status doubtless allowed for a greater readership at the lower socio-economic levels of this demographic than was the case with A1 and likely enabled some downward spread of it as well. Now logically speaking, B1 readers are individuals for whom fascism is a childhood or youthful memory as well as a historical concept received in multiple ways, and the revolution is at most a memory without strong content. They came of age in the post-revolutionary moment, and for them the dynamics of that period and of the national restructuring, including the residue of fascist practices in relation to which the restructuring situated itself, were the major formative elements. They also experienced the periods of consciousness-raising and of subsequent disaffection referred to above. B2 readers, again a subset of B1: members of the intelligentsia with roughly the same demographic profile as B1, a group that, in the main, has found Saramago's work appealing (I base this last assertion on personal contacts and on my reading in the critical record). I suspect that the relationship between B1 and B2 is much more complex than the relationship between A1 and A2, as "intelligentsia" has become redefined in the Western world through changing social structures and increased ease of transportation and communication.

There is little point in thinking beyond generation B, since the effect of the Nobel Prize in 1998 has drastically altered the motivations for reading Saramago's works and hence readership demographics as well.

In terms of sheer numbers, *Baltasar and Blimunda*'s initial readership was probably located relatively evenly in generations A and B, with A, for simple actuarial reasons, providing decreasing numbers thereafter. Groups A2 and B2 are relatively small, though they play important roles as propagators of literary evaluation

Chapter Three

within the society—i.e., they tend to be those who might have a greater effect within the institutional sphere. In short, the original Portuguese readership would have been composed of a mix of young professionals and business people on the one hand and older middle-level people on the other. The latter group will have steadily decreased as time has moved on.

Now it is clear that the generational division will necessarily correlate with differing reception horizons. As has already been stated, generation A produces the "implied" reader of a text such as *Baltasar and Blimunda*: someone so intimately familiar with the culture of fascism as to grasp, for example, that in that novel the characterization of eighteenth-century Lisbon as a mixture of abject poverty in the lower classes and high luxury in the palace, the carefully chronicled religion-based credulity and the workings of an autocratic Inquisition, all functioned—often in considerable detail—both to debunk fascism's notion of a monumental national history filled with enlightened leaders and also to suggest a kind of loose analogical relationship between the depicted era and fascist Portugal itself. They would also be prepared to receive—though not necessarily consciously much less knowing how or why—the complex psychologically liberatory opportunity being offered them as readers of that novel.

As we have seen, passages in *Baltasar and Blimunda* function, structurally speaking, as virtual jokes, told by the implied author to the reader, that rely upon a shared ground of experience of Portuguese fascism for their meaning-making and their impact. A blatant example, in which the narrator and reader virtually share a laugh based on that common ground, is to be seen toward the end of *Baltasar and Blimunda*, when João Elvas, one the novel's minor characters, witnesses a royal procession:

> João Elvas was among the crowd that broke ranks and shouted: Long live the King! as Dom João V, sovereign of all Portugal, went past. If that was not what they were shouting, it sounded very much like it, for one can always tell the difference between acclaim and derision. (278)
>
> [João Elvas estava no meio do povo que abria alas e aclamava, real, real, por D. João V, rei de Portugal, se não era assim que diziam, então seria aquele vozear que só pelo tom permite distinguir entre o aplauso e o apupo … (*Memorial do Convento* 302–03)]

A generation A reader might well identify with the crowd's attitude, which the implied author seemingly allows to be a cheering for authority but—with, again, litotes-like rhetoric—simultaneously hints might in reality be more of what in English would be called a "raspberry" directed at a monarch who would later be treated quite differently in the *Estado Novo*'s "monumental" version of the country's history, only to have the tables re-turned by the 1980s. And the juxtaposition of the two possibilities suggests in and of itself the psychological tension in which the two impulses existed for the reader her- or himself. The pairing of the phonically similar words in Portuguese, '*aplauso*'/'*apupo*,' approximately the English 'cheer'/'jeer,' capsules, then, not only a lexical opposition but a psychological tension, and that tension is activated and used as a part of the reading process. For generation B such allusiveness—especially if it is as straightforward as it is in the above example—may be understood more or less fully because its textual expression is obvious, or because the history is well enough known, or because sufficient characterization of life during the fascist years has been present in the reader's socialization. In terms of the hermeneutic rules, the recognition may include an understanding of the residue of fascist input within the literary institution (perhaps "previously we were unable to say these things or to communicate this way in literature"). But it will not include the vital knowledge of someone who experienced the regime personally, no calling up of the complex, tension-filled relationship to authority.

And, of course, generation B will miss some allusions completely. I once gave a presentation to a large group of primarily generation B Portuguese—young to middle-aged professionals. Mostly, then, group B1 within the above division, though certainly some B2 people as well. That presentation touched on Saramago's *The Year of the Death of Ricardo Reis* and specifically on the references in that novel to Camões, the so-called national poet, of the sixteenth century (Sousa, "Future" in the bibliography to this study comprises a reduced version of that presentation). Those references have principally to do with the novel's representation of the statue of Camões in Lisbon's Bairro Alto area. In conversation after the presentation, several people confessed that, while *The Year of the Death of Ricardo Reis* was their favorite novel (one young man asserted that he had read it at least ten times and in the light of my presentation he was now going to reread it again as soon as he got home), it had apparently occurred to none of them to read the narrator's various remarks about "Camões" as anything more than the registering of urban geography and a bit of the usual poking by "Saramago" at Portuguese sacred cows. They did have a well-formed sense that only recently could a novelist do that in Portugal, but they missed completely that the allusion to the statue of Camões included the ironization of the monumental national history promulgated by fascism, in which Camões was one of the key symbols. Given the total novel context, few generation A individuals and likely no A2 ones would have misunderstood what was being driven at by such allusions, whether they sympathized with the point being made or not. For example, early on in *The Year of the Death of Ricardo Reis*, we see the title character as he walks through the Bairro Alto,[2] feeling "as if he were trapped in a labyrinth that always led him back to the same spot, to this bronze statue ennobled and armed with a sword" (*Year* 55) ["como se estivesse dentro de um laberinto que o conduzisse sempre ao mesmo lugar, a este bronze afidalgado e espadachim" (*Ano* 68)]. For most people who had lived through fascism it would surely become clear before long that the represented urban "labyrinth" of Lisbon is also the assemblage of public signals—statues among them—pointing to the regime's view of the national history. It is the "labyrinthine" symbolic (and bureaucratic) network supportive of fascism, and it is no accident that Reis is always "led back to the same spot." For the generation B member, it would not be—and in my actual experience with generation B individuals was not—clear. (We shall see more regarding the labyrinth/network as this chapter progresses.)

The reader–implied author pact examined in the previous chapter would, then, when we give it this demographic profile rather than a phenomenological focus, seem to comprise the overlay of two pacts: one with readers old enough to have experience of fascism and another with readers who at best possess transmitted, and therefore partial, knowledge. As regards my own smile, despite having lived only a small part of my life in Portugal, I fit most easily in generation A, because of my age, because I had direct experience of life under the fascist regime, and because from my upbringing I was aware of Portuguese politics[3] and, at a certain point I initiated study of the *Estado Novo*. I therefore belong most directly to group A2, albeit to a non-Portuguese subset of it (which fact causes me to remove my own reading experience from consideration on matters about which I do not feel sufficiently acculturated to trust myself). My knowledge of generation B readership has come through multiple conversations with generation B Portuguese from many walks of life and from a reading of the outpouring of commentary on, and criticism and interpretation of, Saramago's writings and other analytical work produced by members of that generation.

* * *

Now to the light that the reading of my reception of *The Year of the Death of Ricardo Reis* sheds upon the dynamics of the implied author–reader pact that we have seen at work thus far. As a prelude to—and, to some extent, a first step in—analysis of salient aspects of the novel's reception, a capsule of some of its main points will be necessary. I shall take a bit of time in this process, in part to touch on some replications of features observed in *Baltasar and Blimunda* and the ways in which differences exist within those similarities and also to develop some principal implications of the differences.

In both Portuguese and English the novel is entitled **The Year of the Death of Ricardo Reis**. While the fact can easily escape me as I read, I need to place my emphasis on "the year." That year is 1936, a year of consolidation of the recently established *Estado Novo* and also of the outbreak of the Civil War in neighboring Spain. One feature of the novel is its maintenance of an approximate historical chronology.[4] That chronology is established on the one end by Ricardo Reis's arrival in Lisbon by ship from Brazil on December 28, 1935[5] after a sixteen-year absence from his native country. The chronology is then kept before my eyes by Reis's and/or the implied author's regular reading of daily newspapers (I shall often use the formulation "Reis and/or the implied author," in variant forms, since in the novel's narration the voices of Reis and the implied author are often indistinguishable). I am led to suspect—correctly—that they are real period newspapers and that, in parallel with practice in *Baltasar and Blimunda*, the novel is incorporating them more or less verbatim.

The chronology is bounded by another factor, which comes linked to Reis's relationship with the novel's other main character:

Chapter Three

the ghost of the poet Fernando Pessoa. It has been Pessoa's death on November 30, 1935 that has occasioned Reis's return to Portugal. Here matters become complex: Pessoa is doubtless the most famous Portuguese literary figure of the modern age (see Chapter 1); his work is translated into virtually every major world language. One of the salient features of his work is that he wrote poetry of quite differing kinds and assigned some of those discrete kinds of poetry to names other than his own, which he called his "heteronyms." He gave each heteronym physical characteristics, a biography, etc. One of the principal of those heteronyms is Ricardo Reis, a doctor born in the Portuguese city of Oporto—who in Pessoa's telling, had left Portugal for Brazil. What we have in *The Year of the Death of Ricardo Reis*, with Reis's novelistic return upon Pessoa's death is, then, the return of a fictitious fictional character to a fictitious representation of his deceased creator. To avoid (further) confusion between novel and history, I assure you that the historical Fernando Pessoa did indeed, as *Year of the Death* presumes, die on November 30, 1935. The Portuguese readership would bring this knowledge to reception of the novel. At least some international readership has not understood it (see p. 119, below). The flamboyance of this plot line certainly rivals that of *Baltasar and Blimunda*, with its flying-machine run on Scholastic mechanics. Pessoa explains to Reis early in the novel that just as human beings pass through nine months of gestation before birth, so we have an equal period after death to wander the earth as ghosts before going definitively to our graves. Thus is fashioned a narrative mechanism for measuring the time span of the novel: it lasts from December 28 (or 29), 1935 to nine months after November 30, 1935, which amounts to most of 1936.[6] At the end of the prescribed time period, Pessoa goes to his grave, Reis, presumably because he is Pessoa's creation, follows him, and the novel ends.

During the eight-or-so months between Reis's arrival and their dual entombment, Reis and Pessoa's ghost discuss many things, and multiple examples of Reis or Pessoa poetry are reproduced and remarked about on the page. Reis also establishes a casual sexual relationship with Lydia, the maid at the hotel in which he is staying. While this activity is going on in the foreground, Reis also functions as a figure through which, or in relation to which, I receive a representation of the Lisbon of 1936. Reis/the implied author take in the city; its poverty; the urban renewal that has taken place; the news of the day, including both the doings of the *Estado Novo* at home and the beginnings of the Spanish Civil War; the weather (it was, in point of historical fact, an unusually rainy winter Europe-wide, and there was much flooding); the commercial advertising in the newspapers of the day. Reis, albeit a nonbeliever, pilgrimages to the shrine at Fátima, constructed during his absence. In general, the discourses of the day are laid before my eyes in ways similar to the anthropological techniques employed in *Baltasar and Blimunda*. And Reis and Pessoa—presented as intelligent and reflective men both—sometimes comment dryly on them in their conversations. Generally, however, I get implicit irony from Reis and/or the implied author—again, much as in *Baltasar and Blimunda*.

Throughout this outpouring of detail, the sense is strongly communicated to me that there are things going on that were then, and still are, in need of interpretation and that their understanding is of vital importance to me. Transmittal of that sense is clearly a part of the backdrop of the reader–implied author communication in the novel and just as clearly labels it as a communication taking place at the time of the reading—not a phenomenon inherent in the horizon of the represented 1936—and thus as a central aspect of the reader–implied author pact. Moreover, on this front a basic misdirection operates throughout the novel. I am implicitly asked to look to Reis and Pessoa as the interpreters, but while they do draw some conclusions, it is unclear that they are involved in any general interpretation project. Instead, on this score they function principally to pose issues in need of interpretation. (This attitude is of a piece with that of the historical poet Fernando Pessoa and also with the "contemplative' outlook he assigns to the Ricardo Reis heteronym.) The actual task of interpretation is implicitly assigned to me the reader, virtually by default: interpretation is urged and there is no other locus of interpretation beyond myself—in tandem, again, with the implied author. While I continue to look to the characters for information, I am gradually forced to take on the interpretive project myself.

Much as in *Baltasar and Blimunda*, none of the characters, not even Reis, is highly developed in the usual sense of literary characterization. And even more than in *Baltasar and Blimunda* those figures resist any attempt on my part to identify with them facilely. Moreover, the events in which they are involved take on the character of enigmas: What are motivations for them? What effect do individual human actions have in this represented world—or in the world in general? How can we know what has caused something to happen? Indeed, the implied author makes much of the idea of puzzles and labyrinths, regularly referring to a book entitled *The God of the Labyrinth*, by an author named Herbert Quain, whose last name, because of eerily close phonic similarity, he likens to "quem," which is the Portuguese interrogative "who?" (12 [23]). (In this case, by the way, the allusion is not one to a historical book but rather to a fictitious one, taken from "Examen de la obra de Herbert Quain," a short story by Jorge Luis Borges [Borges].)

In comparison with *Baltasar and Blimunda*, then, the basic reader–implied author pact is shifted: the implied author, rather than acting primarily as my companion/leader, spends some time presenting me with puzzles for interpretation in a kind of intellectual game-playing that continually asks me to decipher, to seek to understand, and that task is accorded urgency by the novel's very rhetoric. It becomes clear as *The Year of the Death of Ricardo Reis* progresses that the questions posed generally about history, causality, and interpretability both refer to the social scene of 1936 Lisbon and also, as in *Baltasar and Blimunda*, apply generally—and that they receive no clear answers. Hence the puzzle or labyrinthine quality of the novel's texture. We can say that just as 1936 Lisbon presents itself as something of a puzzle to Ricardo Reis, so *The Year of the Death of Ricardo Reis* presents itself as a puzzle to me the reader and that very fact suggests general epistemological applicability.

This new emphasis does not drastically alter the terms of the reader–implied author pact as it was explored in the last chapter. It does, however, produce a more intellectual narrative than I encountered in the prior novel. And if the overriding readerly emotion elicited by *Baltasar and Blimunda* was a kind of joy, here I find myself facing an inconclusiveness and, occasionally, a grimness that is paramount in only a few passages of *Baltasar and Blimunda* (e.g., pp. 64–68, above). While in the earlier novel the characters' violation of orthodoxy contributes to an experience of joy for me as I read, in *The Year of the Death of Ricardo Reis* the sense of all-pervasive suspicion on the part of social authority that orthodoxy might be challenged contributes to a sense on my part of vulnerability and insecurity. I even grow to fear that Reis is going to be (unjustly?) condemned by the *Estado Novo* authorities of the represented 1936.

Generation A readers are likely to have their own anxieties and/or uncertainties summoned up retroactively by this interpellation—in a process of memory-elaboration that, in a kind of inverse parallel to the seriatim seeking of pleasure in the reading of *Baltasar and Blimunda*, could for some individuals amount to the Freudian *Nachträglichkeit*. As for myself in this regard, I still understand that I am being asked, as one of the bases of reading, to confront the Freudian obstacle, but, given the degree to which both the installation of the *Estado Novo* and representations of its workings are directly thematized upon the page, the "obstacle" is now patent: it is the texture of the novel itself—while also continuing to be present within the hermeneutical rules for the novel's reception.

Now the term *obstacle* is derived from the Freudian joke economy, the one model we have been using thus far. In the light of the content of *The Year of the Death of Ricardo Reis*, its appeal to me might be better understood as the admixture of the joke economy and the economy of the Freudian castration complex. In that complex, seen simply, the individual experiences a sense of loss and resultant powerlessness that he or she may seek to overcome in specific acts—such, for example, as the telling/receiving of jokes! Given the historical references to experience under the fascist regime, in *The Year of the Death of Ricardo Reis* the joke "obstacle" can thus be seen to function as the sign of castration—or, because the "memory" of that experience is actually summoned up by the novel content and texture, we should speak of an "induced" or "re-induced" castration trauma (that any such retroactive trauma would necessarily have to be "induced" or "re-induced" [cf. Laplanche 88] should not bother us for present purposes). This summoning-up is likely to occur, in the sense that it is presented here, for generation A readers only, of course, though generation B readers may be appealed to in analogous ways, as we shall see.

As the epigraph to this chapter suggests, Jacques Lacan takes Freudian castration and makes of it not an individual-subject complex but part of an understanding of human be-ing as unstable, or split. This is the famous "Lacanian constitutive lack," which brings with it the subject's repeated efforts to find a way, in Ragland-Sullivan's terms, to "appease" it. In this novel, then, I as reader am asked to experience, in the repeated novelistic summoning-up of the insecurity and opaqueness—for consistency's sake, let us use "impotence" as a generalizing term—that characterized life for many Portuguese under the fascist state, the serial re-induction of a basic castration trauma.

For generation A readers such re-induction depends on some aspect of what we call "memory"—in traditional Western terms (at least since Augustine) a primary area in which we understand that we construct and retain our "self" (Taylor 131–39). In the critical literature there is—understandably—much work done on the "historical" novels' engagement with "national memory," a term understood and developed in that literature in a number of different ways (for an overview, see Martins and her references). It is not my purpose here to participate in examination of the issues involved except to clear a way through them in my smile pursuit. Teresa Cerdeira da Silva, for example, has argued gnomically that all of Saramago's writing "is a site of memory" ("On the Labyrinth" 75), a phrase that provides a useful touchstone to that end. Only in some very specific senses, of course, does "memory" in *Year of the Death* have centrally to do with the concept of "memory" as traditionally understood or with the human capacity to recall, today the object of a great deal of empirical study. It has much more to do with narration and the social power and use of narratives, as Cerdeira da Silva signals with her phrase. I add that it also has to do with the narratives' reception. In the case of *The Year of the Death of Ricardo Reis,* "memory," considered schematically, necessarily involves a processing of input from the reader's past experience as a part of his or her reception of the novel texture. But what construal of "past" and what kind of "processing"? In effect, the novel offers itself as a symbolic labyrinth/puzzle involving the early years of the *Estado Novo* (though it produces some historical anachronisms in anticipation of the regime's later years) and urges me to deal with my trauma related to that era by dealing with it, the novel texture, centrally investing, as Iser postulates I must, my own experience, my own subjectivity, in that process. That is, the novel supplies the "symbolic realm" and offers up to me its own reading as the activity through which "appeasement" of impotence can be sought. Jonathan Boulter, with different goals than mine in mind, nonetheless sums up the various factors involved as I read them as the result of my reception: "… I am wondering ... if Saramago's novels ... wish, at least at one level, to negotiate an understanding of how ... , in Freudian terms, the past continues to work itself out through the subject in the present" (Boulter 140).

Some quotient of "memory" so understood thus comes bound up with the re-induction of the "trauma" of fascism. The function assigned this "memory" can be conceived to an extent useful for present purposes by recourse to Walter Benjamin's analysis of allegory (Benjamin, esp. 163–67)—because, in a first instance, this memory involves the creation of meaning from the dialectical relationship between two narratized or (potentially) narratizable systems—here on the one hand, the novel's texture and the "history" to which it alludes and, on the other hand, readerly subjectivity and the experiential baggage that it brings with it. The novel is filled with names, places, and represented events that function as signs for the civil and symbolic order that, in 1936, was being put in place by the incipient *Estado Novo* and would continue for decades to come. It is that texture that triggers and channels my subjective investment. I do not "remember," in some mimetic sense, the specifics of the events represented or alluded to in *Year of the Death* or the feelings those particular events engendered; we are not dealing with some retention as mneme. Human beings "remember" in relation to narratives we tell ourselves and/or have told to us (Kahneman 386–90). And indeed, if truth be told, in the publication year of 1984 most of even generation A readers would not have been old enough to have experienced those specific events of 1936 and feelings related to them. As Benjamin suggests in his analysis of allegory, it is not through reproduction of past happenings that I "remember" as I read. Rather, the novel's puzzle/labyrinth calls up my existential connections and trades on the fact that I am necessarily creating a sense retroactively rather than calling one up—and that I am doing so precisely against an awareness of the absence of sense. In the specific case of our reader/text relationship, sense is "absent" historically as well—because any possible historical "sense" was both occluded by the power of the *Estado Novo* and as a consequence also repressed or otherwise psychologically fraught within the individual. The attempt to fashion a narrative to account for disinformation or partial information is itself a traumatic undertaking. Such "absence" is, of course, only an instance of sense's general structural "ab-sense"-and-creation in

Chapter Three

the act of "memory"—in Benjaminian terms, an act consisting of the inevitable violent "petrification" (166) of apprehension into "sense." What the novel presents in its open-ended labyrinth/puzzle texture urging interpretation is precisely an "ab-sense-calling-for-sense." I, in reading-for-appeasement, am thus impelled to create a psychologically useful meaning under the sign of the combination of meaning's impossibility and its historical repression and am doing so at the site of both that repression and its historical lifting. The "signs" of which the texture of the novel is made thus function as linearly arranged cues for an act of "memory" necessarily carried out subjectively, with a resultant content that is subjective and affective. Nevertheless, it is created as a response to the need to "appease" this particular, historically fetched "impotence." "Memory," in this case, is thus both a constituent part of reception and a product of it, both the trauma of impotence re-induced and the effort to appease that trauma.

This reception economy forms the basis of a dynamic that—much as does *Baltasar and Blimunda*, in which it exists as a dark underside to the liberatory "joy"—strings together seriatim moments of release and trades on a drive in me the reader continually to go back, to try to find out more from within the novel's labyrinth. It is amazing how many readers of *The Year of the Death of Ricardo Reis* speak of reading it, all or in part, many, many times; recall the young man at my lecture, pp. 91–92 above. I know that I have gone back to reread it, hoping to "find more"—which act, of course, is not carried out for that purpose at all, except as "find more" is a synonym for "appeasement." If we follow Lacan's thinking, then, this attempt is one made to appease the unappeasable, since the need ultimately derives from our sense of incompleteness in general. *Year of the Death*, then, trades on insecurity, on an unknowability that nonetheless urges its resolution in order that I the reader can feel fulfilled. In so doing it demonstrates that the need to "appease" is the central engine of the novel's reception. (I should make it clear that in using terms like *impotence* and *trauma* I am not attempting to pathologize the reader's role in the novels—though psychopathological reactions are clearly possible in some readers; I am merely attempting to sketch out in skeletal terms the psychology of the reader/novel interaction.)

And as though to heighten the sense of individual "performance of memory" in the face of the trace of repression, the novel gives us the character of Victor, the domestic spy who follows Ricardo Reis. Victor is presented through appeal to the sense of smell: he smells of onions, and, in what is a clever way of suggesting the invisible pervasiveness of the domestic surveillance (as well as accomplishing other effects that we shall presently see), I am occasionally told that the odor of onions has been left lingering in the air in one place or another in Reis's wanderings. For most human beings, specific memories are linked to the sense of smell. It is not, of course, that mention of the smell of onions would trigger memories in readers but rather that appeal to the sense of smell, in this case in addition to characterizing the pervasive working of domestic espionage, calls up "memory" categorically.

In short, in ways structurally similar to *Baltasar and Blimunda* but psychologically different from it, I as reader of *Year of the Death* am not urged simply to invest myself in some "normal" performance of a meaning (I do not wish to be understood as presuming that any such de-contextualized instance could ever actually exist). I am instead urged to perform a meaning at the site of trauma involving meaning's overt repression. That performance, then, must at some level continually suggest itself as a performance carried out with the understanding that the resultant meaning is purely heuristic.

Ellen Sapega has argued (*Consensus and Debate* 23) that one of the fronts opened up by the *Estado Novo* as, in the 1930s, it sought to install itself fully, involved the studied creation of "public memory sites." The sites' state-created attached narratives ratified—and, with entrenchment in the public memory, would keep on ratifying—the *Estado Novo* view of the nationality. The process, as she analyzes it, can be thought of as a studied effort to construct what, after Fredric Jameson, we have come to call a social "political unconscious" (*Political Unconscious*). Hence the generation-after-generation "presence" of fascist "memory." In this connection Saramago's three historical novels, and especially *Year of the Death*, can be looked at as efforts to create the ground for a possible retroactive counter-memory based precisely on the residual fascist-created memory—as long as we understand that there is no one counter-memory being promulgated but rather that "counter-memory" refers not to a content but to a kind of performance.

The entire development around "memory" further complexifies much of what we have seen in the previous chapter about *Baltasar and Blimunda*. To begin, it adds dimensions to the terms *repression* and *heuristic*. In the case of the former, the stakes involved in seeking the release of pleasure in the overcoming of the fascist-hermeneutical "obstacle" are substantially redefined to include as well a repetitive seeking to overcome impotence or other psychic disturbances structurally subsumable under that rubric. And such dynamics as rhetorical allegory/displacement-in-reading can now be seen not as simple features of reception or mechanisms of readerly joy but also as sites for the re-induction of castration trauma. "Heuristic," as it applies to *Year of the Death*, is the repetitive creation of an existentially based "sense" out of past experience, a sense somewhere understood to be a fiction in mimetic terms but functionally the appeasement of a categorical need-for-"sense." This "need" should, of course, be included as a factor underlying the hermeneutical rules in question in the reader–implied author pact operating in both novels. "(Re-)writing in the institutional sphere" is thus assigned an urgency that was not easily seen in *Baltasar and Blimunda*. The attitude "let's ransack together" is now not simply the free, celebratory one dominant in that novel. Indeed, its dimension of repetitive joyful release now appears with an underside involving a compulsive, repetitive seeking to overcome impotence. And work in the institutional sphere now takes on the aspect of struggle in which the "obstacle" becomes more internalized in the receiver and less easily tractable than in our view of it in the preceding chapter.

To this complexification of some key terminology it should be added that in *Baltasar and Blimunda* the reader's apprehension of the title characters' love relationship likely receives some of its emotional charge from the presence of the obstacle. It is now obvious that a part of the "meaning" made in reception of the love dimension comes from the presence in the reader of an obstacle constructed along the lines that we now envision. Likewise many of the acts of "hermeneutical violation" that we saw in *Baltasar and Blimunda* invite interpretation—according to the version of the obstacle brought by the reader to the encounter with the text—as something like acts of resistance that bear an emotional charge with them.

Hence the value of the presentation of the "obstacle" in these novels: it is not there in an historical manner only; it is also powerfully there within the individual reader. And conversely, this state of affairs highlights the stakes in the institutional sphere: the struggle is one for (re-)definition there—perhaps because it is there that change of a major sort is feasible, while change within the individual reader is at best ephemeral in socio-historical terms and is, more likely than not, "change from," or "change against," with the obstacle remaining relatively intractable.

Many of these features of *Year of the Death* come together in one or another (of the several) narrative lines that can be traced through the novel's labyrinthine texture. Let me trace out one of those narrative lines—the most obvious—and draw conclusions from it that illustrate the impact of all. As Reis disembarks in the novel's opening scene, the implied author chooses to remark on the presence of several Portuguese torpedo boats in the harbor, including among those he lists, the *Dão*. Some few (Portuguese) readers might know that, in point of fact now substantially erased from history, several Portuguese naval vessels, the *Dão* among them, mutinied in Lisbon on September 7, 1936, a date toward the end of the time period encompassed by the novel. That mutiny represented an unsuccessful attempt to join the Spanish Republican forces in the fight against the Spanish Fascists and perhaps to open up an anti-fascist front in Portugal itself. At that point in the novel it is suggested to me the reader that this connection is not casual, for the already intrusive implied author remarks about the *Dão*: "perhaps we shall have news of her later" (*Year* 6) ["acaso tornaremos a ter notícias dele" (*Ano* 16)]. Alerted as I now am to this pending issue, I follow its thin, wandering trace through the novel's narrative labyrinth, hoping that it will provide for the making of (some) sense. Now Reis is being followed throughout the novel by the odious/odiferous Victor. Eventually Reis is interrogated by the police, apparently under the suspicion that, in his return to Portugal, he has subversive intentions (159–65 [187–93]). I learn much later in the novel that Lydia's brother is a crewman on one of the ships that will seek to mutiny at novel's end; as a consequence I am forced to ask myself—significantly, without being able to answer—if that is why the spy has been following Reis all along or, conversely, if general espionage upon the newly returned Reis has been what has led to the uncovering and foiling of the mutiny. The overriding sense that I get—or, really, create for myself—is that, especially if the latter was the case, the discovery may well have been an accidental one based on mistaken,

Chapter Three

almost random but highly resolute, domestic espionage within the police-state-in-formation that was the *Estado Novo*. The effect is a kind of heartsickness à la Orwell's *1984*: the state is everywhere, clumsily but effectively enforcing its view over people who have no contrary orientation (as far as we know in Reis's case, though there is some reason to suspect him [see n5]). The characters are, however, powerless to resist state logic—just as I am powerless to create any satisfying sense to appease my impotence. All of this adds yet more weight to the general obstacle/re-induced trauma of impotence that I am forced continually to seek to appease as I receive the novel's "symbolic" texture.

* * *

The following extended passage provides one vantage point upon the novel's putting-in-place of the fascist symbolic order and its articulation with the reader on that score. In the passage, the putting-in-place is accomplished by following Reis's acceptance of a suggestion, made by another of the guests in the hotel where he stays upon arrival in Lisbon, that he read a specific book in order to understand what is happening in Portugal under the new regime. The other character is an enthusiastic apologist for the regime. As are considerable portions of *The Year of the Death of Ricardo Reis*, the passage in question is rendered in a style in which reported interior monologue on the one hand and narration/implied author commentary on the other are indistinguishable:

> The very next day Ricardo Reis went out and bought the slim volume ... [The] cover ... shows a woman in a raincoat and cap walking down a street by a prison, the barred window and sentry box eliminating any doubt about the fate of conspirators.... Everywhere there is flood and famine, but this little book will tell how a woman's soul launched itself into the noble crusade of restoring to reason and to the nationalist spirit a man whose mind became confused by dangerous ideas. ... The plot is as follows, a university student ... gets into some mischief, is arrested, locked up in the prison of Aljube, and it is the daughter of [a] senator who with patriotic fervor and missionary zeal will move heaven and earth to secure his release, which is not all that difficult in the end, because to the astonishment of the man who brought her into the world, this senator who belonged to the democratic party but is now an unmasked conspirator, she is

much esteemed in the upper spheres of government, a father can never tell how his own daughter will turn out. (*Year* 118–19)

[Ricardo Reis logo no dia seguinte foi comprar o livrinho ... [A] capa ... nos mostra uma mulher de gabardina e boina, descendo uma rua, ao lado duma prisão, como se percebe logo pela janela gradeada e pela guarita da sentinela, ali postas para não haver dúvidas sobre o que espera conspiradores. ... [H]á cheias por toda a parte, destruições, fome de rabo, mas este livrinho irá dizer como uma alma de mulher se lançou na generosa cruzada de chamar à razão e ao espírito nacionalista alguém a quem ideias perigosas tinham perturbado, sic. ... [C]erto moço universitário ... meteu-se em rapaziadas, foi preso, trancado no Aljube, e vai ser a ... filha de senador quem, por puras razões patrióticas, por missionação abnegada, moverá céus e terra para de lá o tirar, o que, afinal, não lhe será difícil, pois é muito estimada nas altas esferas da governação, com surpresa daquele que lhe deu ser, senador que foi do partido democrata e agora conspirador ludibriado, um pai nunca sabe para o que cria uma filha. (*Ano* 142–43)]

The passage touches on so many issues that it would take page upon page to discuss them all. For example, the word *famine* serves to bring up and establish at the outset a contrast between, on the one hand, the actual social conditions—scenes of want and public begging compounded by the floods and resulting food shortages of early 1936 have been registered several times over in the preceding pages of the novel, often through the reading of period newspapers (e.g., 101 [119–20])—and, on the other hand, the language of the "noble crusade." The contrast between material poverty and idealistic nationalist language that refuses to acknowledge that poverty but instead offers itself as a substitute for it was a feature of both the fascist historical vision and the day-to-day experiencing of the *Estado Novo*. The implied author regularly touches on the language, the experience, or both, and in this passage invites me to bring up and deal with the disparity between them and to use recognition of that disparity and control of it through the activity of reception as a part of the process of appeasement-seeking. As the passage continues, that basic contrast is further played upon, with heavy irony:

[S]uch a benevolent, kind-hearted police force here in Portugal, and little wonder, since they have an informer in the enemy

Chapter Three

camp ... Family traditions have been betrayed, but all will end happily for the parties in question if we take the author of the work seriously. Let us now hear what he has to say, The situation in our country has been discussed with enthusiasm in the foreign press, our economic strategy has been upheld as a model, there are constant admiring references to our monetary policies, throughout the land industrial projects continue to provide employment for thousands of workers, every day the newspapers outline governmental steps to overcome the crisis which, on account of world events, has also affected us but when compared with that of other countries the state of our economy is most encouraging, the Portuguese nation and the statesmen who guide her are quoted worldwide, the political doctrine we pursue is being studied abroad, and one can confidently say that other nations regard us with humility and respect, the world's leading newspapers send their most experienced journalists to discover the secret of our success, the head of our government is finally coaxed out of his persistent humility, out of his stubborn aversion to publicity, and is featured in newspaper columns throughout the world ... In the face of all this, which is only the pale shadow of what could be said, you must agree, Carlos, that it was utter madness to become involved in university strikes which have never achieved anything worthwhile, are you even aware of the trouble I'm going through to get you out of here. (*Year* I 19–20)

[Generosa, benevolente polícia esta de Portugal que não se importa, pudera não, está a par de tudo, tem uma informadora no arraial inimigo ... , porém tudo acabará em felicidade para as partes, desde que tomemos a sério o autor da obra, ora ouçamo-lo, A situação do país merece à imprensa estrangeira referências entusiásticas, cita-se a nossa política financeira como modelo, há alusões às nossas condições financeiras, de modo a colocar-nos numa posição privilegiada, por todo o país continuam as obras de fomento que empregam milhares de operários, dia a dia os jornais inserem diplomas governativos no sentido de debelar a crise que, por fenómenos mundiais, também nos antingiu, o nível económico da nação, comparadamente a outros países, é o mais animador, o nome de Portugal e dos estadistas que o governam andam citados em todo o mundo, a doutrina política estabelecida entre nós é motivo de estudo em outros países, pode-se afirmar que o mundo nos olha com simpatia e admiração, os grandes periódicos de fama internacional enviam até os seus redactores categorizados a fim de colher elementos para conhecer o segredo da nossa vitória, o chefe do governo é, enfim, arrancado à sua pertinaz humildade, ao seu recolhimento de rebelde a reclames, e projectado em colunas de reportagem, através do mundo ... , Perante isto, que é apenas uma pálida sombra do que podia ser dito, tem de concordar, Carlos, que foi uma loucura irresponsável meter-se em greves académicas que nunca trouxeram nada de bom, já pensou nos trabalhos que eu vou ter para o tirar daqui ... (*Ano* 139–40)]

The implied author/Reis, who is reading as I "overhear," has all along been poking fun at the little book quite savagely, in a sort of deconstructive mode. Published by one Tomé Vieira, *Conspiracy* (*Conspiração*) was indeed a popular booklet in 1936—one with a melodramatic plot and a diction supportive of the regime. In characterizing Marília as an informer, the implied author/Reis is exploding the language of innocent patriotic dedication that the little book seeks both to attribute to her and to project generally. That characterization suggests much about the actual workings of the state—and infers a parallel to Reis's own situation with Victor. As one might have expected, the novel's description of *Conspiracy* is accurate down to such physical details as its description of the little book's cover (see figure 2). And, as was the case with the Gomes volume for *Baltasar and Blimunda* (one could choose several other documents for either novel), such lines as the ones that begin "the situation in our country ..." and end "in newspaper columns around the world" constitute a near-verbatim reproduction from it (Vieira 99–100). Nor is that the only near-verbatim stretch from *Conspiracy* within the extended passage. Other kinds of inclusions too dot this part of *Year of the Death*, mostly individual words from *Conspiracy* used as mentions. The clear implication is that, whatever their intention, state policies led to the economic situation under fascism and that I can read the passages from *Conspiracy*—and could by extension, read the whole novel—in such a way as to reveal the failings, or the hypocrisy, of the concepts that the regime propagated for its self-legitimation and thereby seek to "appease" my "impotence." Generation A readers would be able to add to reception of those passages that they heard precisely this sort of language contained in *Conspiracy* publicly repeated by the regime on multiple occasions, even after it was clear that that language bore little relationship either to the actual functioning of the society and the economy or to the experience of those who lived subject to them.

Chapter Three

Figure 2. Cover of *Conspiração*, by Tomé Vieira [Alberto Tomás Vieira], Lisboa: n.p., 1936. Reis/the implied author does a surgical job of explicating in a couple of lines (pp. 104–05) the cover's immediate "scare quality." An aspect not touched on in that explication involves the little novel's characterization of the city itself as a place of conflict and of fear while in the country in general and the village in particular the sun shines and harmony—or at least collaborative exchanges of language—reigns. That contrast is taken all the way to mode of dress: in the "scary cospmopolitan" environment of the cover image, the figure wears cosmopolitan clothing, while many country scenes involve traditional dress.

Reading the Labyrinth

The passage concludes as follows:

> This conversation takes place in the prison, in the visitors' room, but in a village ... [a] farmer, the father of the sweet girl whom this Carlos will marry toward the end of the story, explains to a gathering of subordinates that there is nothing worse than being a Communist, the Communists want neither bosses nor workers, they don't accept laws or religion ... In another four chapters and in the epilogue, the gentle but Valkyrian Marília rescues the student from prison and the political scourge, rehabilitates her father who abandons his subversive activities once and for all, and declares that within the new corporative plan the problem is being resolved without hypocrisy, conflict, or insurrection. The class struggle is over and has been replaced with a system of good values, capital, and labor. To conclude, the nation must be run like a family with lots of children, where the father imposes order to safeguard their education, because unless children are taught to respect their father everything falls apart and the household is doomed. ... God need not have bothered expelling us from His paradise, seeing as we have succeeded in regaining it so soon. Ricardo Reis closed the book, it hadn't taken him long to read it. ... Such stupidity ... (*Year* 120)

> [[E]sta conversa passava-se na prisão, no parlatório ... Lá na aldeia ... outro lavrador, pai da gentil menina com quem Carlos há-de vir a casar-se mais para o fim da história, explica numa roda de subalternos que ser comunista é pior que tudo, eles não querem que haja patrões nem operários, nem leis nem religião ... Em mais quatro capítulos e um epílogo, a suave mas valquíria Marília salva o estudante da prisão e da lepra política, regenera o pai que definitivamente abandona o vezo conspirativo, e proclama que dentro da actual solução corporativa o problema resolve-se sem mentiras, sem ódios e sem revoltas, a luta de classes acabou, substituída pela colaboração dos elementos que constituem valores iguais, o capital e o trabalho, em conclusão, a nação deve ser uma coisa assim como uma casa onde há muitos filhos e o pai tem de dar ordem à vida para a todos criar, ora os filhos, se não forem devidamente educados, se não tiverem respeito ao pai, tudo vai mal e a casa não resiste ... afinal não valeu a pena ter-nos Deus expulsado do seu paraíso, se em tão pouco tempo o reconquistámos. Ricardo Reis fechou o livro, leu-o depressa ... Que estupidez ... (*Ano* 144–45)]

Chapter Three

Again the language of *Conspiracy*, and through it some of the claims of the regime, are being pilloried by their contextually ironic inclusion here. This passage in the novel is the product of two passages from *Conspiracy* (Vieira 66–67, 70). Those who lived through the regime, especially group A2 intellectuals, would have recognized the persistent Salazarist replacement of "class struggle" with the image of a nation structured along the lines of the stereotypical traditional family under legalized patriarchal power and would have recognized as well the discourse attached to that image. Indeed, for them (I include myself here), the sarcasm would point up the persistent contradictions in the regime's self-presentation (e.g., "the gentle but Valkyrian Marília"). And the blatant irony replicates within the novel structure the situation of virtual thought control and the national *isolat* and argument of international exceptionalism that the regime promulgated (albeit principally at a time somewhat later than the 1936 represented in the novel). Those parallel passages function in relation to my reading activity much like the passages from *Baltasar and Blimunda* examined in the previous chapter: a private communication between the implied author and me produces a series of libidinal releases of pleasure in some admixture with both a (memory-based) sense of trauma and appeasement of the resulting impotence.

The clause "unless children are taught to respect their father everything falls apart and the household is doomed," for example, works very much like the structural irony of *Baltasar and Blimunda* save that in the context of *The Year of the Death of Ricardo Reis* it is much more complex and much more provocative. It is clear that the implied author/Reis is skeptical of such thinking, whether because of disagreement with the "family" metaphor, whether with its extension to include characterization of unwanted behavior as in effect "childish," or for other reasons. It should be borne in mind that, historically speaking, by the time of the novel's publication in 1984 Reis/Pessoa had been canonized (to some considerable degree by the *Estado Novo*) as a penetrating intellect. And to think that in *Year of the Death* I am actually invited to join him in reception and thus to read critically along with him the reported language of *Conspiracy*! But the added touches of things "falling apart" and of "doom" raise the psychological stakes considerably. Indeed, the discourse of *Conspiracy*, like that of the regime itself, plays a double-edged game that Reis/the implied author implicitly analyzes—or, in Reis's case, at least takes note of—and leads me to do the same. That game is one in which that discourse is used to proclaim that unorthodox behavior "dooms" society but also clearly suggests—a suggestion reinforced by the plot of *Conspiracy* as well as by the police actions of *The Year of the Death of Ricardo Reis* and the historical police actions with which a generation A reader would to some extent be familiar—that "society" also intends to protect itself by punishing behavior strictly for its failure to bow to the orthodoxy. The game is, then, one in which the language can simultaneously warn against violation of orthodoxy and threaten against it—i.e., the warning is a veiled threat. Again, a phenomenon not unfamiliar to the generation A reader.

Finally, the remark that "God need not have bothered expelling us from His paradise, seeing as we have succeeded in regaining it so soon" works much like "God ... when He so chooses, has no need of men, though He cannot dispense with women" in *Baltasar and Blimunda* (see Chapter 2, pp. 45–46 ff.). The former functions to invite me to engage in a line of thought in deconstruction of the *Estado Novo* mix of Christian and political rhetoric.

In general, for a generation A reader like myself, the overt contrast between the regime's self-promotion on the one hand and day-to-day reality on the other and the implicit debunking of the former in the context of the novel re-resolve the tension that I bear bound up with those issues and release the energy used to keep that tension in place. That is—at least in the Freudian terms introduced in the last chapter—they have the effect of producing something like my own recurrent smile, though, as we have seen, it is now not simply the joyous smile of liberation identified in my reading of my reception of *Baltasar and Blimunda*. It is also a release associated with a Lacanian proleptic making-whole through a making-"sense" that provides "appeasement."

Meaning-making in the act of reading *The Year of the Death* is thus a psychological triumph of sorts, fleeting though it may be. It is a triumph over the "memory" of the historical trauma functioning as constitutive lack. That that triumph really exists only anticipatorily and that the effort to bring it to full fruition leads to what could be termed "compulsive" returns to the text merely define the kind of triumph this is; they do not violate it. In effect, in reading a passage such as the paraphrase/pillory of *Conspiracy* above, I can have the past traumatic psycho-social situation re-rehearsed, find libidinal release (again) from its root tension, and also feel myself (about to be) the victor (!) over the situation, a being (about to be) made right. As was the case with *Baltasar and Blimunda*, the scenario is not one of direct confrontation with the socio-political conflict: it is rehearsal of it through seriatim acts of reading staged in the relative safety of the post-revolutionary era, with that safety being one of the constituent elements of the experience. But here, especially given the thematics of *The Year of the Death*, the removes are fewer: the *Estado Novo* is there, close, and cultural "memory" figures strongly in the constitution of the obstacle/sign of impotence. If we think of the (post)Freudian analysis of the role of constitutive lack in the interpellation exerted by the Freudian fetish object, then Saramago's "historical" novels can, in this one sense, be seen as elaborate and sophisticated fetishes holding out to the reader the (illusory) possibility of overcoming impotence, of making-whole through the reading of the novel.

* * *

Examined in these dimensions, the act of reading has about it the aspect of a process of subject-construction understood very generally. As we have seen, the very texture of *Year of the Death*—the labyrinth/symbolic network in which there are no answers to questions of history, causality, etc., but rather a sense of uncertainty, of vulnerability, of impotence—provides the social symbolic. The reader, especially the generation A reader, can read the labyrinth—in, of course, the highly specific way outlined above. Reading—and rereading—the labyrinth is in effect the exercise of a form of triumph through control in the face, both textually represented and psycho-internal, of "remembered" vulnerability and uncertainty.

For generation B readers, however, the same basic process surely finds a different thematization. The tension represented textually by the structural irony analyzed above is likely to come in implicit reference to "the parallel state" of the late 1970s and the 1980s—a state that represents measures that it cannot or will not enforce but in patently engaging in non-enforcement inserts itself fully into the lives of the parties involved and the populace as a whole, thus appearing to have unclear motives, and therefore has little or no credibility. Indeed, in terms of the rhetoric of its self-presentation, the state virtually says as much. Sousa Santos summarizes:

> One of the most striking features of the official discourse of the Portuguese state is its antistatism. Throughout this period state agents have been claiming that the state is a poor administrator and an even poorer producer, this being the main reason to strengthen civil society and private enterprise. This masochistic discourse is, however, not self-indicting because the concrete state, in so discoursing, distances itself from the abstract state, the real (and thus unreal) bête noir. Because the state has also to intervene in order not to intervene, the antistate discourse is self-defeating. The centrality of the state reproduces itself through the discourse of the marginality of the state. (56)

This state is an implicit contemporary referent for the citizen's sense of uncertainty and vulnerability, the consequent disaffection, the refusal to be "deceived," and the taking of refuge in, among other matters, the personalistic outlook of a "craftsmanship of ideas" (see above, p. 87). (One might profitably compare Jameson's characterization of the subject under late capitalism, as he sees it, as a figure unable to organize its past and future into coherent experience [*Postmodernism* 25].) In this process of displacement-in-reading, the fascist content of the obstacle/sign of impotence functions as both the historical precursor and the effective analogy of the parallel state. One seeks to make oneself whole through overcoming that situation by being able, through the act of reading, to work conceptually with symbols of the nationality as an individual reader. In effect, the scene of reading is thus also the scene of the building of a post-revolutionary subjecthood in relationship to symbols of the nationality referentially past but inferentially present and ongoing. Generation A readers, of course—since they will have had to confront the parallel state in their present-day lives—engage in this reading process simultaneously with the one ascribed to them above. The two readerships, then, more or less coincide in basic motive and in the subject-constructive opportunities they provide but diverge considerably in content.

The two readerships have a number of additional features in common. Those features prominently include a sense that through work with the inherited symbolic in the act of reading one can

Chapter Three

return to an originary moment, to the basics of existence, and control the symbolic through one's own conceptual processes. This sense is given weight by the text of *The Year of the Death of Ricardo Reis*, for, as we have seen, it presents questions that it poses as both Portuguese ones and universal—hence timeless—ones simultaneously. In the national dimension of that double-sided scenario the reader receives the illusion—fostered, indeed, in all three of Saramago's historical novels—that she or he occupies a space either before decisions have been made about national narratives or outside the sphere of their socialization and that he or she therefore has the power to unmake them, make them his or her own way, see their relativity or transposability, etc. (As we shall see in the ensuing chapter, *History of the Siege of Lisbon* goes a step further and thematizes that illusion.)

This set of convergent/divergent processes between the two readerships can be exemplified in relation to the extended passage from *Year of the Death* reproduced above. The remark "a father can never tell how his own daughter will turn out" combines with the later remark about "family traditions" being "betrayed" to remind generation A readers of the care they had to maintain against denunciation to fascist authorities, even by family members—the irony being clear with reference to a regime that promulgated "family." Or at very least it served to remind them of the tales (which I personally heard with some frequency during the fascist years) about such intra-familial denunciations. The "joke" discourse of the novel, which depends upon fascist institutional-level prohibitions for its functioning, allows such readers to smile/laugh at such a fear as they read. And they affirm/build their post-revolutionary subjecthood in the process. (By "subjecthood" I do not refer to any psychological theory of the subject. For my purposes here and henceforth, "subject" needs mean little more than, in literary-reception terms, Iser's "reader"—as long as we add that that "reader"/subject is ever under construction-in-reading and therefore that no stable entity called "subject" is ever created [cf. Belsey 52–61]. In this version, Iser's "reader" is—obviously—variously inflected by such psychoanalytical [and, in my next chapter, psychological] concepts as I develop in passing. Alternatively, in sociological terms, the "reader" is merely the site of confluence of social forces seeking to inculcate one or another notion of subjecthood.)

Generation B readers, to the extent that that portion of the passage about parents and children would interpellate them, would likely undergo a somewhat different process, one having to do with the opposition between trust in the state and trust in themselves. The process would be roughly the same as with generation A save the Freudian "obstacle" would likely include an allegorical overlay of fascist symbolic system and parallel state opaqueness, and the subject-construction would involve securing the ability to control/make one's own relationship to society during the post-revolutionary period. Thus the two reading processes diverge considerably in relation to this set of allusions.

By contrast, the references to Salazar, the "head of our government … finally coaxed out of his persistent humility," doubtless provide the basis for convergent readings, with the generation A reader having more experiential input directly into the content while the generation B reader would have an historical viewpoint upon the fascist leader and might also conflate him psychologically with distrusted contemporary leadership, individual or generic.

In the case of both groups of readers, the processes outlined above are, of course, ones that may vary, along several axes, from individual to individual. They are more easily analyzable in *Year of the Death* than in *Baltasar and Blimunda* but, in the divergent ways we have seen, they are open to activation in the reading of either. Generation A readers will be engaged in a detachment from the sense of themselves fashioned under fascism—through confrontation and overcoming of fascist practices both textually represented and contained within the history of literary institutionality called up for them by their interaction with the printed page. Generation B readers may engage in a touching of that issue but do so in a distanced way.

* * *

Now let us look at the second issue that at the outset of this chapter I promised to explore: that of reception beyond Portugal—both for what it tells us about the various ways in which Saramago novels can be received and also what it tells us, by way of contrast, about the specificity of reception within Portugal.

I once gave a lecture to an American academic audience about Saramago's historical novels, specifically about *The History of the Siege of Lisbon*, outlining aspects of the argument about the role of the reader–implied author pact in that novel that I have made to this point in the present study. When I was finished, I had a question from the audience that went approximately: "Can we conclude from what you have said that non-Portuguese appreciations of Saramago's work are based on a misreading of it?" (There are, to be sure, even more difficult questions that can be posed in this area. I shiver at the prospect that someone will ask if, in proposing the concept that *Baltasar and Blimunda*'s ideal reader is someone who experienced Portuguese fascism, I am in effect doing nothing more than reinscribing Portuguese fascist hermeneutic localism upon the texts in a new register.) The way I chose to answer the question posed by the audience member was to discuss the multiple ways in which literary reading can be analyzed. I concluded with the relatively standard statement that while there can be misreadings when the reader violates the authority of the text, variant readings that do not violate it are legitimate readings that merely bespeak a particular meeting of textual authority and readerly activation. We then discussed the impact of cultural differences in producing such variant readings. In effect, I shall be engaging in a variety of that same discussion in the next few pages.

It is telling that the reception of *Baltasar and Blimunda* outside of Portugal has fixed on the romance between the two characters and subordinated the other plot elements: the flying machine, the Inquisition, the building of Mafra, and the implied author's flamboyant self-presentation, among others. This is not to suggest that the love element is not focused on in Portuguese readings as well; it is merely focused on less absorbingly. Even in neighboring Spain, where Saramago is as much celebrated as in Portugal, if not more so, overwhelming focus falls on the romance-novel aspect. Indeed, in a discussion I once had with Basilio Losada, the novel's Spanish translator, that was all he could talk about. I tried several times to steer the conversation to the *passarola* or the Inquisition—to no avail. He, like Saramago and Corghi in writing *Blimunda*, had made his choice. The most interesting aspect to this is that Spain underwent its own "fascist" experience, namely, the rule of Francisco Franco from 1939 to 1975. And yet the role of the fascist experience in the textual economy of *Baltasar and Blimunda*, not to mention specifically the liberatory reader–implied author pact, were barely acknowledged by the translator. To be sure, he was understandably more interested in the "plot" than in issues of reception, but even so I found the reaction surprising in one who, as its translator, had struggled with the texture of *Baltasar and*

Blimunda. Moreover, in my conversations with (many) Spanish Saramago fans, I have found little variation in that reception.[7]

The questions raised by foreign concentration on the "love aspect" are, however, much larger ones, and they involve two important issues. The first of those issues has to do with the presence, or creation, of a narrative core as one of the bases of the reading of narrative. My simple, ad-hoc term *narrative core* is equivalent, with emphasis on narrative, to Iser's "gestalt groupings" within what he calls "consistency building" as a constituent part of reading a text (*Act* 118–22). The second issue has to do with reading as a reader-character identificatory process. Let us take the issues in order.

Seen in relation to the issue of a narrative core, what we have observed thus far in this study suggests that, for the reader that the texts seek to create, the narrative core of Saramago's historical novels is provided by, or at least prominently includes, the implied author–reader pact and the various transfers of a quotient of emotion—joy and impotence combined—(re-)induced there. This is necessarily true of *Baltasar and Blimunda* in particular, for it is composed of quite disparate, though interconnected, plot elements. In effect, as we have seen, the coherence of the novel is provided by a statement something like: "José Saramago is telling me a story about some things we have in common"—though we must now add that those common elements may differ modally between generation A and generation B readers. Despite the many differences, such is the case in *The Year of the Death of Ricardo Reis* as well, though plot conciseness would enable the reader of the latter work to latch onto other narrative cores if the implied author's sheer level of activity were not present.

What happens with *Baltasar and Blimunda* in Spain and elsewhere can be thought of as follows. The reader–implied author pact is not strongly enough received to provide the core, because the receiver is not culturally prepared to recognize it as such. As a result, another core is fixed upon: the romance between Baltasar and Blimunda. Indeed, the post-Nobel English-language editions play up, on their covers, the "romance" or "erotic" element of both *Baltasar and Blimunda* and *History of the Siege of Lisbon*. For the latter, the cover prose, after referring to the novel as a "multifaceted tableau involving meditations on historiography, the uses and abuses of language, and life under authoritarian rule," concludes by labeling it "[a] rollicking love story" (*History* 1998). I could proliferate examples, but it is clear that for such as the writer of that advertisement, the "romance" angle furnishes the novel's narrative core and her/his caption instructs the (potential) purchaser that it can—or should—be read in that manner.

This replacement leads in multiple directions. I have examined the reader reviews on amazon.com from 1997 to early 1999 (stopping at that time to try to minimize the Nobel effect), and for *Baltasar and Blimunda* the "romance-novel" focus is clear. Almost all the reader reviews invoke it. Indeed, so much so that the burning question in those reviews was whether the novel met the readers' expectations in that area. While there were those who enjoyed the "romance," the overwhelming answer within that admittedly unscientific sample was "no" (which, I am sure, would have astonished my Spanish colleague!). The common rationale: there is too little passion shown between Baltasar and Blimunda, they are too vaguely drawn as characters, and so on. Indeed, a number of English-language readers—and at least one entire book club—refer to abandoning the book in mid-read, angry at the relative absence of the promised "romance." In short, for the majority of those readers (clearly, the sample was small and exclusive to those who were willing to venture forth, albeit anonymously, on the Internet) the "romance" was the core, and in this case it was an unsatisfactorily realized core.

What was really happening was as follows: if one wishes to engage in a reading process that involves that core (some of the disgruntled readers seem to have been expecting something to be read much as one reads a Harlequin romance), elements of the narrative that coordinate with the implied author–reader pact—namely, the characters as enigmas and the anti-identificatory hermeneutical instructions in the text—represent direct conflicts with the core. As a result of that choice of core, then, the various elements of the novel begin to disqualify each other reciprocally.

As regards reading as a reader-character identificatory process, we have, of course, already seen that one of the efforts in both *Baltasar and Blimunda* and *Year of the Death* is to deny both simple identificatory reading and also any reader identification with the texture of the work based on pre-grounded national commonality. The implied author does everything he can to force the reader to take up a critical stance with regard to plot and history as she or he reads, a gesture that should serve to counteract to some degree any identificatory reading process. In an amazon.com reader review from Portugal (written in English) we see clear recognition of that fact through a reading consistent with it. After dealing with the romance in *Baltasar and Blimunda* the writer goes on: " … history is rewritten as an ironic, sometimes painful parable for all kinds of religious fanaticism and despotic power" (9 Oct. 1998). The writer was likely a generation B Portuguese reader, given that the historical critique is seen first and foremost as generally, rather than just "nationally," applicable, indeed susceptible of becoming a "parable" (a remark that anticipates one of the principal directions in Saramago's novel production after *History of the Siege of Lisbon*). But the entire passage, especially in its invocation of the concepts of irony and parable, bespeaks the reader position of someone who has not identified with the "romance" element or any other but rather has kept the distance to which the novel seeks to assign her/him.

When the readership is not Portuguese, however, reader-character identification becomes a central reading mode, both for those who enjoy the novels and those who do not. One reviewer from the United States, for example, clearly identifies with the plight of Ricardo Reis, seeing him as attempting to stabilize himself within the labyrinthine world of 1936 Lisbon:

> The ending … leaves one thinking about what really goes on in Ricardo Reis' mind: did he have enough, or did he realize that, by just contemplating the theatre of the world around him, he wasn't going anywhere? Did he have, in the end, a moment of sincerity with himself? Those are questions that the reader should answer for himself. (24 Mar. 1999)

The reviewer is someone who may not quite have understood the "reason" for Reis's "death," perhaps because he or she did not know—since it is cultural information that the reader must bring to the reading—that Reis was a product of Pessoa's imagination and therefore ultimately could not survive him. But he or she clearly sees Reis in an existential light and equally clearly identifies with the character so construed, thereby foregrounding hermeneutical rules grounded to some extent in that approach to novel-reading. The questions that the novel poses are, for her or him, ones to be taken on by putting oneself in the position of the literary character who stands at their confluence.

There are even mixtures of anti-identificatory and identificatory gestures in foreign readings of the novels. Here is a reader review from the United States that engages in both gestures, one after the other, albeit creating *sui generis* formulations that reconfigure the reader–implied author pact in interesting ways. In writing about *History of the Siege of Lisbon*, that reviewer says:

> I'm not one of those people who throws around words like "brilliant" and "genius." But Saramago seems to me to have created a new form of writing here. The language is astonishing, exhilarating, its twists and turns some kind of sorcerer's spell. A mischievous, laughing conjurer of irony. His frequent asides to the reader, abashed corrections of his own turns of phrase—I don't know, maybe this turns off some people, but it drew me even further [in] …
>
> The day after I started reading the book, it was announced that Saramago had won the Nobel Prize. Then I learned that he is a leading Portuguese communist, and that made me even happier. Then the Vatican issued a stinging denunciation of the Nobel committee for giving the prize to an atheist. Saramago held a news conference and said he'd sooner give up the prize than renounce his atheism. So not only is he an innovator on a par with the greatest artists—but he's one of us, a worker, one of the few remaining artists who refuses to sell out, renounce his class, or let bourgeois norms dictate his art. (20 Jan. 1999)

We shall return in the Conclusion to the matter of "communism" and its problematic relationship to Saramago's work. Here suffice it to say that, in the first paragraph, this one American reader sees (aspects of) the implied author's self-presentation quite clearly, pinpoints its anti-identificatory character, and then, in the second paragraph, actually turns completely around and identifies with aspects of the author-myth that the construct of the implied author holds out to us. The aspects identified with, however, are those that point outward from the textualized implied author to José Saramago, novelist and public figure, some of which would not have been available to her/him in the United States without the serendipitous timing of the Nobel announcement. A version of those mythifying author-aspects would, of course, have been available to a large percentage of Portuguese readers all along and, as we have seen, figure in the author-myth for the Portuguese reader, though, in the ideal reader at least, not in a way that would have so thoroughly overridden the anti-identificatory discourse of the novels.

Finally, one other note is struck, generally from outside Portugal, to create a way to read the historical novels absent the implied author–reader pact: the concept of the post-modern as narrative style (see Chapter 1). One American reader review speaks of *The Year of the Death of Ricardo Reis* as containing "deep insight on life in the post modernism world [*sic*]" (28 Jan. 1999). And voices from other quarters have proclaimed Saramago's style "post-modern" (e.g., Fokkema). The argument here is that the distinctive core of the novels—what holds them together—is a way of writing. Mentioned are such features as writing about the past to invent new facts or even new laws (ways of the social world and/or physical laws) or "forgetting" inherited ones; seeming non-selection/randomness in creating textual features; deviation from accepted logical inferences; hyperrationality leading to logical but unexpected conclusions; and fragmentation instead of "modern-style" internal "coherence" in the literary work (Fokkema 298–301). Application of the category "post-modern" to Saramago is not somehow "wrong," of course. But it generalizes upon a writing practice that, as we have seen, is meaningful precisely because of its specific relationship to its projected readership—and, I think we can now say, to at least some segments of its actual readership at the time of publication as well. To presume a generic "post-modern" narrative practice—i.e., a post-modern "style"—is, then, precisely to miss the point. Indeed, since the post-modern, at least to the mind of Jean-François Lyotard, prominent promulgator of the term within critical circles (Lyotard), is, among other things, precisely the local and the specific rather than the universal, to presume that a generalizing statement can be made by calling a kind of writing "post-modern" and stopping there is to miss the point doubly.

Much more could be done regarding the non-Portuguese reception of the historical novels. The foregoing overview suffices to make the point from a different perspective that the novels find a specific organization around the dynamics within the institution of literature in Portugal, while the loss of that organizing core leads to a number of substitute strategies. The novels' international

Chapter Three

reception, in its illustrative opposition to a reading from the viewpoint of hermeneutic investment in Portuguese literary institutionality, thus casts a strong light on how that investment works within the novels.

* * *

In one sense, then, *Year of the Death*, in its complexity and its extension of the implications developed with reference to *Baltasar and Blimunda*, shows that the historical novels function as imaginative sites within which issues of institutionality are made the objects of (re-)construction and I as reader am assured I have the authority and the ability to engage in that (re-)construction with few if any fixed limitations upon me. Also, that (re-)construction project provides vehicles for me to overcome past trauma and/or to build a sense of my abilities in the face of present imponderabilities—or both at once. The novels, then, are, among other things, loci of a subject-(re-)creation that uses past subject-status—or at least the official version thereof—as the given and allows, or pushes, me the reader to make my own way through the symbols of the supposed nationality that have previously sought to inculcate that specific subject status upon me. This process not only enables a subject-building away from the identificatory nation-grounded subject fostered by fascism but constitutes a subtle but potentially powerful means of popular consciousness-raising.

Chapter Four

Mastering the Culture's Tool Kit, or "Is the City Still Taken?"
The History of the Siege of Lisbon's
Self-Invited Reader

> [O]ur ... transactions and the regulatory self that executes them ... is [*sic*] given a larger-scale map on which to operate by the culture in which transactions take place, and ends up being a reflection of the history of that culture as that history is contained in the culture's images, narratives, and tool kit.
> —Jerome Bruner
> *Actual Minds, Possible Worlds*

As though it were intercepting the course of this book at the present juncture, the third novel, *The History of the Siege of Lisbon*, seems to acknowledge openly many of the issues heretofore developed on the basis of my reading of my reception of the first two novels. First and foremost, it acknowledges the centrality of reading in Saramago's work, as well as the highly transactional nature of the role that work assigns to me, the reader. It does so in the first instance by textualizing a reader figure—and what is more, one who reads the Portuguese past in a critical, albeit an idiosyncratically critical, manner. In this novel, instead of being recruited by the implied author to ransack history in his company or challenged by him to read the fascist labyrinth in order to appease historical trauma, I am from the outset invited to take my lead from another, textualized reader, one who will turn out to be my guide, my model, and/or my proxy within the text, though, as the ensuing pages will demonstrate, none of those roles is as simple as recitation of those categories suggests. Nor does the implied author cease to play a central role in relation to me because of the appearance of the textualized reader. It is the case, however, that I come to know what/how the latter sees (the principal reader figure is male) and also can both share his outlook and diverge

Chapter Four

from it. Furthermore, since throughout the novel much is made of writing and writing's reception, the text frequently uses the word *reader* to refer to me as the active reader, to the aforementioned reader figure, to the collective readership that the novel presumes for itself, and also, frequently, to the reader (of literature) in general (e.g., *History* 1996 3–21 [*História* 11–29]). The four overlap, converge, and diverge according to the passage being read. In that dynamic the principal effects are reciprocal reinforcement of the role of reading and also continual reflection upon the act of reading in the very process of its being carried out. My readerly activity—or, really, its implications—are thus doubled, or trebled, before my own eyes.

Secondly, the textualized reader figure, while representing both reading in the abstract and me/all of us as readers, demonstrably functions also as a figure of regress to the institutional sphere; indeed, he openly operates in that sphere. He thus reveals to me in yet another perspective the institutional stakes involved in the very activity that I am carrying out, as well as broadening my entire readerly relationship to institutionality in ways that this chapter will help elucidate. In sum, I encounter "meta" echoes in virtually every passage I read in *The History of the Siege of Lisbon*.

All but needless to say, the considerable modification in my relationship to the text relocates a number of matters that were relatively uniform within the reader–implied author pact across *Baltasar and Blimunda* and *The Year of the Death of Ricardo Reis*. Most obviously, the reader–implied author relationship is affected. The implied author is as intrusive, breezy, irreverent, and nearly as digressive as before, and the invitation made to me to accompany him remains in force, but now there comes in addition the aforementioned invitation to contemplate on my own part, in a mode that, in comparison with the prior two novels, can only be called "intellectual," the very task of readership. Furthermore, in keeping with *History*'s "intellectual" nature, the remarks that the implied author makes for my readerly consumption—more often than not still Portuguese "in" jokes—lack the sense of intimate communication that characterized the prior two novels. As irreverent as before, they nonetheless seem to be present to be analyzed as either encapsuled comic observations made in relationship to the country the implied author and I share or as part of an intricate text to be deciphered more than to be received as though "José

Saramago were speaking to me" in the present time of my reading. For example, the implied author places into the mouth of the first Portuguese king, as he addresses an assembly of crusaders, a comically anachronistic apology for what he refers to as the "Portuguese spirit yet to be fully formed" [*History* 1996 139)], which he deems an unfortunate characteristic of his time. It is an obvious—and merciless—comic swipe at the language of "national spirit" and strongly teleological concept of history cultivated by the *Estado Novo*. But it and passages like it come in relative isolation and thus, while still serving to identify and characterize the figure of the implied author, contribute much less to the building and maintenance of a foreground pact between that figure and me the reader than was the case in the earlier novels. In short, the reader–implied author pact is both shifted and reconfigured to feature a more nearly autonomous reader and a reader–implied author communication that, in comparison with the prior two novels, can only be termed "attenuated."

Conversely, my relationship to Portuguese history, a staple of the first two titles, is even more centrally thematized in *The History of the Siege of Lisbon*—because exploration of the entire matter of how "history," in particular "national history," comes to be constructed, and where, is one of the bases of the novel. As a consequence, as we shall see, the entire issue of my confrontation with national history is carried on and intensified from its initial development in the two preceding novels, though at the same time, as far as confrontation of the historiographical dimension of the historical trauma of Portuguese fascism is concerned, its import is somewhat weakened through intellectualization. Indeed, in *History*, while the residual historical memory/trauma and the effort to "appease" and find "joy" that I bring to the reading task are still motivators for my meaning-making in reading and are still summoned up by the text as it enlists my subjectivity in that meaning-making, they are not invoked as often as before. Instead, as a result of the novel's plot, I am invited to do something a bit different: to contemplate some of the dimensions of that residue of fascist cultural politics that I bear with me in post-fascist times and to reflect on its relationship to myself. If my reading of *Baltasar and Blimunda* trades upon what is predominantly a joyous, somewhat self-contained reaction to fascist hermeneutics and my reading of *The Year of the Death of Ricardo Reis* trades upon my confronting

Chapter Four

of one moment in fascist history as a trauma/obstacle repeatedly to be appeased to projected liberatory ends, then *History* features on its very surface the more intellectual question of in what ways and to what purposes that history was created. As we shall see, however, the detached readership role that the novel urges takes on a specific character and is given very precise circumstances within which to operate. It thus ends up making demands of me that, in scale and intensity, are just as stringent as those of the first two historical novels.

* * *

Because this novel approaches the above issues by presenting them in relation to a conventional "plot," something like a skeletal plot summary can be used to inventory those issues and to outline the stakes at play for me as reader. The next few pages are built around such a summary—although in it I take the opportunity to develop some of the key issues as they arise, those issues being more important for present purposes than plot summary per se.

The History of the Siege of Lisbon involves a short period in the life of one Raimundo Silva, an anonymous copyeditor—in Portuguese, the word is *revisor* (literally, "reviser" or "re-seer"), and the word's many implications are played on throughout the novel. Raimundo—the name suggests "king of the world"—works, in undefined contemporary times, for a Lisbon publishing house. One day he is given a book manuscript to edit entitled "A História do Cerco de Lisboa" ("The History of the Siege of Lisbon"). It is a book of history about a key moment in consecrated Portuguese history, the 1147 taking of Lisbon from the Muslims by siege as a part of the medieval carving-out of the geographical contours of what would become contemporary Portugal. It is an event and date that every Portuguese schoolchild memorizes in the same way that an American schoolchild memorizes 1775 and the battles of Lexington and Concord. Now for reasons that are not wholly clear but have to do with, among other factors, depression, free-floating disaffection from his work, oppositional thinking, intellectual arrogance, and mid-life crisis (the important implications of this seemingly inconsequential last item will become clear as this chapter progresses), Raimundo takes it into his head to subvert if not national history then at least national-ist historiography. He has a strong sense of the gravitation of fascism's "monumental" history, though he apparently makes little of the specific politics involved. He seems more preoccupied instead with abuses of historiography in general. The reader, especially the generation A reader, is likely more concerned with, and invested in, the political use to which that history was put under fascism than is Raimundo himself; I certainly am.

Be this as it may, the "history" is as follows. Historically speaking (or so we are told!), the Christian taking of Lisbon in the aforementioned year was decisively aided by a large number of crusaders, principally Norman, Flemish, and English, who had stopped at Lisbon before proceeding on to the Holy Land to fight in the Second Crusade. Raimundo, when it comes to the relevant passage in the book he is copyediting, chooses to add the negative adverb *não*, thereby producing the statement that the crusaders decided *not* to aid the proto-Portuguese in their quest to take Lisbon (40 [50]).

That basic plot deployment touches anew a number of issues that we have seen at work in the prior two novels. First, while the issues are treated so matter-of-factly that the effect is easily missed, I see the received monumental version of Portuguese history and its allied hermeneutical rules propagated by fascism summarily dismissed, usually by the implications of the very design of the plot, though occasionally the point is driven home with some directness, as when Raimundo grumbles to himself about the corrupting presence of an informing "patriotism" in the manuscript "History" he is reading (31 [40–41]). What he is given to edit makes some claims that are impossible to document—and others are verifiably false—but they are repeated from retelling to retelling of the siege of 1147 as a part of the mythologizing of history (30–33 [40–42]), and Raimundo reacts angrily to the lack of anything new to justify this new manuscript as well as to the unverifiability of many of the suppositions it claims as historical facts. (One is justified at this point in seeing the cause of his exasperation in the static character that the *Estado Novo* sought to impute to its "monumental" history, especially its effort to create a permanent national past [Sapega, "Consensus" 37–45; Matos 2: 203–04].) To Raimundo, a group A2 Portuguese in action, the claims in the manuscript represent a mythification of the country's past merely to glorify the "nationality." He thus raises very directly for me the issue of nationalistic thought in Portugal, if not of nationalistic thought in general. In the preceding pages I have seen fascist nationalistic thought repeatedly touched on, but here it is directly textualized—in what is clearly a critical manner. Not so much as fascist thought but as nationalism *tout court*. Raimundo's gesture of negation is quite literally a "no" vote with regard to such thinking. Specifically, the *não* constitutes his declaration of independence from the practice of publication of such intellectually empty material as that which he has been given to edit. And I am implicitly invited to accompany that declaration of independence in much the same way that the implied author invited me to accompany him in the prior two "historical" novels. If truth be told, however, Raimundo's seems less an abstractly principled declaration than one informed by his own considerable idiosyncrasies. Indeed, the more principled stand is my own.

Second, it is important to spend a minute considering Raimundo's strategy as regards the specific nationalist practices he confronts. Save for the pure myth-making—or, really, myth-repeating—that he finds, he does not attack specific issues of historical fact and historical interpretation. His *não* is directed more generally: in its categorical fictionality, it represents an attack upon the fascist master narrative itself, the set of basic institutional-sphere assertions that sought to legitimize and inculcate the monumentalized national history and underpin the hermeneutic expectations that come linked to it: the notion of the "epic" past, the motifs of chosenness and extraordinary status, the claim of hermeneutic localism and international exceptionalism, and the making of this model of understanding the national a matter of Portuguese national-responsibility-in-reading (this last item will be developed more nearly fully later in this chapter). Through the addition of the one word *não*, which in effect constitutes an opening he creates for himself to access the institutional sphere where the hermeneutical rules that correlate with such assertions are lodged, he questions their authority claims. It is not that counter statements are propounded (save for the implicit caveat against the "monumental" construct and the purposes to which it had been put); rather, it is that the institutional is thematized as questionable—and changeable—in contrast to the fascists' static construct. That is the import of Raimundo's activity as a figure of regress to the institutional sphere: it gives just about everything in the novel having to do with Portuguese history and nationalism—which is, in one way or another, just about everything in the novel—indelible institutional-sphere implications.

As regards plot traditionally conceived, from the perverse addition of the *não*—or, perhaps, the perverse subtraction of the crusaders—all else in the novel flows. The title becomes multivalent: a novel title that repeats the title of a book on a subject highly worked by nationalist mythology (it is referred to by Raimundo/the implied author as "almost sacred" [99 (113)]) in the process of being undone in the novel itself. I am not going to summarize the many dimensions of what we read. Suffice it to say that Raimundo's *não* gets him the attention of his (female) editor, with whom he ends up establishing an intimate relationship built to some degree on her attraction to what she sees as his originality, if not iconoclasm (the latter may be making too great a claim for him, although, as we shall see, he grows into something like that role as the novel progresses). As a part of that relationship, the editor, Maria Sara, challenges Raimundo to write a "history" of the siege of Lisbon presuming his "not" and all that it brings with it, thus actually providing him the unique opportunity in effect to "*re*-write" a particular key moment in the monumental history in a mode that we can refer to as "in the institutional sphere"—and providing me with the opportunity to accompany him in that undertaking.

A portion of the novel is, then, the record of Raimundo's writing of his own "siege of Lisbon"—i.e., as a part of the novel's texture I am given, verbatim, extended passages of the text-under-construction of Raimundo's "siege" as it passes through his mind and out onto the page. In this way I witness the fashioning of an institutional-sphere re-authorization of sorts and thus see my own activity of meaning-making-in-reading registered as "written also" in that sphere. Indeed, if I follow the novel's invitation I rehearse that reauthorization in my own individual manner through the process of my meaning-making (I use the term *invited reader* to characterize this somewhat unfettered, contemplative mode of readership that *History* requests of me; many of its specific features will be compiled as this chapter progresses—and I shall eventually be adding a reflexive dimension to it as well.) My reading thus deals as much with institutional questions as it does with the traditional "plot"—or, more precisely, in reception of the latter

I perforce address the former as well. In short, I am "invited" to engage consciously in "*reading* in the institutional sphere," an activity that in the process obviously calls institutional-sphere rules and constraints directly into question. Thus, in the context provided by *History*, recourse to the concept of "writing in the institutional sphere" is shown to be more than a means of revealing disturbances in that sphere and hence potential areas of its reformulation, which is how we have seen it to now. It is also the indicator of a wide area of potential reformulation-in-reception. In essence, I as reader cannot but think of the very logic of received national history when I see that logic being painstakingly overturned, especially as I have an ongoing emotional entanglement with that prior logic.

In one sense, this new text of the siege, the value of which lies expressly in its fictionality, is analogous to Padre Lourenço's functional flying machine or to the existence of Ricardo Reis as fictitious fictional main character. They are all flamboyant fantasies that serve within the narrative as complex rhetorical gestures—fictional steps in an analysis that interrogates what is presumed to be factual (cf. Vaihinger), rhetorical foils that lead to useful revelations, and the like—to the end of casting light on the construction and constructedness of what is said to be "real." In the present case, the principal "reality" being put into question is the "reality" of the fascist version of Portuguese history and Portuguese nationalism.

Once again Gonçalo Mendes Ramires of Eça de Queirós's *The Illustrious House of Ramires* (see Chapter 1) offers an illustrative figure of comparison. In ways very similar to those applying in that novel, I am presented with a main character who not only is a reader but on the basis of his reading becomes an author (of sorts), writing a historical text (of sorts) based on reception of a prior text (of sorts). And I confront a text being written within, and as a part of, the text I am reading. There are many other parallels with *The Illustrious House of Ramires*, including the expectable passages in which Saramago's text seems self-consciously to echo Queirós's (e.g., 285 [318]). Indeed, the parallels are so intricate and deploy themselves in such a manner that I (not, in this case, "I reader" but rather "I literary scholar") have elsewhere argued that the relationship between the two texts is that of a palimpsest: *The History of the Siege of Lisbon* is, figuratively, written over *The Illustrious House of Ramires* ("José Saramago 'Re-vises'"). It follows many of the forms of its predecessor as though it were being structured by it, but at the same time it turns them in such a way as to represent a critique-by-alteration of its predecessor's logic, thereby suggesting a logic of its own.

One example illustrates that process. Among the parallels between the two novels is the presence in each of a "tower" that provides the character/author with a vantage point from which to look out over the very same place that is the setting for some portion of the history that he is reading about and of which he is writing. A point of irony is that, while for Gonçalo Mendes Ramires that tower is his ancestral "Tower of Ramires," in *History* the tower is the neighborhood of Raimundo's apartment, including his own terrace, which are located at a vantage point that would, in 1147, have been a tower on the Lisbon city wall and therefore, since at that time Lisbon was being lived in by the besieged Muslims, Raimundo's positional counterpart in history would have been an Arabic *almuadem* (*al-muadhdhan*), or muezzin, in his minaret. Gonçalo's historical counterpart, by contrast, would have been one of his own ancestors. So in his narrative Raimundo creates a muezzin, or perhaps elaborates on one he finds present in the "History of the Siege of Lisbon" he is "revising." By custom, the novel asserts, the muezzin would have been blind, so he is created accordingly (11 [19]). The correspondence—or lack thereof—between Raimundo and the blind muezzin, the crier who cannot actually see what is happening in relationship to the language that he utters, is played on throughout the novel with manifest epistemological implications—What can we really know? What is the status of the knowledge we have? How are our language and our knowledge related? (The imagery of blindness also anticipates Saramago's next novel, *Ensaio sobre a Cegueira*, of 1995, translated into English simply as *Blindness* [1998]—though sight and its metaphorization have been played upon in Saramago novels since the introduction of Blimunda and continue to be so even after *Blindness*.)

While Raimundo palimpsestically reinstantiates Gonçalo, and his narrative trajectory both reacts to and "revises" Gonçalo's narrative trajectory, in one key respect Raimundo is Gonçalo's complete inverse, and the palimpsest serves to point out the inversion. While *The Illustrious House of Ramires* establishes a history of

Chapter Four

ancestral vigor that Gonçalo has to meet on his own terms in order to enter modernity, Raimundo, by contrast, has set for himself an almost logical problem: much like Descartes demonstrating the function of "doubt," he has to show in his new version of the siege of Lisbon how it might have been possible for the Christians to take the city even without the aid of the crusaders. Let me hasten to reassure you (in case, as a "proper" bearer of Western culture, you were worried): after considerable trial and error, on both the Christians' part and Raimundo's—theirs, of course, being a representation of his—, a way is found, and Lisbon is still taken (a truly interesting verbal phrase as regards time reference, and one indicative of the complex temporal structure of the novel; I shall use it several times more).

The basic pattern described by Gonçalo's dialogue with the past in *The Illustrious House of Ramires* is that of the "talking cure": when the subject is able to articulate a clear, exteriorized depiction of the problem (in his case, when Gonçalo is able to fashion a critical outlook upon his family/"national" heritage), a self-activating reason comes to the fore and works to overcome that problem, emancipating itself in the process. In terms of pattern, the "talking cure" describes what is effected in me by the reader–implied author pact in both *Baltasar and Blimunda* and *The Year of the Death of Ricardo Reis*—save that, as we have seen, exteriorization is not a requisite and what comes to the fore in those novels, instead of "reason," is merely another, likely transitory, psychological category—which result puts the very concept of "cure" into question. With *History*, by contrast, that quantity *is* a reason of sorts, though, as we shall see, hardly modern Western "reason." The palimpsestic contrast reveals that in many respects for Raimundo inherited nationalist thought and allied national history, instead of a cultural (or family) inheritance as it was for Gonçalo, a force psychological or ethnic in some manner to be identified with, is a set of rhetorical and logical possibilities with individual- and social-psychological entailments. The contrast, first of all, constitutes an advisory statement against the nationally grounded identificatory hermeneutics that fascism sought to impress upon the Portuguese populace. Raimundo himself meditates on some of the issues involved when he receives his new editing assignment after having performed his (yet-undiscovered) act of negation on the manuscript of "History of the Siege of Lisbon":

Mastering the Culture's Tool Kit

Back in his study and curious about his new assignment, Raimundo Silva examines the manuscript Costa has left him, heaven forbid that it should turn out to be *A Comprehensive History of Portugal*, bringing further temptations as to whether it should be *Yes* or *No*, or that even more seductive temptation to add a speculative note with an infinite *Perhaps* which would leave no stone unturned or fact unchallenged. After all, this is simply another novel amongst so many, he need not concern himself with introducing what is already there, for such books, the fictions they narrate, are created, both books and fictions, with a constant element of doubt, with a reticent affirmation, above all the disquiet of knowing that nothing is true, and that it is necessary to pretend that it is, at least for a time, until we can no longer resist the indelible evidence of change, then we turn to the time that has passed, for it alone is truly time, and we try to reconstitute the moment that passed while we were reconstituting some other time, and so on and so forth, from one moment to the next, every novel is like this, desperation, a frustrated attempt to save something of the past. Except that it still has not been established whether it is the novel that prevents man from forgetting himself or the impossibility of forgetfulness that makes him write novels. (*History* 1996 47)

[No escritório, só para tomar conhecimento do novo trabalho, Raimundo Silva examina o original que o Costa lhe deixou, oxalá não me saia uma História de Portugal completa, que não faltariam nela outras tentações de Sim e de Não, ou aquela, quiçá ainda mais sedutoramente especulativa, de um infinito Talvez que não deixasse pedra sobre pedra nem facto sobre facto. Afinal, é apenas um romance entre os romances, não tem que preocupar-se mais com introduzir nele o que nele já se encontra, porque livros destes, as ficções que contam, fazem-se, todos e todas, com uma continuada dúvida, com um afirmar reticente, sobretudo a inquitação de saber que nada é verdade e ser preciso fingir que o é, ao menos por um tempo, até não se poder resistir à evidência impagável da mudança, então vai-se ao tempo que passou, que só ele é verdadeiramente tempo, e tenta-se reconstituir o momento que não soubemos reconhecer, que passava enquanto reconstituíamos outro, e assim por diante, momento após momento, todo o romance é isso, desespero, intento frustrado de que o passado não seja coisa definitivamente perdida. Só não se acabou ainda de averiguar se é o romance que impede o homem de esquecer-se, ou se é a impossibilidade do esquecimento que o leva a escrever romances. (*História* 56)]

Chapter Four

There is, of course, something metatextual about this novelistic use of comparison with the novel in order to make the point about the nature of historiography. The comparison is, however, by no means unusual: theoreticians of history have long discussed the ways in which historiography relates to fiction-writing (e.g., White). Here the principal purpose is to introduce the concepts of doubt and indeterminacy, which are, in Raimundo's reckoning, constitutive of both genres but admitted to be such only in the novel. Hence the implicit charge that history seeks to occult the fact that it too is basically a rhetorical modality, indeed one created against the insecurity of not knowing (cf. LaCapra, *History and Criticism* 71–94). The suggestion is that novels are more honest in these respects. And, of course, that entire set of questions is trained on *Portuguese* nationalistic historiographical practice in the above passage's first lines, as Raimundo speculates ironically that this new task might involve a "comprehensive" historical book, which would only compound his options and thus bring not one but multiple temptations—which, instead of eliciting a "no," might be allayed by a categorical "perhaps."

It is quite clear as Raimundo and Maria Sara conceive the re-writing project "in the institutional sphere" and he begins to carry it out, that at stake are what are appropriately understood as a set of probabilities: Raimundo has to ask himself how Lisbon can "still be taken" without the manpower and military expertise that the crusaders represent. He literally has to calculate military odds and plan strategy. He is able to do so by walking in the area in which he lives and looking over what was the actual terrain of the siege of 850 years earlier or by looking out from his own terrace. He comes to think of that scene as a large chessboard (e.g., 207 [233–34]). By now it is clear that, despite his character, there is a sense in which Raimundo is aptly named: in this specific cognitive sense, in relation to these specific sorts of operations he is the "king of the world," albeit a world of his own creation, one that, as I follow him in my reading, I see him wresting from inherited (fascist) institutionality itself—indeed I follow along as he does so. The irony is that this "king of the world" is a lowly, and lonely, copyeditor, symbol of how each person, no matter her or his location in life, (potentially) relates to institutionality, the key variable being the degree of agency—in effect, the terms of the subject-construct—that each brings to the task. Indeed, in (re-)writing history Raimundo "becomes" King Afonso Henriques,

Mem Rodrigues, and other Portuguese historical personages, as well as fictitious characters he creates in carrying out his project. The novel dedicates a great deal of time to analysis of how he "becomes" such figures (e.g., 112–13 [128–29]). Within the novel, the controlling metaphor for that process of becoming an-other, of in effect dialoguing with institutionality about the conditions of subjecthood, is one that can best be called "cyber-historical"—in very specific ways.

At first glance, the linking of something that might be called "cyber-history," or "cyber"-anything, and a 1980s Portuguese novel would seem to be nonsensical. Portugal was hardly the home of advanced computer culture at the time; no *Neuromancers* had come out of Lisbon or Oporto, or seemed poised to do so any time soon—though *History*'s implied author tantalizes me with several short meditations about computers (e.g., 18 [26], 221 [248]). And on its very surface the novel has something to do with phenomena otherwise linked to the role-playing games and MUD's of about the time of its publication.

Throughout the historical portion of *History* I witness a process of calculation of the strengths and leadership abilities of personages in a world principled by rules according to which the probabilities of success or failure of possible operations are analyzed—much as in role-playing games. I also see psychological projection, identification, and the like on the part of Raimundo become the narrative and rhetorical gestures necessary for getting Lisbon "still taken." In terms of model, then, rather than chess, Raimundo is actually playing something like the classic "Dungeons and Dragons" or the early online "Ultima." As a result, his negation of the rules governing inherited historiography has the effect not of replacing one "story" with another but rather of moving the writing and receiving of history away from a "modern" model characterizing it as controlled by a self-actuating and self-sufficient instrumental reason, with the product of which one is asked to identify, and to a model based on video-game-like structures of interactivity and changing realities. Raimundo is thus not—or not only—changing key institutional-sphere narratives; more importantly, he is changing some of the basic assertions, the building-blocks if you will, of the institutional-sphere script itself and doing so before my eyes.

That modal shift is so much the case that, out of the many personages that the inherited history offers him, Raimundo quite openly chooses one "character" to "play." What that means in

Chapter Four

game culture is, first and foremost, that the game-player creates the game world—or co-creates it with other players—according to rules that he or she must subsequently obey in playing the game. He or she then has an effect within that world through the actions of a "character" or "characters" with whom he/she identifies to some extent and in some ways. The usual means of describing this effect in the world of the game is to say "*I* want to do this," or "*I* expect that," etc., in which formulas the pronoun "I" is a combination of the player and the character but corresponds to the character's motives and actions within the game world. Lest there be doubt that Raimundo's choice of "his character" involves a process like this, a relevant passage:

> Raimundo Silva, whose main concern is to defend as best he can the unorthodox theory that the crusaders refused to take part in the conquest of Lisbon, will be as satisfied with one character as with another ... He was drawn by young Mogueime's lack of inhibition, if not actual brilliance, in relating the attack on Santarém. ... Therefore Raimundo Silva takes Mogueime as his character. He holds, however, that certain points ought to be clarified beforehand, so that there will be no misunderstandings that might later prejudice ...
>
> [A Raimundo Silva, a quem sobretudo importa defender, o melhor que souber, a heterodoxa tese de se terem recusado os cruzados a ajudar à conquista de Lisboa, tanto lhe fará uma personagem como outra ... No moço Mogueime atraiu-o a desenvoltura, se não mesmo o brilho, com que relatou o episódio [da tomada de Santarém] ... Aceita portanto Raimundo Silva a Mogueime para sua personagem, mas considera que alguns pontos hão-de ser previamente esclarecidos para que não restem mal-entendidos que possam vir a prejudicar, mais tarde ... (*História* 189–90)]

In the last lines of that passage Mogueime's "powers" (a term from game culture) are being established, as when a character is created and given so many exponent "points" for strength, for cleverness, and other characteristics. Mogueime is thus being chosen as "Raimundo's character" in exactly the sense that MUDders and D and D players have used the term.

It takes little foresight to imagine that the combination of Raimundo/Mogueime will come up with a love interest within their combination of history/game world (remember, according to the

English-language cover, this is a "rollicking love story"). Her name is Ouroana. Nor does it take foresight to imagine that that phenomenon will allow for a cyber-pairing with Raimundo and Maria Sara. Indeed, such is the case to the extent that the developing narrative (in which Maria Sara reads along as Raimundo writes, thus becoming yet another reader-figure) structures their lovemaking and their developing relationship and, inversely, their lovemaking and relationship become a source of material and motives for the eventual crusader-less conquest of Lisbon (actually, a few crusaders decide to stay). For example, in a blatantly transferential relationship to his own developing intimacy with Maria Sara, Raimundo conspicuously kills off a Germanic knight in order to open the way for the relationship between Mogueime and Ouroana to develop (251–86 [282–319]). Other psychic processes of Raimundo's—and of Maria Sara's as well—also work transferentially to have Lisbon "still taken." In general terms, neither realm, the contemporary "reality" or the history/game world regularly, occupies a master role: they model each other interchangeably, decision-making in one affecting decision-making in the other. Indeed, this interchangeability operates to the point where, by the end of *History*, virtually any event taking place in one world serves as a metaphor for something in the other. This standing transferential relationship is a textual feature with which I repeatedly have to deal in reception.

A scene in which Raimundo and Maria Sara have met in downtown Lisbon for dinner before going on to Raimundo's apartment textualizes that relationship. It does so in abstract, philosophical terms characteristic of the novel but ones nonetheless permeated by the presence of the characters' own intimate relationship:

> ... she asked how the history of the siege was coming along ... Three [more] lines would be sufficient if I were to adopt the formula of then they married and lived happily ever after, or as in our case, the Portuguese with supreme effort took the city, or I set about listing the arms and baggage, and then I shall never get to the end, one alternative would be to leave the text as it stands, now that we have met each other, I'd rather you finished it, you must resolve the lives of that Mogueime and Ouroana, the rest will be less important, in any case we know how the story must end ... When we return home I'm going to read it from the beginning, Unless we happen to be doing something more interesting, We have all the time in the

Chapter Four

world, dear Sir ... when you set me this task, you knew that I was nothing more than an ordinary, run-of-the-mill proofreader with no other qualities ... What did you have in mind when you talked me into this, what were you looking for ... it's now quite obvious that I was looking for you ... A man ... who had realized that the distinction between *no* and *yes* stems from a mental operation that is only thinking about survival, A good enough reason, It's a selfish reason, And socially useful, Undoubtedly, although everything depends on who the owners are of that *yes* and *no*, Let's be guided by norms based on consensus and authority obvious as it is that any variation in the authority varies the consensus, You give no leeway, Because there can be no leeway, we live cooped up in a room and paint the world and the universe on its walls, Don't forget that men have already gone to the moon, Your claustrophobic little room went with them, You're a pessimist, Not quite, I'm simply a skeptic of the radical kind, A skeptic is incapable of love, On the contrary, love is probably the last thing in which the skeptic can still believe, He can, Rather let us say he has to. (*History* 1996 266–68)

[... ela quis saber como ia a história do cerco, ... Poderia acabá-la em três linhas, no género depois casaram e foram muito felizes, no nosso caso os portugueses num supreme esforço tomaram a cidade, ou então ponho-me a enumerar as armas e as bagagens, e nunca mais chegarei ao fim, uma alternativa seria deixá-la ficar tal qual está, agora que já nos encontrámos, Preferiria que a terminasses, tens de resolver as vidas daquele Mogueime e daquela Ouroana, o resto será menos importante, de toda a maneira sabemos como a história terá de acabar ... Quando voltarmos para casa vou pôr-me a ler desde o princípio, Se não estivermos ocupados em questões mais interessantes, Temos muito tempo, caro senhor ... quando me meteste nestes trabalhos sabias que eu não passava de um normal e modesto revisor, sem outras qualidades ... Que ideia tinhas tu na cabeça quando me desafiaste, que buscavas ... (A)gora é evidente que era a ti que buscava ... Um homem ... que percebera que a distinção entre não e sim é o resultado duma operação mental que só tem em vista a sobrevivência, E uma boa razão, E uma razão egoísta, E socialmente útil, Sem dúvida, embora tudo dependa de quem forem os donos do sim e do não, Orientamo-nos por normas geradas segundo consensos, e domínios, mete-se pelos olhos dentro que variando o domínio varia o consenso, Não deixas saída, Porque não há saída, vivemos num quarto fechado e pintamos o mundo e o universo nas paredes dele, Lembra-te que de que já foram homens à lua, O

Mastering the Culture's Tool Kit

> seu quartinho foi com eles, Es pessimista, Não chego a tanto, limito-me a ser céptica da espécie radical, Um céptico não ama, Pelo contrário, o amor é provávelmente a última coisa em que o céptico ainda pode acreditar, Pode, Digamos antes que precisa ... (*História* 298–300)]

At this point, as far as Raimundo's history of the siege is concerned, Maria Sara's interest has clearly been captured by the Mogueime-Ouroana relationship—that is, by their own relationship as registered through it transferentially. But that is not the only front on which history and present are linked in their discussion. They both agree intellectually that history functions as an area onto which present-time interests and purposes are retrojectively cast. That is, the presence of the two transferentially linked timeframes allows them to link past and present—and, for that matter, to project into future as well. Of course, the two characters "skeptically" agree that the "interests" involved are ultimately wider than individual ("everything depends on who the owners are of that *yes* and *no*"). But they also see those interests as individually borne, holding that one's opting for *no* or *yes* constitutes "a mental operation that is only thinking about survival." By that logic, knowledge comes in service to the outcomes that it can reasonably be assumed to perform. And Maria Sara and Raimundo extend the proposition thus entertained to questions of understanding in general, at which point in the above passage they literally redo Plato's cave metaphor in their own register. And with conclusions opposite to those we have attributed to Plato for the past two-plus millennia: the figures on the walls are not reflections of a self-identical language—i.e., of "truth." They are instead the arbitrary products of our own, human "painting." The result is a view of understanding as something akin to that presented in Einstein's famous watch parable but in a version in which the performative dimension is emphasized. The parable has it that one possesses a sophisticated but unopenable watch. The owner can observe the face, all of the information provided, the changes in information over time, and so on, and create theories to explain how the watch can do all that it does. But because the watch is unopenable, one can never be sure that one's current theory is accurate. Indeed, if a new, superior explanation were to be advanced, one would have to accept it. The watch, of course, is the universe. Raimundo and Maria Sara's cave metaphor works similarly save that what is of greatest import is not the power of the explanation but rather the social and/or psychological role that it plays: the culture it creates and the individual's transactions with that culture. All the while this exchange between the two interlocutors is taking place, its texture is working as an aphrodisiac for them. Thus, I note to myself as I read, another, less intellectualized sort of transference is being demonstrated and another, less intellectualized "survival instinct" is at play in the exchange.

The novel draws to a close as Lisbon is "still taken," though not without wrangling among the proto-Portuguese over whether or not the spoils of victory will be shared equally amongst them (the outlook for which Mogueime becomes the common soldiers' spokesman before the king) or given to the nobles and the crusaders alone (305–08 [340–43]). Mogueime's leadership clearly registers transferentially Raimundo's personal growth and increased self-assurance attained over the novel's represented timeframe. Moreover, the entire confrontation is linked to the time of the novel's reception by the implied author's reference to the ultimately successful petition by the common soldiers that the sharing be equal as an "Armed Forces Movement," which was the self-assigned title of the organization within the military that carried out the 1974 Revolution. (Thus, in Raimundo's telling, Portugal "begins" on something like an egalitarian basis [cf. Frier, *Novels* 128].) At novel's end Maria Sara and Raimundo, together in bed at 3:00 AM, meditate about the future that might "logically" be assigned to "Ouroana" and "Mogueime" (311–12 [346–48])—though, as I read it, I am quite clear that the logic involved is one based on the standing transferential relationship.

Such is *History*'s basic plot, and such are the obvious connections with, and differences from, its two predecessors in the areas relevant to my pursuit of an answer to my smile question.

* * **

In order to be able to delve further into the novel's multiform interrogation of nationalist historiography and my readerly involvement in that interrogation, a further area of inquiry—one several times suggested in the prior pages—must be developed. Let us begin that task by supposing for a moment that Raimundo and Maria Sara are historical persons rather than literary characters. How would the "history" that they would have received through their upbringing and education and, like all generation A readers, would have brought with them to their encounter with historiography actually have sought to impose itself institutionally?

There is a great deal stated or presumed in contemporary criticism that very much underreads the texture of the *Estado Novo* historical politics launched to that end. To be sure, the regime did fashion and did propagandize its own grandiose version of the inherited history. But such acts were not generally ones grounded in simplistic evasions of the knotty problematics of historiography. Indeed, quite the contrary. Both state spokespersons and unofficial apologists for the regime meditated on the subject, often in public media, at remarkable length and with considerable complexity. Indeed, if one includes the work dedicated to the issue of so-called Portuguese philosophy (see Chapter 1)—which, amongst other things, represented a front upon the issues of "national history"—it is likely that, between the end of World War II and the mid-1960s, Portugal was the place in Europe where the problems of history were discussed publicly at greatest length. And much of what we think of as the bases of the contemporary critique of modern historiography was well understood by the principal actors of fifty, sixty, even seventy years ago in Portugal: that, thinkers like Ranke notwithstanding, history is a human narrative, not a constituent feature of temporal duration somehow "out there" to be discovered; that the narrative varies with the narrator (White); that the concept of a para-scientific causation provides an inadequate model for historiography; that national historiography is not (merely) a "factual" matter but rather can be—and has been—as well a powerful instrument of social cohesion. The logic of an Álvaro Ribeiro or an António Quadros (Chapter 1) or even that of an official *Estado Novo* spokesman like Rodrigues Cavalheiro or Gustavo de Fraga is one in which the incommensurable varieties—and, in some senses, the arbitrariness—of history are often dealt with directly.

Let me reproduce a quote that will be useful in this regard:

> Facts ... are inert and dead, submerged in a time long gone; they were the products of organisms and circumstances of which we can no longer have experience ... they can be revived, can take on a meaning, when they are referred to a concrete experience of the real, to a living intuition of time and of movement ... (Quadros, *Teoria* 93)

Chapter Four

The passage points to the often-observed tension between, in its own terms, past "factuality" on the one hand and what we would call historiographical thematization on the other. The author of the above words, the often-aforementioned António Quadros, already has in mind a way to resolve that tension, as the passage's phrasing suggests. His diction, especially in the notions of "revival" and of "intuition," manifests as much. The starting-point with "dead" factuality is clear. We today, instead of constituted "facts," would probably speak of "sources" or "data"—which terms actually refer to concepts derived from sources and data—but that is basically what Quadros means. Clear too is the necessity of human narrative to effect the "revival." I am not going to go through Quadros's exposition in any detail; suffice it to say that he will argue (I refer to his argumentation in *Teoria* 12–96, 241–50) that historical knowledge is teleological by nature and that that fact must be accepted as one of its constituent features. He will then say that the telos that *he* accepts is a version of Christian eschatology. With that acceptance, to be sure, he begins to smuggle in a whole set of scholastic notions about the immanent purposiveness of things' existence, but that is really not a necessary part of his argument. His answer to the historian's dilemma is that an eschatological theory will enable the fashioning of historical knowledge out of "dead facts" with no sense that the knowledge produced will be universal as regards content. In effect, what anthropology might see as an imperative to order, or psychology see as a security drive, he—in many ways like Maria Sara and Raimundo in the passage reproduced above (pp. 137–39)—posits as a psycho-cultural realm in which epistemological patterns are forged. And to think that he could not have made an argument to that end with reference to the European anthropological and psychological theory of the day and to contemporary work in philosophy and theory of history would be very much mistaken—though the psychology in particular would now be rejected and many of his readings are, in my judgment, more appropriations than readings.

The move that Quadros makes locates the historian, not the realm of "facts," as the primary system; in effect, he follows Kant in seeing teleology as a regulative principle rather than a constitutive one—though he then proceeds to blur that distinction by virtually equating the telos emerging from the epistemological realm that he designates, the historian's narrative, and supposed constitutive features of the "facts." (Too he ignores the "language problem" that we today would see immediately, though he could, I believe, easily accommodate it.) He ends up arguing that while many philosophies of history are to be seen within the traditions of Portuguese historiography, they are all reducible to construction around a teleology like that provided by his Christian eschatology. (Hence his familiar incorporative gesture [see Chapter 1, pp. 25–26].)

Quadros also—almost needless to say for anyone who knows the intellectual figure he cut in the 1950s and 1960s—suggests that patterns of commonality within diversity that, to his mind, are revealed as he sets forth the teleology betoken a latent "genius" for a variation that is somehow also, at some remove, unifiedly and uniquely "Portuguese." Ribeiro, his intellectual mentor, would wish to add to that argument, as we have seen (above, p. 22), that there is a national symbolic realm that underlies and informs the national language itself, and the specific symbols and symbolic values derive from the national experience and therefore are peculiar to Portuguese and open to understanding by Portuguese alone.

The general effects of such discourse—which was continually promulgated at the time, especially in relation to the "aesthetic" realm—are several. First, it locates a virtual responsibility for history inside the "national" individual, rendering it a part of psychic make-up. (This is not to suggest that liberal historiography had not already initiated a somewhat similar move.) Second, it poses the problems of history in such a way as to promote the sense of a complex psychological relationship between national historical "facts" and the individual Portuguese human being—as though "national history" constituted a set of vital elements binding the individual to it in a mutually defining and confirming dialectic. Third, it urges the individual to seek to recognize the ground of that dialectic in his or her daily life and, as we have previously seen demonstrated, most especially in the reception of cultural products. I can no longer estimate, for example, the number of Portuguese who have sheepishly confided to me that they "don't understand" or "can't read" *The Lusiads*, the sixteenth-century epic poem publicized for the past two centuries as "the national epic." The questions they should be asking themselves, of course, are, first, according to what (or—better—whose) logic they would expect to understand a long, erudite Renaissance poem in the first place and then—even more importantly—why they feel guilty for not being able to do so.

The argument for Portuguese uniqueness in many respects anticipates the post-modern argument for epistemological localism—save, of course, that for such as Quadros all localisms will finally show up in some coordinated relationship to each other at the *eschaton*, where Portuguese commonality is confirmed. (He argues, then, both sides of the same proposition: localisms within Portuguese space will be overcome while the localism/exceptionalism of Portuguese uniqueness in the world cannot.) Thus is promulgated—within formal institutions as well as in the media—an invisible commonality and an invisible hold on Portuguese precisely *through* examination of the complexity of the creation of historical knowledge.

Far from avoiding the problems of history, then, some in the *Estado Novo* camp actually nationalized and psychologized them—albeit in a fashion that seeks to employ abstract, symbolic, even para-theological argument to capture individual psychology. I should add that this précis, which is admittedly quite selective and thus necessarily reductionistic, gives specific definition to what I have heretofore been referring to with a series of terms all reduceable to a formulation such as "fascist hermeneutics based on identification with the nationality." The identification that the fascist regime sought to foment was not mere receptor self-projection upon features of a cultural product as the basis of receiving it but rather one that also freighted that self-projection with the added weight of "*the* national past" and quite literally a sense of individual psychological responsibility for that past in present time. To be Portuguese, for such as Quadros and Ribeiro, was in effect to be psychologically responsible for a specific heritage—and to be guilty of personal failure, even malfeasance, if you did not carry out that responsibility. That psychological compulsion was the force that sought to direct Portuguese to the identificatory hermeneutics of which we have been speaking. This précis complexifies my exposition of "nationality" introduced in the first chapter above and regularly invoked thereafter. It should be understood as complexifying and deepening psychologically my characterization of fascist identificatory hermeneutics in Chapters 2 and 3 as well.

Mastering the Culture's Tool Kit

* * *

If we think for a moment simply in dry, intellectual terms, response in kind to such phenomena as the *Estado Novo* psychologization of "national history" as exemplified by António Quadros might take several routes: it could deny the projected closure represented by Quadros's *eschaton*—though if it does it may have difficulty in coming up with a non-teleological alternative. While in practice we tend not to follow out the question, modern "history" as a concept is constituted teleologically to the point that it would be difficult to extract the telos and remain with something we would recognize as history. Perhaps a more fruitful route would be to interrogate the features ascribed to the teleology, for Quadros does not allow himself to think of it in other than uniform, definitive terms: in his theorization, the teleology has ultimately to be authoritative; from that necessity, all else follows. But what if it is there less definitively, as, say, a working hypothesis purposely held as such, or as the organizer of an ordering drive that is accorded only behavioral value? In either case—and the two are neither exclusive of each other nor the only alternative options—difference from thought such as Quadros's would come not in the acceptance or rejection of the teleology but in the character and operativity accorded it. In many ways *History* "invites" me the reader to entertain multiple options approximately to that end in reading.

Now let us return to the concept, developed in previous chapters, that Saramago's historical novels work in a "heuristic" manner because they invoke hypothetical or patently fictitious elements, advance their own self-presentation and direct their own reception. As regards the presentation of history in *History*, the novel urges me to read heuristically the fictional account that Raimundo's *não* produces and its intersection with his life: the various acts by his "historical" characters—we get long speeches seeking to steel soldiers before battle as well as camp scenes, views of intimate life, and so on—are there on the page I read obviously not as attempts to represent events I will consider creditable. In fact, *precisely* not. They are instead points of departure urging me to think about, among other matters, how historical events are constituted and how they come to be regarded as creditable. (Also, of course, within Raimundo's developing narrative, they function as means for having Lisbon still taken.) Indeed, in the scene where Raimundo humorously thanks his lucky stars he has not been given a comprehensive history to read (above, p. 133), the reference to the necessity to "pretend that" something is true, "at least for a time, until ... ," is a capsule definition of the heuristic mode that *History* itself cultivates. As with the prior two historical novels, I am invited to read a text that presents itself in a mode in which it simultaneously sets itself forth and takes itself apart—or, better, asks me to receive it in constative and performative modes simultaneously. Very much, then, as in the possible responses to Quadros that I suggest above, I come to understand through my reception that with this novel, history can be characterized as something that we have in a mode that has psychological value for us and has that value in part because we participate in its making, which in turn has to do with our self-making (see the exchange about "interestedness" in Raimundo and Maria Sara's "cave conversation," pp. 137–39 above). *History*, then, has the effect in the first instance of inviting me to think about my/our investment in history and history's investment in me/us. In opening up that individual-psychological dimension, the novel at the same time opens up a space within which I can deal both with the internalized monumental history that I bring with me to the reading and with the assignment of responsibility for it to the individual Portuguese—I can, that is, deal with the centerpieces of the fascist hermeneutics. Arrayed against them are Raimundo's "no," the rewriting project in which he and Maria Sara engage using an approach emphasizing a creative role for the individual, and ultimately myself, the reader, invited to participate in a similar manner.

Across the three historical novels, the space of response to constituted history is created by a series of narrative strategies that have in common the overt questioning of the status of the inherited telos. Quadros's "dead facts" are patently present within *History*'s design: the manuscript "History of the Siege of Lisbon" that Raimundo and Maria Sara are "re-vising" and other texts like them, as well as several identifiable documents of Portuguese history, among them medieval chronicles that deal with the siege of Lisbon, and the famous participant account of the siege contained in a crusader letter/report, written in Latin, given the title of "De expugnatione Lyxbonensi." Indeed, predictably, the implied author plays with the text(ure) of that letter (in a way that suggests research into such issues as the knotty question of its authorship). Also predictably, passages in *History*, virtually from the novel's first pages, play on the text of that account (for a passage where the interface between the two texts is clear, see 287 [321]).

The History of the Siege of Lisbon is thus in one sense the elaborate staging of an opportunity for me to ruminate on the construction of historical discourse (cf. Cerdeira da Silva, "José Saramago: A ficção reinventa" 175)—and, by implication, of the entire received cultural heritage. Indeed, not merely an "opportunity" but one urged upon me. In seeking to negotiate the text, I come to entertain the sense that while Quadros's "dead facts"—be they the historical documents poured into *History*, the newspaper passages of *The Year of the Death of Ricardo Reis*, or the parallel passages in *Baltasar and Blimunda*—have formerly been put to use in one mode of historical narration, I am now able to imagine their being narratized according to another mode, *some* other mode, with no definitive *eschaton* in operation ultimately to decide among modes. I conceive this heuristic narrative arrangement as involving, then, a mix of "dead facts" and the continual implicit (sometimes explicit) holding-out of means to reject a step such as Quadros and other *Estado Novo*–connected thinkers take to give history a univocal, not to mention specific, structure—or at least means to do something other as I see fit. Thus the simple appearance of documentary material, set forth as it is within this novelistic context that questions claims of authenticity and/or univocity made for it, is also the signal of a space not only for me to practice irreverence but also for me to (re-)think.

If, within the course of reception, I harken back to the cyber-metaphor that describes Raimundo and Maria Sara's "new" attitude toward history, I can now take a further step and say summarily that *The History of the Siege of Lisbon* invites me to "cybernize" Portuguese history through the suggestions that that history can potentially be received and organized in any number of ways, that those alternative organizations owe as much to the receiver/organizer and his or her circumstances as to the content (cf. Raimundo and Maria Sara's updating of Plato's cave), and also that such organizing operations represent potentially useful modes of knowing—the word *useful* signaling that their value is not to be found in some modern "truth" concept but rather in

Chapter Four

their operativity. The task I am asked to perform as the receiver of history constructed through my transactions with this novel is, then, not incorporation of a "given" history to myself or projection of myself upon it—literally, in Quadros's terms, a project with the goal of "reviving" "dead facts." It is rather the invitation to look upon history as a highly constructed practice and to receive it in a way that takes into account that it is in my power to do some quotient of the construction as a part of the reception. In this connection the implied author's commentary, rather than leading me as it did in the prior two novels, functions as a reinforcer, modeling an attitude toward issues developed in the text that I am "invited" to take up.

The reader of *History*, then, has the potential to intercept the identificatory hermeneutics advanced under fascism and turn it 180 degrees. Instead of a mode of reading that urges identification with aspects of a text on the basis of a supposed shared "nationality" and the induction of guilt if that course of action does not immediately spring forth, the novel asks me to carry out a mode that literally complexifies the process by instantiating a reader-text relationship that, as in the computer games referred to above, admits the rhetorical value of a kind of identification, namely, identification with a character in the game world, but at the same time suggests that the identification should be one in which the reader/game-player role is consciously developed and understood. It should, then, be an identification that is provisional or partial, that reserves both the possibility of redoing itself and also contains options for changing direction. Such is the specific configuration of the heuristic in *History*. It is one that, read back into the two preceding chapters of this book, adds further to the complexities of the heuristic as it has been developed up to now.

Let us get down to specifics. The outlook I have just set forth is profiled in more or less these terms as Raimundo responds to Maria Sara's questioning when she first reads about Mogueime and Ouroana. To her question about who they are, Raimundo's response is:

> I'm still not sure, he said and fell silent, after all, he should have guessed that Maria Sara's first words would be to inquire who these two were, these, those, whosoever else, in a word, us. Maria Sara seemed satisfied with the reply, she was an experienced enough reader to know that the author only knows what

> his characters have been, even then not everything, and very little of what they will become. Raimundo Silva said, as if he were replying to an observation made aloud, I doubt whether they could be called characters, People in books are characters, objected Maria Sara, As I see them they belong somewhere in between, free in a different way, so that it would not make sense to talk either about the character's logic or about the contingent necessity of the person ... (*History* 1996 235–36)

> [Ainda não sei bem, disse, e calou-se, afinal deveria ter adivinhado, as primeiras palavras de Maria Sara teriam de ser indagar quem eles eram, estes, aqueles, outros quaisquer, em suma, nós. Maria Sara pareceu contentar-se com a resposta, tinha experiência suficiente de leitora para saber que o autor só conhece das personagens o que elas foram, mesmo assim não tudo, e pouquíssimo do que virão a ser. Disse Raimundo Silva, como se respondesse a uma observação feita em voz alta, Não creio que se possa chamar-lhes personagens, Pessoas de livro são personagens, contrapôs Maria Sara, Vejo-os antes como se pertencessem a um escalão intermédio, diferentemente livres, em relação ao qual não fizesse sentido falar nem da lógica da personagem nem da necessidade contingente da pessoa ... (*História* 263–64)]

After identifying the cyber-pairs—"in a word, us"—Raimundo goes on to see the former of the pairs in much the way I have described cyber-characters above: neither as simple tokens in a logic-bound fictional world nor as modern, world-creating human beings, but "somewhere in between." In effect, like cyber game-players, Raimundo and Maria Sara come to read in such a way that, in the process, they on the one hand reflect on the role of the reader-function in the making of the world of possibilities that is the novel and on the other hand understand and reflect upon the impact upon themselves of that very readerly activity. And my "invitation" to engage in a similar process, should I accept it (though, as we shall see, I have really already done so in order to get this far in my reading), in effect has me become thereby a reader/game-player as well. The most effective way I can read *History*, I am, then, virtually forced to understand, is creative dialogue with it and with the "history" that it deals with, and/or with the latter via the former.

Seen as a commentary on history, *History* thus suggests—indeed, virtually states—that notions about the past should be received as a bundle of information variably narratizable and differentially meaningful across whatever diversity describes the receivership and, conversely, its formative impact on the receiver should be recognized in reception. The palimpsestic contrast on this point with *The Illustrious House of Ramires* functions to put that suggestion in strong relief: Gonçalo's strategy involves the mere re-definition of the terms in his static relationship with a history understood as already constituted. And Quadros's strategy means to hold that history in its assigned place. Raimundo's, conversely, is based on a present-time-oriented mutability of the terms of the relationship itself and thus projects into the future rather than, as the *Estado Novo* configuration would have it, being cut off from the future through continual redirection back into the past.

History, then, carries further a set of issues that lie at the core of the reader–implied author pact in both *Baltasar and Blimunda* and *The Year of the Death of Ricardo Reis*. The narrator/implied author continually whispers to me something like: "you and I have been told all our lives to see this matter this way; let's instead see what happens if, free to do so, we try to see it entirely differently. This is my way." Or perhaps "… This is my way at this moment." To which might be added such questions as: "What do you think of it?" or "What is *your* way," or "What is your way at this moment?" And Raimundo Silva exemplifies that outlook.

History's narrative arrangement, narrative texture, and very specific cultivation of its reader, then, combine to suggest over and over again the possibility of erasure of the inherited telos of fascist national historiography and simultaneous structuring, using that inheritance as a rhetorical foil, of something else at its site, the two acts being, really, a single compound act. In the final analysis, a principal role I am invited to play is that of agent of a project of erasure. It is a role cast according to the logic of the cyber-game.

* * *

My transactional relationship with the text does not stop there, however. Indeed, the opportunity to erase (and replace) includes several additional, more concrete dimensions, ones not exclusive of the foregoing, being, indeed, constituents of it. Allow me to explore some of those additional dimensions. (Because of the sheer density of the issues, the ensuing pages will involve some—I hope, excusable—repetition of analyses advanced before, albeit casting them in a new light.)

Let us begin by recalling what I have dubbed the "cave conversation" between Maria Sara and Raimundo. The version of that conversation reproduced above (pp. 137–39) is in fact highly selective: in it I have excised almost everything that did not relate to the issue then at hand, namely, the interchangeability between contemporary "reality" and the history/game world and the far-reaching implications derivable therefrom. As I mention in introducing that highly edited passage, the conversation, improbably philosophical though it is, takes place in a very concrete setting: the two are having dinner at a downtown Lisbon restaurant. As they converse, they do things other than philosophize. Indeed, the philosophizing comes interspersed with references to their relationship, their immediate surroundings, the historical entailments of those surroundings, their day-to-day lives, their own motives in acting as they have, and other like matters. They comment on the fact that they are dining in what is, in the terms developed in these pages, a "still-taken" Lisbon and on what that fact means for their rewriting project; allude to what awaits them sexually later in the evening; banter about who should pay the check in the light of the "institutional" disparities between them; comment on each's sense of her/his own quirkiness; establish their present location in relation to where events might have occurred/occur in their "history/game" ("the boats probably passed this way carrying the corpses of those who lost their lives when storming the city gates" [266]); and then after dinner take a lovers' long summer-evening stroll through the city before reaching Raimundo's apartment (where they had spent the previous night together), there to engage in their writing/reading project and its transferentially linked sexual referent. Thus, when they speak philosophically of what I have called their particular "interestedness," singular and plural, they are simultaneously quite aware that they do so from a historical-material positioning that they are actively living—one peculiar to themselves.

A parenthetical gloss of the word *historical* used here: it does not refer back to the words *historical/history* as I have been using them to this point. Indeed, in many ways its reference is one made to a concept of "history" that stands opposed to my prior usage of the term. Here it refers to the complex locatedness of the individual human being in space and time, the unique "historicity" (the term I shall prefer hereafter in this regard) that belongs to each of us. In Raimundo and Maria Sara's case, their social linkages and obligations; their social relations, past and present; the change that has taken place in their lives since they met each other; their respective senses of self and their intimate desires. Indeed, the entire extended "cave conversation" can be seen as a face-off between, on the one hand, "history" as a set of abstract, teleologically constructed discourses with attached social functionality and, on the other, "historicity" as locatedness in the world and in life. And in this context the latter holds out the possibility of escape from the weight of the former, specifically from the form that it takes in this novel and in the characters' lives, one roughly equatable with the "internalized" *Estado Novo* version. Such escape could come from foregrounding, instead of "history," an understanding of one's own position, one's legitimate needs in life, and making them the principal factors one takes into account as one engages in her/his daily transactions with his/her culture and its legacy. (To be clear: an outlook involving absorbing self-interest is not—necessarily—being entertained in that proposition; as a part of a transactional process, a taking-into-account can both involve the recognition of one's own disposition and needs as a part of a culture and also recognize and react to that culture's expectations of its members. What such a taking-into-account stands in opposition to is not an exaggerated egotism but, in this case, the attitude that says that a narrative lodged elsewhere than in the life of the individual must be allowed to co-opt that individual's transactions. [One might profitably compare this profile with Almeida's discussion of his findings of "mild individualism" in 1980s and early 1990s Portugal (Almeida, "Evoluções" 64–65; "Society and Values" 157–58)].)

Let us look at the passage set forth at greater length (it is all one paragraph):

> They dined in a restaurant in the Baixa, she asked how the history of the siege was coming along, Reasonably well, I'd say, considering how absurd it is, How soon do you expect to finish it, Three [more] lines would be sufficient if I were to adopt the formula of then they married and lived happily ever after, or as in our case, the Portuguese with supreme effort took the city, or I set about listing the arms and baggage, and then I shall never get to the end, one alternative would be to leave the text

Mastering the Culture's Tool Kit

as it stands, now that we have met each other. I'd rather you finished it, you must resolve the lives of that Mogueime and Ouroana, the rest will be less important, in any case we know how the story must end, the proof being that here we are dining in Lisbon, being neither Moors nor tourists on Moorish territory, The boats probably passed this way carrying the corpses of those who lost their lives when storming the city gates, When we return home I'm going to read it from the beginning, Unless we happen to be doing something more interesting, We have all the time in the world, dear Sir ... when you set me this task, you knew that I was nothing more than an ordinary, run-of-the-mill proof-reader with no other qualities, But enough to take up the challenge, Provocation might be the better word, All right, let's call it provocation, What did you have in mind when you talked me into this, what were you looking for, At the time, I didn't see things too clearly, however much I might have justified them to myself, or to you ... it's now quite obvious that I was looking for you, For me, for this thin, serious man with badly dyed hair, as sad as a dog without a master, A man who had deliberately committed an error he was obliged to correct, a man who had realized that the distinction between *no* and *yes* stems from a mental operation that is only thinking about survival, A good enough reason, It's a selfish reason, And socially useful, Undoubtedly, although everything depends on who the owners are of that *yes* and *no*, Let's be guided by norms based on consensus and authority obvious as it is that any variation in the authority varies the consensus, You give no leeway, Because there can be no leeway, we live cooped up in a room and paint the world and the universe on its walls, Don't forget that men have already gone to the moon, Your claustrophobic little room went with them, You're a pessimist, Not quite, I'm simply a skeptic of the radical kind, A skeptic is incapable of love, On the contrary, love is probably the last thing in which the skeptic can still believe, He can, Rather let us say he has to. They finished their coffee, Raimundo Silva asked for the bill, but it was Maria Sara who, with a quick gesture, drew a credit card from her wallet and placed it on the saucer, I'm your boss, I can't allow you to pay for the dinner, there would be no more respect for the hierarchy if underlings were to start outshining their superiors, I'll allow it this time, but don't forget that I'll soon be an author, and then, Then you won't pay under any circumstances, whoever heard of an author treating his editor to dinner, really, you know very little about public relations, I've always been led to believe that editors lunch and dine off their wretched authors, Such shameful slander, a base display of class hatred ... (266–68)

Chapter Four

[Jantaram num restaurante da Baixa, ela quis saber como ia a história do cerco, Menos mal, creio, para o absurdo que é, Ainda te falta muito para terminá-la, Poderia acabá-la em três linhas, no género depois casaram e foram muito felizes, no nosso caso os portugueses num supremo esforço tomaram a cidade, ou então ponho-me a enumerar as armas e as bagagens, e nunca mais chegarei ao fim, uma alternativa seria deixá-la ficar tal qual está, agora que já nos encontrámos, Preferiria que a terminasses, tens de resolver as vidas daquele Mogueime e daquela Ouroana, o resto será menos importante, de toda a maneira sabemos como a história terá de acabar, a prova é estarmos a jantar em Lisboa, não sendo mouros nem turistas em terra de mouros, Provavelmente passaram por aqui as barcas que levaram ao cemitério os mortos do ataque às portas da cidade, Quando voltarmos para casa vou pôr-me a ler desde o principio, Se não estivermos ocupados em questões mais interessantes, Temos muito tempo, caro senhor ... quando me meteste nestes trabalhos sabias que eu não passava de um normal e modesto revisor, sem outras qualidades, As suficientes para teres aceitado o repto, Deverias chamar-lhe antes provocação, Seja provocação, Que ideia tinhas tu na cabeça quando me desafiaste, que buscavas, Naquela altura não o via com muita clareza, por muitas explicações que pudesse ter dado a mim própria, ou a ti ... agora é evidente que era a ti que buscava, Este tipo magro e sisudo, com os seus cabalos mal pintados, vivendo fechado em casa, triste como um cão sem dono, Um homem que me agradou logo que o vi, um homem que fizera deliberadamente um erro onde estava obrigado a emendá-los, um homem que percebera que a distinção entre não e sim é o resultado duma operação mental que só tem em vista a sobrevivência, E uma boa razão, E uma razão egoísta, E socialmente útil, Sem dúvida, embora tudo dependa de quem forem os donos do sim e do não, Orientamo-nos por normas geradas segundo consensos, e domínios, mete-se pelos olhos dentro que variando o domínio varia o consenso, Não deixas saída, Porque não há saída, vivemos num quarto fechado e pintamos o mundo e o universo nas paredes dele, Lembra-te que de que já foram homens à lua, O seu quartinho foi com eles, És pessimista, Não chego a tanto, limito-me a ser céptica da espécie radical, Um céptico não ama, Pelo contrário, o amor é provávelmente a última coisa em que o céptico ainda pode acreditar, Pode, Digamos antes que precisa. Acabaram de tomar o café, Raimundo Silva pediu a conta, mas foi Maria Sara quem, num gesto rápido, tirou da carteira e colocou no pires o cartão de crédito, Sou a tua directora, não posso permitir

Mastering the Culture's Tool Kit

> que pagues o jantar, acabava-se o respeito das hierarquias se os subordinados começassem por aí a querer botar figura contra os seus superiores, Admito por esta vez, em todo o caso lembro-te que estou a caminho de tornar-me autor, e nessa altura, Nessa altura é que não pagarias de todo, onde já se viu o despautério de pagar o autor o jantar ao editor, realmente não sabes nada de relações públicas, Sempre ouvi dizer que dos infelizes autores é que fazem almoço e jantar os editores, Calúnias indecentes, manifestações inferiores de um ódio de classe ... (298–300)]

Aside from the obvious fun the implied author pokes at the relationship between authors and editors—José Saramago having become a very well known author by the time of *History*'s publication—the conversation manifests a number of important features. Let me touch on just two. First, the characters demonstrate a considerable facility in dealing with social constructs. Indeed, they grotesque them (e.g., "class hatred"), banter using them, and think from them—or from what they have made of them in their serio-comic exchange—all in a highly flexible way. Certainly not in a way that merely accepts the given in that area of their lives. (Regarding "the craftsmanship of ideas," see Almeida, "Evoluções" 68–70; Almeida, "Society and Values" 160–61.) Second, the discourse I am calling "philosophical" does not come separately from their thinking about the implications of their own historicity but rather precisely in relationship to it. The problems they introduce derive from their taking stock of their presence before each other, their immediate attraction to each other, with all it implies. Indeed, their discourse is ultimately rooted in their lives and regularly refers to their separate and shared historicities and then extrapolates from them to reach the philosophical register. In short, the scene acts out some proposition such as that philosophy depends upon what I have been calling historicity, while, by contrast, the inherited "monumental history" is constructed in such a way as to render historicity dependent upon *it*.

Now passages such as this one and the others like it that occur with some frequency in the novel's end sections can be read in a number of ways. This "cave conversation," for example, can be seen as the continuation of several elements of plot conventionally understood, as a rudimentary sketch of some dimensions of a materialist concept of social regulation, or as hermeneutic instruction—as, then, a site of regress to the institutional sphere.

Seen as the last of those alternatives, it presents me with features important to take into account for present purposes. As the reader of these pages of mine has doubtless noticed, in this chapter I have had frequent recourse to such phraseology as "the text asks me the reader to …," "the texts suggests," "the reader is invited to … ," "what is demonstrated to me the reader is … ," and other like formulations. What all that urging, suggesting, inviting, and demonstrating itself suggests is that the reader of *History* is being presented with something akin to a morality play—not in terms of content but in the relationship that she/he is asked to set up with the characters and in the possibility of using that relationship to do an adequate reading of the text. The relationship the reader is "invited" to assume involves just enough simple identification to make a reader-character connection but at the same time the maintaining of a contemplative distance that enables reader instruction to be drawn from the novel's pattern and the characters' activity. Such a relationship is inculcated upon *History*'s reader in considerable part by the implied author's practice of referring to Raimundo and Maria Sara principally by their names—in Raimundo's case, usually last name as well as first: "Raimundo Silva." Indeed, if content did not somewhat mitigate the effect, because of that factor alone one could read *History* as a case study—or, better yet, a radio play in which a diegetic narrator continually speaks of, or to, one of the characters by repeatedly using her/his full name. Despite the fact that as reader I know something about their psychological processes, then, I am still asked to keep Maria Sara and Raimundo at arm's length, as though they were objects of contemplation for me just as they seem to be for the implied author even as he produces the novel's text. In short, for all their specificity in one sense, in this other sense they *exemplify*. And one of the things they exemplify is the attitude toward Portuguese cultural history that I have just characterized, namely, that "history" can be jettisoned in favor of "historicity," rhetorically at least. Just as the two characters contemplate the inherited history in their curious way, the implied author asks me to receive them as examples of the contemplation of that history. In this case, then, the reader–implied author pact again functions as a mechanism seeking to locate reading, albeit in a manner considerably different from that obtaining in *Baltasar and Blimunda* or *The Year of the Death of Ricardo Reis*. In the case of *History*, it does so by inviting me to imitate the implied author's schematically outlined example and construe the characters as something like *exempla*. This effect is, of course, another version of the anti-identificatory hermeneutical instruction the presence of which we have seen in the prior two novels. (A similar practice of character reference through repeated use of all or part of their name(s) is in force in the prior novels as well, but in *History* its implications come most strongly to the fore.) *Exempla* are designed to be followed; thus is it suggested that I could choose to look quite consciously at Portuguese history not in the received manner but from the view of my own historicity as receiver/bearer of that history.

As the novel progresses, the reader sees through their interactions that Raimundo and Maria Sara become conscious of their own historicity and then theorize about that historicity as it applies to them. Their conversations, as well as some of Raimundo's musings to himself—virtual soliloquies—involve a mix of registering the concrete happenings of their daily lives and the specific conditions within which they lead those lives (complete with such touches as Leonard Cohen music coming out of apartment windows along the street) and attempting to draw conclusions about it all. "Love," which seems to be the last philosophical redoubt in the "cave conversation," clearly encompasses not "love" in some abstract sense or even just the love relationship continually building between the two characters and helping shape the development they undergo; it refers more generally to a self-conscious engagement with life's immediacy, of which the evolving personal relationship is only the central feature and exemplar.

Unlike its two predecessors, then, *History*, in presenting this very concrete, very human-focused route to erasure, actually sets out a transformative possibility—though, if one looks back to *Baltasar and Blimunda*, some constituents of the "space" for entertaining other historical options are described there as well in relation to the lives—and, again, the "love"—of the two title characters. That earlier text, however, does not support our reading Baltasar and Blimunda as possessing transformative possibilities. This is so in considerable part because the characters themselves do not reflect upon those factors in any generalizing way and thus do not signal the reader that it is appropriate for her/him to do so.

Now to be sure, I can legitimately doubt the efficacy of the transformative possibility that *History* presents, suspecting that it can even be entertained only because the novel's very peculiar, contrived context has it that the (middle-class) characters/examples/proxies occupy a position with regard to institutionality that is wholly ungeneralizable. But at very minimum what is pointed to is a place in which I can plausibly break into inherited "history" and set up opposition to the role it has virtually forced me to allow it to play in my life. I can do so by repositioning my life itself and using that repositioning to rescript the creation of history—acts that would, because of their interdependence, be effectively simultaneous.

In sum, the interplay between registering the day-to-day and theorizing about it that increasingly constitutes *History*'s texture as it unfolds creates "historical" beings within the novel world and ones whose historicity seems necessarily to involve self-reflexivity. In Raimundo's case, his very self-aware characterization of himself in the "cave conversation" stands in contrast to how he evaluated himself at the novel's outset. (More about that self-reflexivity presently.) I the invited reader of the novel, when that attitude is demonstrated to me in the manner we have seen, would be hard pressed to resist entertaining in a similar manner the question of my own historicity while in the act of reading. The novel in effect invites me to consider the proposition that I too have the potential to be—even, am free to be—a similarly "historical" being. It tells me that, within the terms that it develops and in which it involves me, I, as a specific individual, matter.

That point is repeatedly instantiated in a wholly other way as well—and one that is central in my reception of the novel. I refer to the highly distinctive configuration of the reading that I am asked to carry out in order to come to entertain such thoughts as this about my own historicity—and other matters pertaining to myself as well. As has been seen, my reading is located for me at the confluence of, first, past—a past the very construction of which I continually see as highly problematized, which fact freights it emotionally for me—and then a present that simultaneously addresses past and, in complex ways, both takes stock of presentness in relation to past and also projects itself into the future. The interrelations are accurately capsuled in the phrase "the city is still taken."

As I read and read my reading, I realize that I think of this configuration as describing a physical space (I have characterized it that way several times over the preceding pages). In fact, I think of it as a space semi-enclosed by hinged rays coming from a single generally "past" point and opening out to a widening—because less fully defined—future. One of the rays is horizontal, the other rises from the point of the hinge at a modest upward angle. The former ray represents a chronological ordering of the bare "facts" of the Portuguese past, though those "facts" are necessarily chosen from myriad options in some relationship to the "monumental" version of history that is the immediate historical inheritance. The latter ray represents a different version or composite of different versions of something alternative to that inherited "history." The variables contributing to its "difference" might involve varied interpretation, new construction of the interpreter(s), new conceptualization of the relationship between interpreter and "history," or the combination of more than one such factor. Within the configuration I as reader occupy a point on the latter ray that marks the time (and, ultimately, the metaphorical "place" within the graph) of my reception. In effect it is my vantage point upon the whole assemblage and the position from which I invest myself in the making of the text. In the space thus created I use various graphic arrangements to try to keep in mind—one might almost say "keep track of"—the various relationships. The entire configuration is, in one sense, the graphic representation of the transferential linkings that Raimundo and Maria Sara create in their effort to hold precisely those same relationships together and to explore them through—and because of—their own relationship. I re-create it in this formalized way of mine in following their lead and end up using it as an aid in carrying out my reading task. I would suppose that few readers organize in this highly graphic way, but they will have to organize to the same ends in some way.

In effect Maria Sara and Raimundo "live" a complex narrative chronotope, one in which the city's "still taking," if you will, is both a dead fact and a present reality that freights—in some senses virtually enables—their relationship. And I do something similar in reading in order to keep control of the novel's constituent parts: the transferential linkages, the character projections, the character interestedness, and so on—and their many nuances. In short, just maintaining the chronotope requires considerable activity on my part as I read, and my clumsy graph is a way I have developed to organize that task for myself.

The implications of my activity do not end there, however, for as I contemplate that activity I realize that the novel's complex chronotope is also, for me, something like a "hermeneutitope," if the neologism can be pardoned—a "hermeneutitope" similar to the chronotope but differing in function, the hermeneutical version being a representation of the activity I must perform in order to read as thoroughly as I can. Not only must I keep track, I must continually modify elements and adjust relationships amongst the various pieces of the configuration as new elements and/or new implications arise. It is a dynamic system, and my reading task requires that I remain active in order to keep the two rays apart, to keep the angled ray from collapsing back onto the horizontal one. To keep, then, historicity, and/or the cybernizing option, the exemplification, and other textual features from being absorbed back into the "easy" national-historical inheritance. In my hermeneutical task, then, I must remain active—even vigilant—in order metaphorically (but not only metaphorically) to "keep the space open," the "space" being both the space of (re-)making of history and also the space in which I act.

In a key sense, then, the repeated "invitation" to see anew that the reading process offers me, that is, the invitation to see yet another set of implications and how they relate to me, how they make yet another connection within my ever-evolving metaphorically spatial conceptualization of my reading arrangement, is one that the novel forces me to extend to ... *myself*. It is, then, less an "invitation" than a requirement—if I am to read the novel as fully as I can. In concert with the text, I have created what amounts to a building—or remodeling—project for myself as I read, one in which I perforce see new connections all the time between past, present, and future—and build them one after another into my hermeneutitope. This is the mainspring of my reading almost from the outset—which means I have had to accept the aforementioned invitation before I even became aware of it as invitation. *History* has "pre-invited" me. I am thus "pre-invited" in order that I may become "self-invited."

Furthermore, while it is beyond the scope of my "smile pursuit" to follow out in detail, this process of continual accommodation of new elements in definition and redefinition of my reading task forces me to create ever-more-complex cognitive maps regarding key dimensions of my outlook upon the history and historicity—presumably not only in novel-reception but in my life transactivity. In effect, to read *The History of the Siege of Lisbon*, to give one's subjectivity to it as Iser says we must in reading, is at a minimum to confront the possibility of cognitive restructuring on one's own part, at least in practice. In fact, the structure of the reading tasks in the novel—their repetitiveness with progressive variation and complexification, their focus on aspects of a central problem, namely, how to deal with the "national" heritage, and their location of my thinking patterns and processes as the key elements—very much resembles the structuring of therapeutic exercises seeking cognitive restructuring in patients (e.g., Beck, esp. 213–62). In reading *History* it would be all but impossible not to be engaging in something like that restructuring—self-consciously or not it wouldn't matter. Like *The Year of the Death of Ricardo Reis*, then, but in a quite different manner, this novel too offers me its own texture as a surrogate for my dealing with the Portuguese heritage. In this case, my dealing with the novel is my learning to deal with that heritage in a manner or manners that emphasize—and exercise—my own role and my own abilities.

* * *

With this overall picture in mind, let us look at a heretofore-unexplored area that I have had to accommodate into my hermeneutitope. In locating me in relationship to a "space" in which other options might be entertained, the text fosters the sense that, along with the implied author and, to some degree, the novel's principal characters, I am somehow immersed in the stuff of historical contingency and possessed of what cognitive psychologist Jerome Bruner has called "culture's tool kit." A part of that sense, as we have just seen, is that in *History* the implied author and I enjoy a position in which we are intellectually—though not (necessarily) historically or psychologically—unfettered as regards the making of history. We have seen similar though much paler versions of this sense in the earlier novels as well (see p. 72 and pp. 113–14). In *History* too, then, a part of the propagated liberatory feeling comes from this sense of unfetteredness. The sense propagated in this novel, however, is markedly different from the varieties offered in the prior two novels. *History* in effect points out that while, as *Year of the Death* suggests, the overcoming may always

Chapter Four

be momentary, at least for generation A readers, it is an option always conceptually available: as receiver I necessarily have had all along a role in determining the character and functioning of the institutional-sphere rules, for those rules function for me only in my employ of them. This, of course, is simply the reverse pole from the emphasis seen before; in either case, I the reader am the agent in the arrangement. This changed emphasis does not constitute an emotionalized option as in the prior two novels, but rather an intellectualized one that I activate for myself in reading.

In this regard, about *History*'s specific project of rewriting the siege of 1147, Bruner provides a useful guide by positing: "we ask of a proposition not whether it is true or false, but in what kind of possible world it would be true" (Bruner 45) (in reference to Saramago writings, cf. Krabbenhoft, esp. 123–27). That is not exactly Raimundo Silva's question, but the modal logic is exactly his, and he rejects the inherited "world" in which "it"—inherited history, or historiography, or hermeneutics, or nationalist narration, or … —was said to be true without question, rejects it for a world, or worlds, in which a variety of potential realities is recognized. Operatively, that attitude represents the opposite of the Freudian obstacle/Lacanian lack; it is actual authorization for me to read "other-wise." In short, Lisbon is "still taken," but the way that Raimundo finds to accomplish the taking is not *the* (new) way but rather merely *a* way; he is talking precisely in that vein above when he ruminates on the need to "pretend" that something is true, "at least for a time" (see p. 133). And I am shown that I can follow suit—but, as in the cyber-model that this novel propagates, follow it for myself.

A key manner in which I am "shown" that I can follow suit is fascinating. For Raimundo's perverse addition of "no" has constituted, among other things, what is referred to in Adlerian psychoanalytical terminology as a "sideshow"—in this case, one in which the national history has been invoked as a transferential dimension for his—that is, Raimundo's—personal life-change process. In his writings the pioneering psychoanalyst Alfred Adler occasionally used the term *sideshow* to refer to a series of phenomena in which an individual faced with a problem in life engages in activity in a life area completely different from the area in which the problem has occurred but in relation to that problem nonetheless (e.g., Adler, *Journal Articles* 17 ff.). (Sometimes Adler describes that strategy or similar activity without using the term *sideshow* [e.g., *Superiority* 133].) The nature of the relationship between the two areas can vary considerably, the constant element being that the activity in the one area is motivated in some degree of specificity by the problem in the other. While it may strain Adler's usage a bit, one can read *History* as suggesting that, at some level of awareness, Raimundo has created the entire problematic with history that underpins the novel in an attempt to attract Maria Sara—not her specifically but someone like her. That is, with his behavior he has sought to attract a vehicle to change his life. It is to this phenomenon that I allude earlier (p. 126) in speaking of the very specific entailments of Raimundo's possible "mid-life crisis." And Maria Sara, as we have seen, openly suggests that at some level of consciousness she sought him (pp. 137–39). Now especially generation A Portuguese readers are likely to read the text not primarily with regard to the two principal characters' "center ring"—i.e., the building relationship between the two of them—but rather with regard to the general and generalizable implications of the "sideshow" of national history (which is precisely what Raimundo and Maria Sara, generation A readers both, are themselves doing, albeit with a growing awareness of so doing). The motivation to read that way is powerful, since the implications of the "past" dimension have to do with the readers' vital experience—in the issues of reception of the scripts of history and of nationalist ideology and in particular the sense of an individual responsibility-to-history in that act of reception. International readership is probably more likely to recognize both developments but to concentrate on the intimate relationship between Maria Sara and Raimundo—especially when that potential orientation is encouraged in hermeneutical instruction inscribed on the book's cover.

Because of the manner of their linking, the two focuses cannot really be separated. The presence of both the "sideshow" and the "center ring" in *History* underscores that it is inevitable that history exist in relation to us as a function of our interestedness, analogous to Maria Sara's and Raimundo's biographically (and sexually) freighted, complementary, and growing "interestednesses"—in each other, in the historical moment in which they live, in understanding understanding, all of which are ultimately versions of one and the same "interestedness." In terms of cognitive psychology, what I have been calling "interestedness" may equally be termed, from the point of view of its operativity, its "transactionality": roughly, the ways an individual understands the expectations the culture has of him/her and chooses to bear them in her or his interactions as a member of that culture (the "choice" not necessarily being presumed to be a conscious, much less a rationalized, one). In this sense, "transactions" involve the individual's understanding of cultural expectations, her/his interaction with those expectations in a given situation, and the narratives s/he uses to legitimate the choices made. The question, posed directly in the "cave conversation" between Raimundo and Maria Sara (pp. 137–39, above) is whether or not we will have control of the terms of our "interestedness" so understood. Moreover, the trajectory of the relationship between the two characters both guides the reader in reading and models a positive development of "interestednesses."

I have been relating, in my readerly/game-playing manner, primarily to the showy sideshow of Portuguese history that the text presents, with all the complex freighting that comes with it and doing so in roughly the same transferential way that Raimundo and Maria Sara show me they relate to it: as an area of self-making. (This whether or not I accept the task of self-making as regards myself.) I have thus—at least positionally—treated this novel that demonstrates hermeneutic activity centrally featuring self-conscious transference as both a model and also, simultaneously, as a "sideshow" to my own personal "center ring": I have treated it as an area to which I too can relate transferentially. My recognition and acceptance of the transferential relationship that I continually tend is thus also recognition, if not acceptance, of the proposition that I can control my own meaning-making and self-making. I have had, then, to add to my hermeneutitope the representation of a heightened sense of my own potential "interestedness" as I read—especially about past—and as well the similarly heightened sense of my own self-making in that relationship.

Matters must be carried still further, however, and there is still more that I "invite myself" to accommodate. One of the fascinating things about cyber-technology is what can be called its multiple investment of (and in) subjecthood. What *History* does with Raimundo Silva, and in parallel manner with its own readership, has illustrative relationships to conclusions that can be drawn from studies on computer-generated worlds and their relationship to subjecthood and to narration (Murray; Turkle, *Life on the Screen*;

The Second Self). In its insistence on the multiple re-creatability of the historical script on which Raimundo and Maria Sara work and their self-creation through engaging in re-creation, the novel exercises the proposition that subjecthood too can be less fixed and less monocular than has been presumed to be the case both in classical theories of the subject and—what is most important for present purposes—in the identificatory nationalist grounding of subjecthood promulgated by Portuguese fascism. And, of course, the novel asks me—or, really, asks me to ask myself—to entertain that proposition as well. The proposition would have it that potentially we can hold more than one "world" fully in our minds at once and be flexible enough to relate fully to both or all of the possibilities involved rather than giving ourselves over to only one—an attitude that we have seen developing since our analysis of Blimunda in the first of the three novels (see above, pp. 68–70). And that we are continuously being made and re-made through our trans-activity as we receive cultural stuff—in this case, our trans-activity as "transferential" receivers of *The History of the Siege of Lisbon*.

Within the logic of *History*, these multiple possibilities are entertained in the historical imagination psychologized—the characters' and my own. Principal questions that the novel poses are how such scripts and narratives about history as are normally relied upon come into being, second how they work as scripts and narratives, and third what role they play in our (self-)creation. As to the first two of those questions, what *History* seems to presume is that there are merely a handful of received assertions that must be maintained: most of all, of course, Lisbon must "still be taken" on a given date in 1147; some of the personages must be in approximately the same places as in the received documentary record, and certain currently accepted paradigms of probability and verisimilitude have to be observed. All else is narrative discourse, and any rhetoric that upholds the few received verities will do. In effect, then, when I see in *History* a person's rescripting of consecrated events the current official version of which he has just read, I am asked to see that rescripting as an act of the sort that has always been being carried out—from, to be sure, some "interested" viewpoint or other.

As regards the third of the above questions, what the logic that *History* sets out in its recourse to the game model is a subjecthood very different from the classical modern one to which Gonçalo

Mendes Ramires aspires. It is one that trades not on modern-style identificatory processes but rather on examination of alternative realities through an identification that remains ever provisional. Such an outlook coincides in some central ways with philosopher Richard Rorty's contention in effect that at this point in the movement of Western culture we can self-consciously leave off with uniform transcendent "realities" and work on the basis of recognized intersubjectivity and consensus-building (Rorty 1–34). In that model, transcendentals are abandoned for a view of meaning-making as a purely social phenomenon—with, as *History* would appear to see it, the likely Marxist-fetched corollary that the individual subject can potentially be a fully self-conscious actor within both the process of meaning-making and that of social meaning-brokering (to the extent that those are distinct processes) and can understand his or her social agency to depend upon the ability to engage in those processes. And finally he or she can see him- or herself as less fixed and more interactive than inherited notions would have it: a subject capable of seeing options for itself and acting out those options—all in a way that constantly changes it as it proceeds. Even though that change process never reaches any goal, for in this model the very notion of a goal would be an illusion. Hence the epistemological implications of the characters' redoing of Plato's cave. In a sense, then, the logic would have it that we ourselves are—or can be—more like Dungeons and Dragons characters than we have been led to suppose over the past several millennia of Western thought about subjecthood and certainly under the Portuguese *Estado Novo*, save that, as in Dungeons and Dragons, we can simultaneously be something akin to the player who "plays" the character. Like Raimundo, then, I can "become" Mogueime or King Afonso Henriques all the while looking upon myself/them from outside and understanding the entire arrangement as heuristic and constative at the same time.

All but needless to say, by its very set-up this reading arrangement disqualifies *Estado Novo* hermeneutics in my readerly eyes by pointing out, through implicit comparison of this outcome to Raimundo's initial problem with the book he is asked to edit, that all along for political reasons the fascist regime was seeking to strip Portuguese of a potential—and, according to one's political convictions, even rightful—agential role in the interpretation of Portuguese cultural products.

Mastering the Culture's Tool Kit

* * *

So ... with these additional elements—"sideshow" and "center ring," control of one's own meaning-making, cognitive restructuring and suggestion of a non-modern subjecthood—accommodated, what does this highly peculiar reading arrangement "get me?"

First of all, the force of *History*'s plot and its attempt to direct its readership as here described clearly call upon me as reader to entertain within myself the possibility of a subjecthood that seeks a relationship to the cultural heritage in which I am aware of many of the dimensions of my role in the ongoing transaction. In this subject-culture relationship there is no longer an authoritative "national transcendental," a la Amândio César or António Quadros. In the case of the activity in which Maria Sara and Raimundo engage, the subject role is one of potential "mastery" over the inherited cultural symbols of the nationality, which mastery includes flexibility and agential self-reflexivity in manipulating them. This is one step further from the notion, suggested as the underside of the readerly joy of *Baltasar and Blimunda* and traded upon centrally in *The Year of the Death of Ricardo Reis*, that "control" of those symbols—or, really, the achieving of a modicum of self-control through their "appeasement" in face-to-face confrontation with them and their historical appurtenances—is the goal. To be sure, nothing in those earlier novels actually prohibits me, in my self-construction through the act of reception, from conceiving of this sort of "mastery" instead. But the horizons inherent in those works hardly suggest its attainment. In *History*, however, Raimundo and Maria Sara are complexly self-reflexive in the ways that the cyber-metaphor describes, and they investigate how the world seeks to construct them and take that into account as a part of their own trans-activity within the culture. In short, the novel suggests, indeed demonstrates, that mastery of the culture's "tool kit" is at one and the same time also the active self-constitution of a subject capable of that mastery and aware of that capability. Readers (here I do not attempt to differentiate between Portuguese and international readers) can, of course, be less "masterful" and still read the novel successfully, though the interpellative power of the novel's locating of the reader would make it hard, especially for Portuguese, not at a minimum to contemplate taking a path—in effect, a path toward self-construction of what, historically, we can call a "post-revolutionary subjecthood"—somewhat like the one that their reading activity enables them to construct for themselves. (Work has been done regarding literary construction of a post-revolutionary Portuguese subject; see, e.g., Sapega, "Aspectos"). Again, the cognitive-structuring element in the reading arrangement provides a practical route to that end: ideally at least, to read *History* is to build one's subjecthood—in the ways suggested in the preceding pages.

It should be mentioned as well that the "liberatory" gestures that the implied author makes with respect to the reader in all three novels are, in the logic of *History*, given some schematic definition in this regard. The novel clearly does not propose a subjecthood in which, in the style of modern thought, the subject can be "freed" from the socio-historical fetters that restrain it (again, the contrast with Gonçalo Mendes Ramires is pertinent). Instead, liberation is, logically speaking, the achievement of agential status sufficient to be a force within the markers of the culture and the cultural heritage. For generation A Portuguese, the constructing of post-revolutionary subjecthood is likely to involve achieving some degree of mastery of the national "tool kit," with all that we have seen such "mastery" to imply, in opposition to being forcibly limited to the configuration and content accorded that tool kit under fascism. Thus a sense of self-in-opposition to past experience is likely a prime "interest." For generation B readers, "interestedness" is more likely to seek to construe cultural symbols to include and emphasize such valences as freedom to use/reconfigure/reject those symbols in the process of pursuing personal self-interest in the social and economic spheres. In this last respect, unlike its two predecessors *History* would seem to address itself more effectively to the generation B reader than to the generation A reader. For if the conclusions outlined above (pp. 86–87) derived from survey data are accurate, the former is engaged in exploring concepts and their transposibility as a part of making him- or herself effective in the post-revolutionary moment.

What is set in motion with the reader in *History* can be summed up by recourse to several of the locutions partially developed in this chapter. The implied author—and the novel's very self-deployment—present the reader with a means to agency both in the institutional sphere and in general. And the act of transfer of that agency to the reader that takes place in the novel is effected by the flamboyant opening-up of the Portuguese national "tool kit" via the novel's plot and by the making-available of its contents, namely, some of the received symbols of the "nationality" and the record of their prior use, as well as the virtual forcing of the reader repeatedly to invest him- or herself in those elements as a part of the act of reading. The only limitation is that Lisbon "still be taken." In taking up the opportunity to exercise her or his own individual "interest" in the "taking," the reader is at the same time "self-invited" to engage in self-(re-)construction as a cultural being.

Conclusion

What Has the Smile Brought with It?

The most direct manner of bringing this exploration to a conclusion is to return to the smile question and to declare that the foregoing shows the complex etiology of my smile—and, presumably, the smiles of others like me. My smile, it turns out, derives from the very expectations, hermeneutic in the narrow sense and also emotional-psychological bound up with the hermeneutic, that I was accustomed to bring to the reading of a contemporary Portuguese novel. In attempting to read the three novels in question, I encountered a task set out for me in which some of the core expectations I brought to the reading task were, in ways subtler than this bald statement might seem to suggest, labeled "pre-revolutionary" or "fascist." Then they were employed as rhetorical and emotional-psychological foils seeking to have me not only read differently but also engage in many other operations in and through the reading process, operations that began at the outset restructuring my hermeneutic expectations and continued restructuring throughout. The restructuring engaged in during the reading of the last novel was more openly cognitive than in the prior two, though upon hindsight I realize that dimension was present throughout. As I read I was asked/invited/urged/at times virtually forced—the modes of the texts' engagement were many—to do things differently. I was enabled to give my emotionality over to a sense of liberation from the constraints that were a part of the reading expectations I brought with me. I was virtually channeled into confrontation with historical trauma, which confrontation included the ability to fashion what was at best a momentary sense of liberation through the very act of reading. And I found it demonstrated to me through the way I was constructed as reader that I had all along been in control of the expectations I might bring to reading. What is more, I could learn to consciously exercise that control, not only in reading but in other interpretive acts in which I might engage in life. I could attain "mastery" over the inherited symbols of the culture. In sum, I found that Saramago's three historical novels stage—or seek to stage—both the invocation of the immediate hermeneutical legacy and various pushes away from that legacy onto new ground.

This is, to be sure, a highly condensed summary of the preceding pages, and one that gives the misleading impression that a neater progression is to be traced—from free-floating emotional liberation to confrontation of trauma to final, self-conscious contemplation of liberation—than this book evidences. Moreover, the hermeneutical focus of the above summary by and large fails to mention that all of the operations referred to come heavily freighted with cultural and historical factors in such a way that the reader's cultural life, including her/his psychology and emotionality, is bound up with the hermeneutical operations referred to above. Every substantive act of hermeneutical restructuring asked of the reader has strong cultural entailments; when the reader engages in a specific operation in reading, s/he is often engaging in socio-cultural work through that very same act. Hence the intricacy that the foregoing pages sometimes assume.

As for my smile in particular, the issue of mastery represents a last element in its production—and one that I have observed at work as well in some of my professional colleagues who labor on matters having to do with contemporary Portugal, not to mention other Saramago readers. I smile, I think, not only from liberatory joy and a sense of overcoming trauma. I smile as well as I contemplate the modal turn of events that *History* stages—though that turn of events is already hinted in the "release" elicited by *Baltasar and Blimunda* and the self-contradictory opportunity for "control" held out by *Year of the Death*. Moreover, this last, contemplative ingredient in my smile is more general and therefore more fundamental than the others. The Portuguese reader (standing for all Portuguese), after having been subjected to "nationality" and to "history," is being shown that, in one sense at least, s/he can now subject them—through mastery of the national tool kit, with all that we have seen such mastery betoken. This modal turn of events is doubtless the master "Portuguese joke" of Saramago's "historical" novel production. To that motive for smiling I think I personally add another dimension—perhaps a meta-smile: it

What Has the Smile Brought with It?

comes because I sense that my impotence is appeased also through contemplation of this credibly introduced opportunity for general appeasement-through-mastery. This meta-smile, or meta-appeasement, is likely focused on a subset of readers from across groups A1 and B1 in the above readership profile—a cross-generational group the coherence of which has to do with some study of Portuguese society and also a political orientation that at a minimum sees democratic change (a term I use in the widest of senses) in the country as desirable.

As a consequence of the intricacy that my "smile answer" suggests, it becomes clear that many more threads could be traced out in the foregoing pages—considerations brought along as parts of the smile quest—for which some sort of conclusion might be fashioned to complement the "smile answer." The first question that must be asked is which "conclusions" is it appropriate to attempt and which not. In the latter category, I suspect that the reader will agree with me that any review of the "local study" dimension would be reductionistic—and in being reductionistic might well be dangerous as well. Dangerous in the sense that such a review would in effect look like an argument for the concept of the "local study" through declaration that a discrete "local" nature impervious to being abstracted from or generalized upon has been evidenced here and then the parallel declaration about its "sort" of study. Such an outcome would, of course, run the risk of making the "local" into a concept parallel to the "global"—an oxymoronic "generic particularity" as it were—thus robbing these pages of their immediate specificity in the name of yet another overarching critical category into which they can be neatly folded and tucked away with presumably parallel "cases." Better just to say that the foregoing shows what it shows and in the process helps profile some of the determinants of my smile—nothing less or more—though aspects of what it shows can surely be starting points for reasoning in many kinds of critical endeavor.

A number of more narrowly definable issues touched on in the course of my answering of the smile question are currently of some moment, and some of them could hypothetically be "concluded" here. For example, one might consider exploring the implications of the foregoing for reader response criticism. Another possibility: exploring the foregoing in relation to studies in the "postmodern." The problem in both cases is that such an exploration would necessarily be lengthy and quite inapposite to much of the argument that has brought them up. So neither will be engaged in here—though some issues involved with the latter option will be touched on in the ensuing pages in relation to other matters.

Others of those threads, coherently related amongst themselves only in the context of these pages, can, however, be extrapolated upon in such a way as to bring this study to a useful conclusion. I propose to take them serially in an order that creates a coherent narrative.

First, a way to discuss in a wider scope the reception horizon created in these pages. In world-system terms, as we have seen, through the fascist years and well into the post-revolutionary period, Portugal was a semi-peripheral country (I am not implying that it is not one today, though the very terminology seems to harken back to a prior time). It was also the last old-style European colonialist, with, in 1974, the colonial ending up overthrowing the state by inciting a revolution within the military, initiated in Africa, that brought the fascist regime to a sudden end. Portugal's governmental history over the past century has involved: constitutional monarchy into the twentieth century, parliamentary republic after that, then military revolution and military interregnum, fascism, and then the Revolution of 1974 and the current "return" (consciously portrayed as such in Portugal) to parliamentary republic. As we have seen, however, that return has come at a moment in the movement of Western civilization when, unlike the period being "returned" to, the interrelated concepts of "nationality," "national subjecthood," and the power of the concepts of Enlightenment modernity have blatantly fallen into question. The "return" is thus one in terms of general (very general!) governance modality and little more. The operating realities have changed mightily, and Portugal was on the sidelines for much of the change: the considerable industrial expansion of the post–World-War-II years and as well first stages of the loss of the agglutinating power of the discourses that underpinned that expansion. Indeed, during the 1980s—the time period of the reader–implied author communication in the foreground of the novels examined here—Portugal leapt from an enforced pre-modern polity and enforced arrested economic development directly to (forced) consideration of the awaiting "post-modern" socio-economic problematic the text-analytical dimensions of which I have alternately alluded to and skirted in the preceding pages.

What Has the Smile Brought with It?

Some quotient of the texture of that leap has been illuminated by our local study of the institutional dimensions of Saramago's three historical novels. What has been revealed is that, in "returning" to a pre-fascist institutional arrangement as regards literature (and many other matters as well, of course)—that is, in returning to a version of the "autonomy" arrangement developed from the 1820s up to the military period and subsequent long rule of the *Estado Novo*—Portugal simultaneously re-opened a sphere whose very opening and specific configuration could be used as the basis for conceptualizing and reacting to the demands of the era. Our three novels seek to foment a quite distinctive kind of readerly activity, or to support it, or to respond to it, according to the specific reader involved. In any case, that readerly activity sought to renovate (really, "innovate") radically the conditions of individual relation to the social symbolic and to launch a new understanding of the coordinates and possibilities of individual subjecthood.

In this regard, seen as a social operator, each novel provides very specific and complex cues to the reader about how it wishes the reader to receive it and uses that reception as the vehicle for the attempted inculcation of socio-symbolic change. In other words, the novel's ideal readership should, through negotiation of that novel's reading, comprehend something of the "return," the challenges brought with it, and what the renewed institutional arrangements might enable by way of address of those challenges in various arenas of Portuguese life, from the individual to the macro-social. We can therefore understand the operativity that the novels exercise as, in the widest of senses, one of defining and (re-)organizing current options for and within post-revolutionary Portuguese society.

Given the novels' mode of operation—the forging of a complex pact with the reader in the foreground of the novelistic communication; the use, within that communication, of allusions to ongoing "change opportunities" in the institutional sphere; and the focused use of the process of reception as a mechanism of interpellation and as a designated area of reader work and consequent reader socialization—the operation is necessarily one that directs itself to each reader individually rather than, say, to that reader as designated part of a socially defined group. Indeed, in *History* the principal characters, in their joint philosophical meditation on history (see above, pp. 137–39), clearly treat the issues they come up with as ones focused on the individual.

175

Conclusion

A second matter: the complex question of the social future of the directions in which the novels seek to point the reader—i.e., evaluation of the operations' goals. The one surprising matter, given the ongoing suggestion within the novels of a "liberation" of the reader and the author's publicly proclaimed adherence to some variety of Marxism, is precisely the individual focus of the social operations that the novels seek to perform. At first blush, one gets the sense that, in addition to presenting change as coming from within the very specific contours of the national-cultural inheritance rather than, say, through innovation afresh, the novels merely broadcast faith in the individual Portuguese to recognize change possibilities and to carry out changes along the directions indicated. In effect, the novels can be seen as giving say to the "people" (a term created here by synecdoche from the "reader") in determining the future contents and operation of the Portuguese cultural tool kit (that conclusion is one espoused by some scholars of Saramago's work; see, e.g., McNee 65 and his references). At most, such a faith in the "people" can be thought of as coming accompanied by the unspoken Marxist-fetched conviction that those changes will lead to the creation of a popular front that will claim ownership of the inherited culture, from the symbolic to the material. Seen in this way, at best the novels limit their immediate scope of action to a complex form of consciousness-raising, the potential making of every one of its readers into a social agent of the sort we have seen outlined in the preceding pages, notably one who has had pointed out to them the inherited Portuguese cultural "tool kit" and ways it can be approached and utilized.

The most obvious analysis would involve contending that the "tool kit" is being set out for "mastery" by the individual Portuguese as a first step toward the definitive overcoming of the nation-ality itself: the first step in creation of a Marxistic international—or non-national—popular consciousness. Indeed, in *History* some of the implied author's merciless and ongoing poking fun at terms characteristic of the monumental version of the national history promulgated under fascism can be read as supportive of such an analysis (see, e.g., p. 125, above). And one can certainly argue that the novel's very pattern centrally involves rejecting the hail of nationalist ideology. There is, however, no clear discursive element in the texts pointing away from the inherited markers of Portuguese nationality. The strongest argument that can be made to that end is to say that, in the area of the social symbolic, the novels seek to recast the relationship between those inherited markers and the individual in the direction of individual agency and provide no systemic limiting of the scope of future individual action to just the nationality. Thus the rejection/overcoming of nationality is one possible readerly direction, it is not in any way foreclosed by the novels, and it is suggested to the reader, especially by *History*. Should that direction be taken, the irony—albeit one we have seen at work in other applications within the novels—would be that its enabling would have come expressed in nationalistic terms.

This précis leads neatly to a third and final point, which can be taken along with the prior. This last question is: "If this be Marxism, then what sort of Marxism is it?" José Saramago—now not the implied author but rather the historical author—was significantly a partisan of the developments deriving from the 1974 Revolution up to the anti-left revolt within the military. Why, then, no language of class analysis such as was common in Portuguese public discourse up through the mid-1980s, in fact led by the Portuguese Communist Party, of which he was a very public member? Why no registering of the concept of emancipation-in-history? An explanation consistent with the novels is that they are themselves in some way expected to function as the agglutinating force around which a social formation is/can be brought into being, literally *through* literary reception. It seems a weak assertion, however, and, in practical terms, contemporary events have surely not included any such dynamic.

There is also a clear and quite powerful counter-argument: the notions that multiple histories and multiple realities are possible because history, nationality, and even reality are in effect arbitrary language phenomena and that one can engage in recombination and transposition of their elements, not to mention their outright abrogation, would seem to seek to construct a subject attuned to the post-revolutionary capitalist growth directions in Portugal and, even more important, to a capitalist international order in which cultures are all relativized and individual success—i.e., the "goal"—is dependent upon one's mastering and using that relativization to one's own ends. Indeed, one obvious fact is that the "mastery of the cultural tool kit" brings with it no moral dimension (I mean the term *moral* in a structural sense) such as would be necessary to support a rationalized class consciousness—unless one considers the concept of "love" evidenced in the relationship between Baltasar and Blimunda and touched on by the characters themselves in Maria Sara's and Raimundo's "cave conversation" in *History* (pp. 137–39, above) to be the cornerstone of a moral dimension to be built. As it is in the context, however, that concept is too little developed to serve that function.

Moreover, in the classical opposition between the possible aesthetic and critical functions of literature, the three novels, read conventionally, while they invite a reading that foregrounds the critical over the aesthetic, do so with such cleverness that, in formal as well as reception terms, it is difficult to separate the two. One suspects that, as a consequence, the "aesthetic" will eventually assume the dominant position—that is, the cleverness itself, the generally "noisy" surface of the texts, and, probably, the romance (as opposed to "love") angle will be the future focus of reading. We have seen a variety of that focus already with non-Portuguese readership, and I can testify to its presence among generation B and younger Portuguese readers. The novels, very un-Marxistly, do nothing to foreclose such a reception.

There are several possible answers to the questions thus suggested, as well as to others that could be posed along similar lines. One is that these novels are what I have elsewhere called "tactically occasional" (*Voz autoritaria* 91). By that label I have meant to suggest that the horizon of their reception may be limited to the period of post-revolutionary transition—perhaps a particularly complex and fecund moment for symbolic-sphere work, as transitional moments can sometimes be—and that the novels' goals, tactical within that moment (again, please recall that I am not, or not necessarily, speaking of conscious tactics), are likewise limited: to a specific task of consciousness-raising and the linking of it to the multiple suggestions, within the texts, of liberatory action to be taken in relation to the inherited cultural "tool kit." According to that logic, such action was to be taken by and within the individual, not—at least not then—as a part of a societal-level transformation program.

If resolution is individual in this way, then I would suggest, from the still-partial vantage point of 2010, that in this area too the aftermath has not matched the endeavor. In a curious inverse parallel, something like the "aesthetic" has separated itself from the

What Has the Smile Brought with It?

"critical": the novels have won Saramago the Nobel Prize for Literature but the left program has not fared well in Portugal, though, if we use the Portuguese Communist Party as our focus, that program is still, in coalition with the Green Party and segments of labor, a significant participant in national politics and governance and a major force at the municipal level. Perhaps, then, much as they refunction the institutional sphere of the *Estado Novo*, the current place of *Baltasar and Blimunda*, *The Year of the Death of Ricardo Reis*, and *The History of the Siege of Lisbon* involves their availability for future rescue from the realm of the "aesthetic" and their refunctioning for wider social-constitutive purposes.

Such are some of the final considerations brought by my smile. I *am* still smiling.

Notes

Chapter One
Portuguese Fascism and Literary Institutionality

1. The best short-form résumé is in fact to be found in one of the newspaper articles: Cruz Pontes's "O Sim e o Não da Filosofia Portuguesa." The article also provides some references to authors, titles, and bibliographies involved with the controversy.

2. Ribeiro, *Arte* 127. Much of my précis follows his development of issues on pp. 21–51, 121–45, 225–44 of this title. This title, *A Arte de Filosofar* (something like "The Art of Doing Philosophy"), was chosen because of its concentrated presentation, but the basic points of the argument are repeated in other Ribeiro publications.

3. E.g., Ferro, *Salazar: Portugal and Her Leader* 27. This is the expansion and translation into English of Ferro's earlier *Salazar: O Homem e a Sua Obra*, of 1933. The books comprise a set of annotated interviews with Salazar. The passage alluded to is to be found only in the English version, which apparently draws on material not included in the earlier volume in Portuguese. Parallels can be found throughout Salazar's discourse. Two bits of information for one who is unaware of the personalities: António Ferro was Salazar's Minister of Propaganda, and he is the father of the often-mentioned António Quadros (full name: António Quadros Gabriel de Ferro).

4. Quadros, "Livros, Ideias e Figuras," *Diário de Notícias* 29 Dec. 1955: 7–8 at p. 8. During this period, Quadros had a regular column, called "Livros, Ideias e Figuras" ("Books, Ideas, and Figures"), in the *Diário's* weekly (Thursday) literary section.

5. See again Weber 485–86. Weber himself does not miss the irony that a state grounded in the notion that the nation is one *sui generis* nonetheless takes up political thought developed in another country.

6. I think specifically of the affixation of publicity—placards, signs, etc.—which was reserved to the state and its assigns in *Estado Novo* Portugal. And the state did indeed avail itself of the opportunities that this practice offered to publicize itself and its outlook with, especially, a wide array of what amounted to propaganda posters affixed to the walls of Portuguese city buildings (see figure 1 on p. 27).

7. An example chosen because of its reference to Pessoa criticism: the first version of Mário Sacramento's influential *Fernando Pessoa, Poeta da Hora Absurda* was written, in 1953, while the author was in Caxias prison because of his political stance. It was then rejected by publisher after publisher over a number of years.

8. Prado Coelho, "Da Filosofia Portuguesa," *Diário de Notícias* 26 Sept. 1963: 13, 15. The polemic ran off-and-on for many years in several formats. It goes beyond the scope of this study to seek to document it fully.

9. Prado Coelho understood quite consciously that his anti-polemical policy (ironic for one who in his life engaged as a principal in several major

public polemics) served precisely as a strategy to create a space for professional literary criticism within the sphere of literary institutionality as characterized here (personal conversation, 1970).

10. Costa Pinto, *Modern Portugal* 35–36. And, for an overview of the changes in public education under the *Estado Novo,* especially in 1936–37, when, according to the author, "ideology replaced ... pedagogy," see Matos 2: 201–07 (quote at 202). The footnote sources on those pages also provide an excellent entrée into primary critical literature on the subject.

11. The *Estado Novo* can hardly be imagined to be attempting to deal sensitively with the problem of low literacy, since that too fit its overall vision of the nation. In direct contrast to the Republic that it overthrew, which had proclaimed overcoming illiteracy to be one of its principal goals, in the early years the *Estado Novo* was capable of expressing publicly its conviction that public education was not a priority and could even be seen as deleterious to good citizenship (Cova and Costa Pinto 81; Leitão de Barros and Pereira Henriques 149–51).

12. The Hobsbawm reference in the Works section can stand for the many studies that agree on the central points enumerated here.

Chapter Three
Reading the Labyrinth: Text as Obstacle in *The Year of the Death of Ricardo Reis*

1. An expansion and upgrading of the Portuguese educational system had in fact been initiated before the 1974 Revolution. I found myself working, in the United States, with groups of future middle-school teachers from Portugal as early as 1972.

2. One of the features of the novel is its practice of describing, often in some detail, specific locations that Reis visits in Lisbon. At the height of the novel's popularity some tour agencies offered walking tours that followed various of his routes.

3. By "awareness of Portuguese politics," I refer to something very specific: the material regularly sent to people considered "diaspora Portuguese" by the regime. My father's family received such material, it circulated within his group of friends, and from my youth on I saw it quite regularly. By the way, the government also sporadically sent speakers to "diaspora" communities in the United States and elsewhere.

4. The extent to which the novel seeks to characterize the year can be seen in the fact that Saramago kept a calendar of 1936 with many of the events of that year, great and small, entered on it, as a part of his scripting process. See Cerdeira da Silva, "On the Labyrinth" 84–86.

5. In point of historical fact (I looked it up in the shipping itineraries in the Lisbon daily *Diário de Notícias* for the end of 1935), the ship on which the character Reis returns, the British steamer *Highland Brigade*, really did call at Lisbon at that time on its regular route. (And, as the novel states (1 [11]), it really did have a "twin" named the *Highland Monarch*.) Given that—as obviously is his practice—Saramago has done this same research, it is reasonable to assume that the historical date of the ship's arrival is also the date within the novel. According to the shipping itineraries, the historical date of the arrival was December 28, 1935. Reis, however, under interrogation, gives the date as December 29 (161 [190]). Was the ship late in arriving and does Saramago know that, or is Reis lying? Does Reis have something to hide?

6. Actually, the novel stretches that time period by a couple of weeks. Given Saramago's accuracy of detail, I am almost afraid to research the question of whether the historical Pessoa was overdue at birth …

7. I suspect that, while this is first and foremost a case of cultural miscommunication, it also reveals a complex culturally based denial on the part of the Spaniards. The Portuguese have gone through the 1974 Revolution and subsequent events and thus have had a public airing of sorts of the whole question of the fascist past. Spain has not yet undergone anything like that airing, and in my view has thus not yet finished apprehending its own past in this regard and what it says about the present—though work is continually being done that might lead to that end. The three Saramago novels being treated here—and specifically the implied author–reader pact around which they function—in fact represent one dimension of just that apprehension in Portugal.

Works Cited and Consulted

Adler, Alfred. *Journal Articles, 1921–1926*. Vol. 5 of *The Collected Clinical Work of Alfred Adler*. Trans. Gerald L. Liebenau. Ed. Henry T. Stein. Bellingham, WA: Classical Adlerian Translation Project, 2004. Print.

___. *Superiority and Social Interest. A Collection of Later Writings*. Ed. Heinz L. Ansbacher and Rowena R. Ansbacher. Evanston, IL: Northwestern UP, 1964. Print.

Almeida, João Ferreira de. "Evoluções Recentes e Valores na Sociedade." *Portugal Hoje*. Ed. Eduardo Sousa Ferreira. Lisboa: Instituto Nacional de Administração, 1995. 55–70. Print.

___. "Society and Values." Costa Pinto, *Modern Portugal* 146–61.

Althusser, Louis. *Lenin and Philosophy and Other Essays*. Trans. Ben Brewster. New York: Monthly Review Press, 1971. Print.

Arnaut, Ana Paula. "The Subversion of History in *Memorial do Convento*." *Portuguese Studies* 15 (1990): 182–93. Print.

Beck, Aaron T. *Cognitive Therapy and the Emotional Disorders*. New York: International Universities P, 1976. Print.

Belsey, Catherine. *Critical Practice*. 2nd ed. London: Routledge, 2002. Print.

Benjamin, Walter. *The Origin of German Tragic Drama*. Trans. John Osborne. London: Verso, 1998. Print.

Borges, Jorge Luis. "Examen de la obra de Herbert Quain." *Ficciones*. In his *Obras completas*. Buenos Aires: Emecé, 1974. 461–64. Print.

Boulter, Jonathan. *Melancholy and the Archive: Trauma, Memory, and History in the Contemporary Novel*. New York: Continuum, 2011. Print.

Brandão de Brito, José Maria de. "The Portuguese Economy: From Salazarism to the European Community." Costa Pinto, *Modern Portugal* 102–11.

Bruner, Jerome. *Actual Minds, Possible Worlds*. Cambridge: Harvard UP, 1986. Print.

Bürger, Peter. "The Institution of Art as a Category of the Sociology of Literature." *The Institutions of Art*. Ed. Peter Bürger and Christa Bürger. Trans. Loren Kruger. Lincoln: U of Nebraska P, 1992. 3–29. Print.

___. *Theory of the Avant-Garde*. Trans. Michael Shaw. Minneapolis: U of Minnesota P, 1984. Print.

Ceccucci, Piero. "Paródia irónica em *O Ano da Morte de Ricardo Reis*." Medeiros and Ornelas 29–40.

___, ed. *Viaggio intorno al Convento di Mafra. Dal "Memoriale del convento" di José Saramago alla "Blimunda" di Azio Corghi*. Milano: Guerini, 1991. Print.

Cerdeira da Silva, Teresa Cristina. "José Saramago: A ficção reinventa a história." *Colóquio-Letras* 120 (1991): 174–78. Print.

——. "On the Labyrinth of Text, or, Writing as the Site of Memory." Trans. Anna Klobucka. *On Saramago* 6 (Spring 2001): 73–96. Print.

César, Amândio. "Fernando Pessoa, Poeta de *Mensagem*." *Gil Vicente*, 2ª· Série, 19.9–10 (1968): 151–57. Print.

Costa, Augusto da, comp. *Portugal Vasto Império: Um Inquérito Nacional*. Lisboa: Imprensa Nacional, 1934. Print.

Costa Pinto, António, ed. *Modern Portugal*. Palo Alto, CA: Society for the Promotion of Science and Scholarship, 1988. Print.

——. "Twentieth-Century Portugal: An Introduction." Costa Pinto, *Modern Portugal* 1–40.

Cova, Anne, and António Costa Pinto. "O Salazarismo e as Mulheres: Uma Abordagem Comparativa." *Penélope* 17 (1997): 71–94. Print.

De expugnatione Lyxbonensi. Trans. Charles Wendell David. Introd. Jonathan Phillips. New York: Columbia UP, 2001. (Trans. originally published in 1936.) Print.

Eça de Queirós, José Maria de. *The Illustrious House of Ramires*. Trans. Ann Stevens. Athens, OH: Ohio UP, 1968. Print.

——. *A Ilustre Casa de Ramires*. Lisboa: Edição "Livros do Brasil," n.d. [1900]. Print.

O Estado Novo: Das Origens ao Fim da Autarcia, 1926–1959. 2 vols. Lisboa: Fragmentos, 1987. Print.

Fernandes, Ceres Costa. *O Narrador Plural na Obra de José Saramago*. São Luís [Brazil]: CORSUP/EDUFMA, 1990. Print.

Ferreira, Ana Paula. "Home Bound: The Construct of Femininity in the Estado Novo." *Portuguese Studies* 12 (1996): 133–44. Print.

Ferreira, Virgínia. "Engendering Portugal: Social Change, State Politics, and Women's Social Mobilization." Costa Pinto, *Modern Portugal* 162–88.

Ferro, António. *Salazar: O Homem e a Sua Obra*. Lisboa: Empresa Nacional de Publicidade, 1933. Print.

——. *Salazar: Portugal and Her Leader*. London: Faber and Faber, 1939. Print.

Fokkema, Douwe. "How to Decide Whether *Memorial do Convento* by José Saramago Is or Is Not a Postmodern Novel?" *Revista Portuguesa de Literatura Comparada* 1 (1991): 293–302. Print.

Freud, Sigmund. *Jokes and Their Relation to the Unconscious*. Trans. James Strachey. New York: Norton, 1960. Print.

Frier, David G. *The Novels of José Saramago: Echoes from the Past, Pathways into the Future*. Cardiff: U of Wales P, 2007. Print.

___. "Padre Bartolomeu de Gusmão: Inspiration for *Memorial do Convento*?" *Romance Quarterly* 50.1 (2003): 56–68. Print.

Gomes, Joaquim da Conceição. *Descripção minuciosa do monumento de Mafra*. 2ª· ed. rev. Lisboa: Imprensa Nacional, 1871. Print.

Hobsbawm, E. J. *Nations and Nationalism since 1780; Programme, Myth, Reality*. Cambridge: Cambridge UP, 1990. Print.

Howe, Irving. "Fueling the Passarola." Rev. of *Baltasar and Blimunda*, by José Saramago, trans. Giovanni Pontiero. *New York Times Book Review* 1 Nov. 1987: 7. Print.

Hutcheon, Linda. *A Poetics of Postmodernism: History, Theory, Fiction*. New York: Routledge, 1988. Print.

Iser, Wolfgang. *The Act of Reading: A Theory of Aesthetic Response*. 1978. Baltimore: Johns Hopkins UP, 1980. Print.

___. *The Implied Reader: Patterns of Communication in Prose Fiction from Bunyan to Beckett*. 1974. Baltimore: Johns Hopkins UP, 1978. Print.

Jacobus, Mary. *Psychoanalysis and the Scene of Reading*. Oxford: Oxford UP, 1999. Print.

Jameson, Fredric. *The Political Unconscious: Narrative as a Socially Symbolic Act*. Ithaca: Cornell UP, 1981. Print.

___. *Postmodernism, or the Cultural Logic of Late Capitalism*. Durham: Duke UP, 1991. Print.

Jauss, Hans Robert. *Aesthetic Experience and Literary Hermeneutics*. Trans. Michael Shaw. Minneapolis: U of Minnesota P, 1982. Print.

Jusdanis, Gregory. *Belated Modernity and Aesthetic Culture: Inventing National Literature*. Minneapolis: U of Minnesota P, 1991. Print.

Kahneman, Daniel. *Thinking, Fast and Slow*. New York: Farrar, Straus and Giroux, 2011. Print.

Kaufman, Helena. "A metaficção historiográfica de José Saramago." *Colóquio-Letras* 120 (1991): 124–36. Print.

Krabbenhoft, Kenneth. "Saramago, Cognitive Estrangement, and Original Sin?" *On Saramago* 6 (Spring 2001): 123–36. Print.

Lacan, Jacques. *Le Séminaire de Jacques Lacan, Livre XI: Les quatre concepts fondamentaux de la psychanalyse (1964)*. Paris: Seuil, 1973. Print.

LaCapra, Dominick. *History and Criticism*. Ithaca: Cornell UP, 1985. Print.

___. *Writing History, Writing Trauma*. Baltimore: Johns Hopkins UP, 2001. Print.

Laplanche, Jean. *New Foundations for Psychoanalysis*. Trans. David Macey. Oxford: Oxford UP, 1989. Print.

Leitão de Barros, Júlia Teresa, and Raquel Pereira Henriques. "A Educação do Estado Novo nos Anos 30—Com Base na Rejeição de uma Proposta de Livro de 1933." *O Estado Novo* 2: 149–58.

Lima, Afonso de. "Unidade e Revelação Cultural no Mundo Lusíada." *Diário de Notícias* 5 July 1962: 13. Print.

Lourenço, António Apolinário. "História, ficção e ideologia: Representação ideológica e pluridiscursividade em *Memorial do convento*." *Vértice* 42 (1991): 69–78. Print.

Lourenço, Eduardo. *A Nau de Ícaro Seguido de Imagem e Miragem da Lusofonia*. Lisboa: Gradiva, 1999. Print.

___. *Situação Africana e Consciência Nacional*. Cadernos Critério 2. Amadora: Bertrand, 1976. Print.

___. *This Little Lusitanian House: Essays on Portuguese Culture*. Trans. Ronald W. Sousa. Providence: Gávea-Brown, 2003. Print.

Lyotard, Jean-François. *The Postmodern Condition: A Report on Knowledge*. Trans. Geoff Bennington and Brian Massumi. Forward Fredric Jameson. Minneapolis: U of Minnesota P, 1984. Print.

Marcuse, Herbert. *Negations: Essays in Critical Theory*. Trans. Jeremy J. Shapiro. Boston: Beacon Press, 1968. Print.

Martins, Adriana Alves de Paula. *A Construção da Memória da Nação em José Saramago e Gore Vidal*. Frankfurt am Main: Peter Lang, 2006. Print.

Marx, Karl, and Friedrich Engels. *The German Ideology, Parts I & III*. New York: International Publishers, 1963. Print

Matos, Helena. *Salazar*. 2 vols. Lisboa: Temas e Debates, 2004. Print.

McNee, Malcolm. "An Intertextual Intertwining of Mystic Nationalisms; Saramago's Post-Modern Challenge to the Pessoan and Salazarist Discourses in *O Ano da Morte de Ricardo Reis*." *Lucero* 10 (1999): 57–66. Print.

Medeiros, Paulo de, and José N. Ornelas, eds. *Da Possibilidade do Impossível: Leituras de Saramago*. Utrecht: Portuguese Studies Center, 2007. Print.

Mello e Souza, Laura de. *O Diabo e a Terra de Santa Cruz*. São Paulo: Companhia das Letras, 1986. Print.

Miguéis, José Rodrigues. *O Milagre Segundo Salomé*. 1975. 2ª ed. Lisboa: Estampa, 1982. Print.

Monteiro, Nuno G., and António Costa Pinto. "Cultural Myths and Portuguese National Identity." Costa Pinto, *Modern Portugal* 206–17.

Murray, Janet H. *Hamlet on the Holodeck: The Future of Narrative in Cyberspace.* New York: Free Press, 1997. Print.

Oliveira Marques, A. H. de. *História de Portugal.* Vol. 1. Lisboa: Palas, 1974. Print.

On Saramago. Portuguese Literary and Cultural Studies 6 (Spring 2001). Print.

Piaia, Miquela. "Viagens de Saramago ao Passado Português." *Literatura em Debate* 2.2 (1999): 1–10. Print.

Pontes, Cruz. "O Sim e o Não da Filosofia Portuguesa." *Diário de Notícias* 2 June 1966: 17–18. Print.

Pontiero, Giovanni. "The Apotheosis of *Blimunda*: An Opera by Azio Corghi Based on Saramago's *Memorial do Convento*." *Hispanic Studies in Honour of Geoffrey Ribbans.* Liverpool: Liverpool UP, 1992. 335–43. Print.

Prado Coelho, Jacinto do. "Da Filosofia Portuguesa." *Diário de Notícias* 26 Sept. 1963: 13, 15. Print.

___. *A Letra e o Leitor.* N.p.: Portugália, 1969. Print.

Quadros, António. *Fernando Pessoa.* 2ª· ed. Colecção A Obra e o Homem 3. Lisboa: Arcádia, n.d. Print.

___. "Livros, Ideias e Figuras." *Diário de Notícias* 29 Dec. 1955: 7–8. Print.

___. *A Teoria da História em Portugal.* Vol. 2: *A Dinâmica da História.* Lisboa: Espiral, n.d. Print.

Ragland-Sullivan, Ellie. *Jacques Lacan and the Philosophy of Psychoanalysis.* Urbana: U of Illinois P, 1986. Print.

Ramos do Ó, Jorge. "Modernidade e Tradição: Algumas Reflexões em Torno da Exposição do Mundo Português." *O Estado Novo* 2: 177–85.

Ribeiro, Álvaro. *A Arte de Filosofar.* Lisboa: Portugália, 1955. Print.

___. *Escritores Doutrinados.* Lisboa: Sociedade de Expansão Cultural, 1965. Print.

___. Prefácio. *A Nova Poesia Portuguesa.* By Fernando Pessoa. 2ª· ed. Lisboa: Inquérito, n.d. 7–15. Print.

Rorty, Richard. *Objectivity, Relativism, and Truth.* Vol. 1 of *Philosophical Papers.* Cambridge: Cambridge UP, 1991. Print.

Rosas, Fernando. "Salazarism and Economic Development in the 1930's and 1940's: Industrialization without Agrarian Reform." Costa Pinto, *Modern Portugal* 88–101.

Sacramento, Mário. *Fernando Pessoa, Poeta da Hora Absurda.* 2ª· ed. Porto: Inova, 1970. Print.

Salinas, Tomás Granados. "Heterónimos: Los diversos narradores de José Saramago." *Quimera* [Barcelona], 150 (1996): 28–31. Print.

Sapega, Ellen W. "Aspectos do romance pós-revolucionário português: O papel da memória na construção de um novo sujeito nacional." *Luso-Brazilian Review* 32 (1995): 31–40. Print.

———. *Consensus and Debate in Salazar's Portugal: Visual and Literary Negotiations of the National Text, 1933–1948.* University Park: Pennsylvania State UP, 2008. Print.

Saramago, José. *O Ano da Morte de Ricardo Reis.* Lisboa: Caminho, 1984. Print.

———. *Baltasar and Blimunda.* Trans. Giovanni Pontiero. New York: Harcourt Brace Jovanovich, 1987. Print.

———. *Blindness.* Trans. Giovanni Pontiero. New York: Harcourt Brace, 1998. Print.

———. *Ensaio sobre a Cegueira.* Lisboa: Caminho, 1995. Print.

———. *A História do Cerco de Lisboa.* Lisboa: Caminho, 1989. Print.

———. *The History of the Siege of Lisbon.* Trans. Giovanni Pontiero. New York: Harcourt Brace, 1996. Print.

———. *The History of the Siege of Lisbon.* Trans. Giovanni Pontiero. 1996. San Diego: A Harvest Book, 1998. Print.

———. *A Jangada de Pedra.* Lisboa: Caminho, 1986. Print.

———. *Memorial del Convento.* Trans. Basilio Losada. Barcelona: Planeta, 1995. Print.

———. *Memorial do Convento.* Lisboa: Caminho, 1982. Print.

———. *The Stone Raft.* Trans. Giovanni Pontiero. New York: Harcourt Brace, 1994. Print.

———. *The Year of the Death of Ricardo Reis.* Trans. Giovanni Pontiero. New York: Harcourt Brace Jovanovich, 1991. Print.

Schmitter, Philippe C. *Corporatism and Public Policy in Authoritarian Portugal.* London: Sage, 1975. Print.

Schmitter, Philippe, and Gerhard Lehmbruch, eds. *Trends toward Corporatist Intermediation.* London: Sage, 1979. Print.

Schulte-Sasse, Jochen. Foreword. Bürger, *Theory* vii–xlvii.

Sousa, Ronald W. "Europe and the Invention of Fernando Pessoa." *Homenagem a Alexandrino Severino: Essays on the Portuguese-Speaking World.* Ed. Margo Milleret and Marshall C. Eakin. Austin: Host, 1993. 63–76. Print.

———. "The Future of a National Symbol." *Portugal: Strategic Options in a European Context.* Ed. Fátima Monteiro, José Tavares, Miguel Glatzer, and Ângelo Cardoso. New York: Lexington, 2003. 11–16. Print.

———. "José Saramago and the Modalities of History, or Dragging Their Telos behind Him." Medeiros and Ornelas 315–23.

———. "José Saramago 'Re-vises,' or Out of Africa and into Cyber-History." *Discourse* 22.3 (2000): 73–86. Print. (Rpt. in *José Saramago: Modern Critical Views*. Ed. Harold Bloom. Philadelphia: Chelsea House, 2005. 95–108.)

———. "Pessoa Criticism and the Antagonistic Literary Institutionality of the Estado Novo." *Indiana Journal of Hispanic Literatures* 9 (1996): 211–24. Print.

———. *The Rediscoverers: Major Writers in the Portuguese Literature of National Regeneration*. University Park: Pennsylvania State UP, 1981. Print.

———. *Voz autoritaria y experiencia fascista: José Saramago*. Madrid: Ediciones del Orto/Universidad de Minnesota, 2003. Print.

Sousa Santos, Boaventura de. "State and Society in Portugal." *After the Revolution: Twenty Years of Portuguese Literature, 1974–1994*. Ed. Helena Kaufman and Anna Klobucka. Lewisburg: Bucknell UP, 1997. 31–72. Print.

Taylor, Charles. *Sources of the Self: The Making of the Modern Identity*. Cambridge: Harvard UP, 1989. Print.

Turkle, Sherry. *Life on the Screen: Identity in the Age of the Internet*. New York: Touchstone, 1995. Print.

———. *The Second Self: Computers and the Human Spirit*. New York: Simon and Schuster, 1984. Print.

Vaihinger, Hans. *The Philosophy of "As If": A System of the Theoretical, Practical and Religious Fictions of Mankind*. Trans. C. K. Ogden. London: Routledge and Kegan Paul, 1924. Print.

Vieira, Tomé [Alberto Tomás Vieira]. *Conspiração*. Lisboa: n.p, 1936. Print.

Wallerstein, Immanuel. *The Modern World System*. New York: Academic Press, 1974. Print.

———. *The Politics of the World Economy*. Cambridge: Cambridge UP, 1984. Print.

Weber, Eugen. *Action Française: Royalism and Reaction in Twentieth-Century France*. Stanford: Stanford UP, 1962. Print.

White, Hayden. *Metahistory: The Historical Imagination in Nineteenth-Century Europe*. Baltimore: Johns Hopkins UP, 1973. Print.

Wiarda, Howard J. *Corporatism and Development: The Portuguese Experience*. Amherst: U of Massachusetts P, 1977. Print.

Index

Action Française, 20, 24
Adler, Alfred, 162–63
aesthetic function of art, 14–17, 29, 105, 178–79
   in tension with critical function of art, 14–17, 178–79
Almeida, João Ferreira de, 81, 86–87, 152, 155
Ano da Morte de Ricardo Reis, O (The Year of the Death of Ricardo Reis [Saramago]*)*, 79–122
anti-identificatory reader instruction, 50, 56, 59, 70, 76, 118–21, 157
autonomous art, sphere of, 12–18, 24–26, 32, 36–37, 175

Baltazar and Blimunda (Memorial do Convento [Saramago]*)*, 39–78
Blimunda (character), in Saramago's *Baltasar and Blimunda*, 49, 57–58, 68–75, 131, 157, 165, 178
Bürger, Peter, 3, 6, 12–18, 26, 28, 79

Camões, Luís de, 91–92
   The Lusiads, 143
castration complex, 97–98, 102
"cave conversation," in Saramago's *The History of the Siege of Lisbon*, 139, 146–47, 151–52, 155, 157–58, 164, 166, 178
Ceccucci, Piero, 56, 75
Cerdeira da Silva, Teresa, 98, 147, 182n4
César, Amândio, 20–21, 29–34, 70, 167
cognitive restructuring, 167–68
consciousness-raising, 81–87, 89, 122, 176, 178. See *also* post-revolutionary period
Conspiracy (Conspiração [Vieira]*)*, 107–12
constitutive blank, 17, 46, 62
Costa Pinto, António, 24, 35, 62, 81, 83–85
critical function of art, 14–16, 178–79
crusaders, 127, 129, 132, 134, 137, 140, 172
culture's tool kit, 123, 161, 167–69, 176–78
cybernization of history, 135–37, 147–51, 159, 161–62, 164–67
craftsmanship of ideas, 87, 113, 155

"De expugnatione Lyxbonensi" (medieval letter), 146–47
Diário de Notícias, 19, 29, 37, 182n5
displacement-in-reading, 65–66, 69, 75–77, 102, 113

Eça de Queirós, José María de, 11–13, 15, 58, 74
education/educational system in Portugal, 22, 28, 36, 89, 141, 182n10, 182n1
Estado Novo, 19, 23–25, 28, 32, 35, 46–48, 54, 62–63, 66–70, 77, 81, 91–93, 95, 97–99, 101, 104–05, 110, 112, 125–27, 141, 144–45, 150, 152, 166, 175
   role assigned to women in, 62, 81, 110
expectations in reading, 13–14, 28, 33, 40, 74, 118, 128, 171–72

Index

Exposition of the Portuguese World (1940), 32–34

fascism, Portuguese, 11, 18–20, 23, 36, 61–62, 67–68, 71, 73, 76, 79–80, 83, 88–90, 92, 97–99, 101, 103–04, 107, 113–15, 122–23, 125–28, 130, 134, 144, 148, 165–68, 171, 174–76
fascist hermeneutics, 67, 76, 125, 144, 146–48, 152
Fátima, 54, 62, 95
Flaubert, Gustave, 12, 58
Freud, Sigmund, 9, 39, 63, 66–68, 79–80, 97, 99, 111, 114
Freudian obstacle, 67, 79–80, 97, 102–14, 112–14, 126, 162
flamboyant fictions, 94, 130, 168–69

generational divergence in readership, 90–92, 97, 107, 112–17, 162–63, 168, 178
Gomes, Joaquim da Conceição, 44–45
Gusmão, Bartolomeu Lourenço de, Padre, in Saramago's *Baltasar and Blimunda*, 57–58

Habermas, Jürgen, 9, 12
hermeneutic localism, 23, 83, 110, 116, 128, 144
hermeneutitope, 160–61, 164
Historia do Cerco de Lisboa, A (The History of the Siege of Lisbon [Saramago]*)*, 123–70
heuristic mode, 73, 101–02, 145–46, 148, 166
historicity, 151–52, 155–60
History of the Siege of Lisbon, The (A Historia do Cerco de Lisboa [Saramago]*)*, 123–70

Hutcheon, Linda, 5, 7, 49, 53, 73
hyper-nation, 11, 35–36

Illustrious House of Ramires, The (A Ilustre Casa de Ramires, [Eça de Queirós]), 11–15, 130–32, 150
Gonçalo, protagonist of, 12, 130–32, 150, 165–66, 168
implied author, 60–62, 65, 67, 70, 73–79, 90–96, 103, 110, 116–20, 123–25, 129, 135, 140, 146–50, 156–57, 161, 168, 176–79. *See also* reader–implied author pact
Inquisition, 57–58, 65, 67–69, 75, 90, 116
institutional sphere, 11, 15, 23–26, 28, 31–37, 61–63, 68–70, 73–77, 79–80, 102–03, 115, 121–24, 128–30, 134–35, 155, 158, 162, 168, 175
access to, 128
operators in, 34, 68–70, 80, 124
regress to, 73, 77, 124, 128, 155
struggle within, 35
invited reader, 129–30, 145–49, 156–58, 160, 164, 169
Iser, Wolfgang, 3, 16–17, 28, 39, 44, 46, 62, 88, 90, 98, 114, 117

Jameson, Fredric, 7, 73, 101, 113
Jauss, Hans Robert, 16–17, 28
John V, king of Portugal, 40, 47, 90–91
Jokes and Their Relationship to the Unconscious (Freud), 39, 63, 97

Kant, Immanuel, 9, 15, 142
labyrinth, 92, 96, 98–100, 103, 112, 123

Index

Lacan, Jacques, 79, 97, 100, 111, 162
liberatory dimension of reading, 60, 71, 90, 100, 111, 116, 161, 168, 171–72, 176
Lourenço, Eduardo, 11, 48, 84
Lourenço, Padre. *See* Gusmão, Bartolomeu Lourenço de
Lusotropicalism, 19, 84

Mafra, 4, 44, 51–53, 57, 72, 116
Marxism, 33, 84, 166, 176–78
Memorial do Convento (Baltazar and Blimunda [Saramago]*)*, 39–78
memory, 75, 80, 89. 97–102, 110–12, 125
monumental historical narrative, 35–36, 46, 59, 90–92, 127–28, 141, 146, 155, 159, 176

Nazi Germany, 18, 25–26
narrator, attributes of, 46–52, 60

obstacle. *See* Freudian obstacle

Padre Lourenço. *See* Gusmão, Bartolomeu Lourenço de
parallel state, 86, 112–13, 115
Pessoa, Fernando, 19–20, 25–26, 29–32, 70, 94–95, 110, 119
death and Saramago's *Year of the Death of Ricardo Reis*, 94, 110, 119
Mensagem, poems by, 29–32
Plato's cave, 139, 147, 166
Portuguese Communist Party, 37, 177, 179
Portuguese philosophy, 18–26, 28, 141
post-modern, 5, 7, 121, 144, 173–74
post-revolutionary period, 2, 46–48, 75–77, 88–89, 112, 115, 174–75, 177–78

post-revolutionary subjecthood, 113–14, 167–68
Prado Coelho, Jacinto do, 25–26, 29–34, 181nn8–9
psychologization of history, 143–46, 148, 163

Quadros, António, 20–21, 24, 26, 30, 141–48, 150, 167, 181nn3–4

reader–implied author pact, 50–51, 56, 59–61, 70–79, 88, 90, 92–93, 95–96, 102, 110, 115–18, 120–21, 124–25, 132, 150, 174–75, 183n7. *See also* implied author
Revolution of 1974, 48, 81, 83–84, 88–89, 140, 174, 177, 183n7
Ribeiro, Álvaro, 20–25, 28, 31–32, 35, 141, 143–44

Salazar, António de Oliveira, *iv,* 20, 24, 115, 181n3
Sapega, Ellen, 101, 127, 168
Saramago, José
bio, 37
identification with narrator, 60
Nobel Prize (1998), 4, 37, 73, 88–89, 117–18, 120, 179
readership constituencies, 87–93
works
O Ano da Morte de Ricardo Reis (The Year of the Death of Ricardo Reis), 79–122
A Historia do Cerco de Lisboa (The History of the Siege of Lisbon), 123–70
Memorial do Convento (Baltazar and Blimunda), 39–78
Sartre, Jean-Paul, 17, 22
sideshow, 162–63, 167

195

siege of Lisbon (1147), 126–29, 131–32, 139, 162, 165
smile pursuit, 1–6, 37, 39–40, 58–60, 63–64, 68, 71, 77, 92, 111, 140, 160, 171–74
Sousa Santos, Boaventura de, 36, 84, 86–87, 113
space of historical contingency, 72, 113–14, 161
Spanish Civil War, 93, 95, 103
subject construction/reconstruction, 112–15, 122, 160–61, 165–69

tendentious joke, 39, 63, 66–68, 80
transactivity, readerly, 50–51, 80, 123, 148, 150, 160, 164–65, 167

transference, 49, 77, 117, 137, 139–40, 151, 159, 162, 164–65
transtemporality, 46–47

Vieira, Tomé [Alberto Tomás Vieira], 107–12

World War II, 23, 82, 141, 174
writing in the institutional sphere, 33–35, 68–70, 73–74, 102, 129–30, 134
    concept of, 33–35
    rewriting in the institutional sphere, 102, 129, 134

Year of the Death of Ricardo Reis, The (O Ano da Morte de Ricardo Reis [Saramago]*),* 79–122

About the Book

On Emerging from Hyper-Nation: Saramago's "Historical" Trilogy
Ronald W. Sousa

On Emerging from Hyper-Nation represents Ronald W. Sousa's attempt to answer the question "Why do I smile on reading one of Saramago's 'historical' novels?"—Why that reaction of emotional release? To answer the "smile question" the book engages in a critical mode that could be described as "discourse analysis." It combines several critical strains and relies on basic concepts from Freudian and Lacanian psychoanalysis, Adlerian psychology, and contemporary cognitive psychology for their discourse-analytical value rather than as entrees into psychoanalytical reading per se.

The introductory chapter presents some of the concepts that underlie that compound analytical modality and sets out an overview of twentieth-century Portuguese social and economic history. Then, with an eye to answering the "smile question," the book reads Nobel Laureate José Saramago's three novels, *Baltasar and Blimunda* (1982), *The Year of the Death of Ricardo Reis* (1984), and *The History of the Siege of Lisbon* (1989). Or, better, it seeks to read Sousa's own reading of the three works, since focus falls on how each novel seeks to construct both its own reading and also Sousa as its reader.

The discussion brings to light a number of textual phenomena that bear upon the "smile question." Among them are that the novels invoke, often subtly, the fascist hermeneutical heritage remaining from before the Revolution of 1974 as a constituent part of their communication with the reader; that they summon up historical trauma; that they function as Freudian-style "tendentious jokes"; and that, through these various invocations, they seek to constitute a post-revolutionary Portuguese subject. The reading of Sousa's reading, then, ends up being a reading of some of the cultural forces at work in post-revolutionary Portugal.

About the Author

Ronald W. Sousa, University of North Carolina Asheville, is the author, co-author, editor, and/or translator of a number of scholarly articles and books dealing with general cultural criticism, as well as Portuguese-language and Spanish-language cultures. Among the books is *The Humanities in Dispute*, co-authored with Joel Weinsheimer, published by Purdue University Press.

"The book's project is sound and its realization remarkably cogent and ably carried out. The author's analysis of the reception horizon and process, as applied to Saramago's three major historical novels, is useful, insightful, stimulating, and frequently exhilarating in its sharpness and elegance."
—Anna Klobucka
University of Massachusetts–Dartmouth